Fringe First

Pioneers of Fringe Theatre on Record

Roland Rees

First published in the United Kingdom by Oberon Books Limited, 1992

ISBN 1-870259 30 0

Oberon Books Limited
521 Caledonian Road
London N7 9RH
Tel: 071-607 3637
Fax: 071-607 3629

Managing Director: Charles D. Glanville
Publishing Director: James Hogan
Associate Editor: Nicholas Dromgoole

Typeset by O'Reilly Clark Printing Services, Enfield, Middlesex
Printed and bound by The Longdunn Press Limited, Bristol
Cover illustration by Ralph Steadman from *The Floater* programme, Latchmere Theatre, London, June 1991
Cover layout by Lorraine Hodghton

For

Sheelagh Killeen

ROLAND REES directs extensively throughout the theatre in the UK, including the Royal National Theatre, the Royal Court Theatre, Hampstead Theatre, the Bush Theatre, many repertory theatres and commercial theatre. In 1972 he co-founded, as Artistic Director, the Foco Novo Theatre Company with David Aukin and Bernard Pomerance. He is a strong supporter of new writing, introducing playwrights Pam Gems, Bernard Pomerance, Michael Weller, Alfred Fagon and Mustapha Matura, as well as new work by already established writers. Foco Novo toured, as one of the leading national touring companies, for sixteen years in the Regions, Europe and London, until 1988 when the Arts Council of Great Britain withdrew funding from the company.

ANDRA NELKI: All the photographs in this book were taken by Andra Nelki, unless otherwise stated. She is a freelance photographer specialising in the arts, including book illustrations for Penguin Books, Readers Digest, Collins and Weidenfeld & Nicholson.

JOHN HAYNES contributed the production photographs of *The Elephant Man, As Time Goes By, A Man's a Man, The Nine Days and Saltley Gates, Independence, The Lower Depths, The Cape Orchard, Snap,* and *Bloody Poetry.* His production photographs span 21 years, including many for the Royal National Theatre, The Royal Shakespeare Company, the Royal Court Theatre, Hampstead Theatre, and national touring companies, Foco Novo and Joint Stock.

RALPH STEADMAN (cover illustration) has achieved international recognition for his distinctive and original book illustrations, drawings and cartoons. His own books include *Between the Eyes, Strangled Banger, America, I Leonardo, No Room to Swing a Cat, Paranoids, Near the Bone* and *Tales of the Weirrd.*

CHRISTOPHER PEARCE contributed the production photographs of *Sleeping Policemen* and *Black Mas* from the collection owned by Christopher Pearce Associates, trading as The Panic Pictures Library, Croft Cottage, 8 Shorts Croft, Roe Green Village, London NW9 9AN. Tel/fax: 081-905 0868.

ALLAN TITMUSS (freelance photographer) contributed the production photograph of *The Ass.*

SARAH AINSLEY (freelance photographer) contributed the production photograph of *Needles of Light.*

CONTENTS

ACKNOWLEDGEMENTS

All 41 contributors to this book gave freely of their time and to them I am most grateful.

I must thank the many people with whom I worked, particularly those involved in all capacities with Foco Novo productions. In a book of this nature, it was not possible to acknowledge everyone who made that period of theatre so exciting.

I would particularly like to thank Jeanne Griffiths, who read each interview as it appeared, and was a most encouraging and helpful sounding board as the book progressed, and also Dr. Trevor Griffiths and Kathy Rooney for their expert advice.

I am indebted to the theatre photographers, John Haynes, Sarah Ainsley, Christopher Pearce and Allan Titmuss for making their production photographs available.

Andra Nelki's portraits are an integral part of the book and her patience and humour in the face of an ever changing timetable was a great support.

Finally I would like to thank Matthew Carey for his care and advice.

PREFACE

This is a book of conversations about the theatre with people with whom I have worked. The list is selective, inevitably reflecting my own interests and tastes, although not always my own opinions.

Each discussion focuses on a specific show or body of work. This serves an as anchor. From these examples, views and ideas were able to shift outwards, allowing a wider debate. Most of the shows mentioned were produced by Foco Novo in the period 1972-88. However, the book covers a wider span, starting in the Sixties.

Out of the forty participants, there are two exceptions to my having-worked-with rule. They are Mark Long of The People Show, and John Ashford, the journalist and arts administrator. I have known them since the Sixties and feel as if I *have* worked with them. Their individual views and specialist knowledge on those times richly contribute to the book.

Conversations enable the flavour of individual voices to be captured. They also allowed me to enjoy the Socratic process of asking questions to discover. Even though there were prepared questions, inevitably the script was thrown aside. Certain themes and plays crop up in more than one place, casting a different perspective on a subject. This provides a mosaic of experience, as if you had grabbed a lot of snap-shots of people in your hands and then dropped them at random on the floor. What they reveal, what is glimpsed or hidden, is all part of the pattern.

My purpose is to capture a picture of the new theatre, whose genesis lay in the Sixties, through these discussions with writers, actors, directors, designers and producers, and to try to determine its distinctive qualities; to understand how it developed in the Seventies and Eighties and what the future may hold. This is done in the belief that its contribution to mainstream theatre, film and television has been considerable. The personnel, who found their feet working with groups or small theatres, have travelled on and are now leading actors, writers and directors. The emphasis placed on new writing and new work and, less visibly, the fruitful and fresh approaches to the creation of theatre have also influenced practice in the mainstream.

The book is intended as a record to interest people who work in theatre and students of drama, though one hopes it will interest all theatre-goers.

David Schofield in The Royal National Theatre 1980 production of Bernard Pomerance's *The Elephant Man*.

Photo © John Haynes 1980

INTRODUCTION

Theatre whose origins lay in the Sixties I call New Theatre. Fringe theatre does have an historical role to play, but not until the end of the Seventies. John Ashford, first and pioneering Theatre Editor of *Time Out*, says he introduced the category Fringe to the magazine's theatre listings in the late Sixties, naming it after the Edinburgh Festival Fringe. There were those who were invited to play at the International Festival, whilst the the rest, the uninvited, the Fringe came to 'shack up in any old village hall' for no financial gain. This was the sort of theatre emerging in London, which Ashford wrote about for *Time Out*. The terms Fringe and Alternative he agrees, gave the impression that the practice was subordinate and marginal to mainstream theatre. Quite the opposite was the case. Fringe or New Theatre started with its own philosophy and created its own traditions.

New Theatre includes the priority placed on new writing and experimental work, partnered with a desire to tour this work to new audiences, who would not normally have social and geographical access to it. To accommodate this theatrical outburst, new places and spaces had to be created, built or converted for live performance. This became the small scale touring circuit with all its variety of venues – studio theatres, clubs, Arts Centres, pubs, colleges and universities, community, trade and welfare halls. The audiences who came to these venues ranged from students in Birmingham to pensioners in East Ham, from miners and their families in the Rhondda or the Yorkshire coalfields, to the habitués of provincial Arts Centres. A full house could be fifty or 600. The variety and breadth of the new touring circuit was remarkable.

Manifestations of new writing and work include Political Theatre, Feminist Theatre, Community Theatre, Black and Ethnic Theatre, Gay Theatre, Theatre in Education [*TIE*], and a multitude of different types of Performance/experimental/ physical/visual theatre, the seed for which, in one way or another, was germinated in the flourish of the Sixties and early Seventies. Although the conversations do not touch upon all of these categories. In the early stages, the work was focused on groups, companies of actors, often including a director or writer, who chose themselves to work with. This meant New Theatre was not building-based but primarily in origin a touring phenomenon.

There is a super-objective. The explosion of new writing and work in the Sixties was an exciting period in British theatre. The earlier milestone of 1956, *Look Back in Anger*, by comparison, was a date in the mainstream theatre calendar. The diversity of the new theatre, however, was enormous, ranging from performance art on a beach, through new playwriting in a cramped room above a pub to the socialist message of an agit-prop group in a trades hall. It attracted people, who in other times, would never have participated, people not Drama School trained. At this point, theatre was culturally 'where it was at' because it embraced other interest groups and pre-occupations, allowing experimentation to happen on a broad front. A number of the conversations attest to this.

During the next decade, many of those who had gained their apprenticeship in groups and small theatres, naturally, in a free market, moved on. In mainstream theatre you stayed put and got paid properly. This movement of actors, directors, designers, administrators and above all writers provided an important and enduring creative injection into the theatre, film and television business as a whole. Even those who did not make this journey imbibed an atmosphere of its practice by brushing shoulders with those who had taken this route. Ashford tells how he believes that the techniques employed in Shaffer's *Equus*, would not have been possible without the physical work of Freehold. Though Stephen Rea, a former member of Freehold, maintains that nowadays, despite the introduction of those fresh approaches – openness within rehearsal, breaking down of company hierarchy – the traditional defensiveness of actors in rehearsal remains: 'Some actors have no direct experience of working like that. They have not been touched by it.'

Eventually and inevitably this process destroyed the original flame. New Theatre with one or two stout exceptions became colonised. New writing, the most durable contribution of New Theatre, having achieved a special provision within each theatre's budget, found that even this benefit eroded. Some theatres did honour the brief, but in the recession, the good intentions got lost. The result is that the RSC and the Royal National, plus a few small theatres, are becoming the fulcrum for the production of original new plays. Fiona Shaw warns: 'I fear the two national companies could become the sole purchasers and doers of new plays.' The process of producing new work has passed from the comparative poverty of individualistic, and free-wheeling touring groups into the comparative wealth of large institutional buildings.

The philosophy of the new theatre derived from the cultural politics of that time. The inspiration for its work came from its connection with the larger sub-culture which articulated its ideas through political demonstrations, drugs, rock and roll, the underground press and an attitude to the world wholly in opposition to its parents. There was a wide feeling amongst younger people for change. The '68 generation was the first post-war generation that did not need to go to work or go to war. Jon Chadwick says: 'There was an aspiration to do something new and at that time 'new' had a good reputation. You were on the edge of the transformation of political, personal, social and economic relations and you wanted the theatre to be part of that transformation.'

By the Eighties, this had disappeared. Ashford reckons it only existed as a coherent body of work in its purest form for three years. Spin-offs from the original impulse continued through the Seventies, although with diminishing vigour. In the Eighties the Fringe came into its own. Fringe means edge or border and the implication is that those working in The Fringe are on the outside, wanting to get on the inside. Stephen Rea says: 'We started with experiment and now it has degenerated into showcase theatre above pubs. An animated version of *Spotlight*. "Go along and pick them!" It is not about an approach to work.'

The Eighties was the decade of 'choice'. There were more magazines and papers devoting space to listings, more theatres above pubs advertising plays than there had been ten years previously. With the arrival of the Politics of Choice, within an alien cultural framework, the new theatre became divided into separate practices. Nigel Gearing, playwright, entered theatre in 1981 and already realised that he was conscious of a 'whittling down to specific skills and aims in theatre practice.' He compared this to the change in politics from one decade to another. In the Seventies there had been 'a general feel, an overall outlook' but by the Eighties everything had become 'issue based'. So in theatre: 'People were into one kind of theatre or another – Red Ladder or Theatre de Complicité.' Dr. Trevor Griffiths, Chair of Foco Novo Board, points to the 'compartmentalisation' of audiences. There are those who go to the Drill Hall and those who visit the Royal Court. It would take, he says, a 'special kind of show' to attract the habitués of one to the other. This seems to be the paradigm of Thatcher's statement that: 'There is no society, only individuals.' The Arts Council now declares that: 'There is no hierarchy of art forms.'

In the Sixties and early Seventies, one form used to feed off the developments made by others to strengthen its own practice. Writers learnt from the ensemble approach groups made to their work. As Bernard Pomerance says: 'People did talk about each other's work. There was a genuine collegiality of feeling.' John Ashford argues that the writers who worked for Portable Theatre reflected a more 'cinematic and free flowing approach' in their work as a result of this interaction. Another side to this debate, also common within American as well as English experimental theatre practice, is revealed in the spring 1973 edition of the magazine *Performance*. Richard Schechner writes about his experience of producing Sam Shepard's *The Tooth of Crime* with his New York ensemble The Performance Group. There is an exchange of letters. Shepard says: 'Every ensemble group I have seen always works best from a piece which they originate along with a director and writer.' Schechner says, *The Tooth of Crime* is the first regular play they have done. When they have used words before they were 'pushed, pulled, punched out of shape . . . treated operatically.' Shepard replies: 'You gotta understand this play for me is very preconceived.' Schechner: 'We must work long and hard to find our own places within the world of your script.' But they *were* attempting to join forces and the production took place.

Instead, in the Eighties we got a fusion of forms as in music. For theatre this resulted in shows which seemed to inhabit solely, their own theatrical world. Bernard Pomerance: 'Now it is more about enhancing theatre than it is about enhancing life. The quality of the early Seventies was that the theatrical enterprise was a valuable addition to life.'

Performance/physical/visual theatre, for example, gained an ascendancy. It suited the times, with its use of images, not words. Its messages were implicit, not explicit, more abstract, less specific. Playwright, Joshua Sobol: 'Forms favoured and considered avant-garde in the Eighties were primarily physical theatre, dance and performance art. Content took second place.' 'Form is at present the message. But it is obsolete and decadent. Heavily subsidised but decadent.' Sobol is pessimistic about the Nineties, a time of 'dark reaction', but is optimistic that by the year two thousand the primacy of content will have returned, and with it a subversive underground theatre, separated from the 'big houses of culture'. Equally optimistic, Howard Brenton writing in *The Guardian*. 'The conditions for a counter-culture to grow are here again . . . anti-Establishment, unpredictable, beautifully ugly, unafraid of new forms and *plugged into reality*.' [my italics].

From being an important focus of new theatre, new writing became one among the competing forms. It was as if it was dated, faintly embarrassing to those interested in experiment. It was embraced by mainstream theatre. Indeed, even those theatres and companies, who relied upon the use of text, increasingly shied away from new British plays, putting on fresh versions of dead and foreign authors. This was a realistic recognition by theatres, companies and funding bodies alike that audiences were now much more conservative. Mark Long thinks that 'the use of the creative imagination became more limited in the Eighties.' He said that was what audiences wanted and required from theatre and 'theatre does subconsciously respond to that.'

For me an important loss, as a result of this movement of the tectonic plates, was the weight placed on the distinction between text and non-text based work. The growth of performance/physical/visual theatre ensured that. Not because it gained a higher profile – why should it not? – but because it was placed in separation from and in artificial distinction to text-based work. Theatre without a word spoken does have a 'text'. Such work, if it is good, has an inner narrative or development, depending on the same qualities inherent in a text. Mark Long speaking of The People Show: 'We would generally start with a theme, an idea . . . narrative in terms of plot would not be a primary concern . . . that the show makes sense would be.'

Different approaches to experiment existed before. But there was a creative diaspora within which this work occurred. In the Eighties, theatre was again exclusive. Hence the Fringe. The great attempt of the Sixties was to be inclusive. For a moment, it happened. That's why non-theatre people were attracted to theatre. When specialisation set in, the generosity of the diaspora disappeared. We were back to normal, pursuing separate interests.

The politics of choice engenders specialisation. The gathering commercialisation of the arts achieved it. Marketing targets a practice and then sells that commodity. Funders also like it. It makes their job easier. Categories are introduced which favour specific forms of theatre. It is advisable to fit a pigeon hole, have a job description. Dr Trevor Griffiths points to the contradiction: 'If you wanted to get out of the pigeon hole you were not allowed to, and if you stayed in it, you risked being shot.'

Howard Brenton found the bureaucratisation of the arts by the Eighties very striking. In the Sixties, the Arts Council 'had no structure then of how to distribute money to a new, small company. By the end of the Eighties, when Foco Novo folded, there were endless structures.' He says that Foco Novo like others became institutionalised. 'Because we got so worried about the position of the company . . . this worry took over all the theatres, the RSC, the National, the Court, and you end up worrying more about the grant than you do about the audience.'

Jenny Waldman, former administrator of Foco Novo, Arts Council Drama Officer and now Director of Arts Centre Projects at the South Bank, points out that: 'In the late Eighties, the Arts Council decided that theatre companies should derive 50 per cent of their income from sources other than their funding, such as sponsorship. Suddenly this was a decision. A company like IOU or Foco Novo would never have a chance of making up 50 per cent of their turnover from earned income.' Over a longer period of time, Waldman adds, the venues, created from the earliest days to receive the newly funded theatre companies, began to adopt their own policies. They wanted autonomy of their resource. Consequently they started to book cheaper companies; non-Equity companies, who did not have a wage structure. The established touring companies, who presented new writing and work, were also not picking up the audiences. The next phase of companies offered more saleable fare – versions of well known classics and novels. Preferably, as Waldman says, by 'dead authors'. So in two ways, the established companies producing new writing and new work found themselves deprived of their livelihood.

The difference between the New Theatre and the Fringe is institutionalisation. Now the Fringe is part of the mainstream. This does not mean the work is any better or worse. Probably it does mean that it is more technically adroit. But it does not contain the quality of: 'I have a very urgent story, which you have not heard before, and which it is important for me to tell you.' This is Bernard Pomerance. He is talking about films but he is making a clear analogy to theatre, his first love. He says films from Africa and from Central Europe provide this urgency. They have a story to tell. He says, we in the First World produce good films, but they are in a catalogue of many good films. They are just another film.

The exciting theatre of the future will emanate increasingly from non-English speaking parts of the world which lie beyond the Eurocentric model of culture. A number of the conversations here indicate that same sentiment. Yet, ironically, at the same time, the English language and European culture are increasing their hold on those parts of the world. There is a contradiction for those who desire to make theatre in this climate. It was continually present to me when I directed black actors in plays by black writers. The form used for the construction of a play inevitably was inherited. That was what was known. It did not necessarily best serve the play.

Thelma Holt speaks of World Theatre, comparing it to 'World Music': 'Something you can make accessible to anybody.' John Ashford disagrees. World Music, he says, is a cross-over between local, indigenous, probably African music and European sound. It is the mixture or paste-on of the pre-electric with the post-electric. World Theatre has yet to experience cross-over in this manner. What of its desirability if it was to occur? The strongest music and theatre comes up through the cracks in the pavement and earth. It is about specifics, however experimental the approach. Joshua Sobol calls World Theatre, Festival Theatre. It is 'important for theatre people. It does not concern the wider audience. Festival Theatre has to be approached with scepticism.' John Ashford: 'I'm against Festival culture. Culture is not for holidays, it is for every day. Western culture is being festivalised in an unhealthy way.' One of the prime motivations of New Theatre was to take the work to those who were not served socially and geographically with the type of theatre we were producing in the Sixties and Seventies.

Howard Brenton: 'Theatre has to be particular and go for its nights. Foco Novo was the middle ground. Wasn't prestigious like Shakespeare or, on the other hand, flashy like performance art, but it tried to capture the sounds and overtones of the mess of what was happening at the moment and anything good only comes out of that.'

Recently I have worked through the British Council in Kenya and Zambia with actors from those countries. They wanted the workshops to prepare the first three scenes from *Hamlet*. What they learnt was European expertise. What I learnt was that such a play made immensely more sense within their culture, socially and politically, than it does in mine. Warriors and Kings, Ministers and Queens, blood and family, ancestral spirits and political putches, revenge, all came to life in a way that made me aware how culturally rich the potential was in comparison to British Shakespeare productions.

Shakespeare was spurred to write his plays from the vantage of a country whose political importance and centrality to the world as a whole meant that, at the time of writing, he and his peers spoke with great cultural confidence. English speaking writers now, in the 1990's, do not share that confidence because Britain, despite its history, is now not in a position of political centrality. It is an off-shore island to mainland Europe. The momentous events unfolding on our television screens are usually not a direct part of our history. They are somebody else's history. The New Theatre must take on board our own view of these events, write about them and produce the work to take us into the twenty first century.

EARLY DAYS

Early Days is a personal recollection of the motives and influences which drew me to theatre, covering the years I spent in New York, from 1965 to 1967, and how that experience shaped my outlook. It also describes my own early endeavours amidst the new theatre sprouting up in London from the mid-Sixties.

The People Show was a foundation stone of this movement. Mark Long offers insight into how that company worked and what lies in the future. Stephen Rea covers his time with the influential group Freehold, playing in the Foco Novo production of Brecht's *Drums in The Night*, and his recent work with Field Day Theatre Company. In the final conversation, David Aukin and Bernard Pomerance, with whom I co-founded Foco Novo Theatre Company in 1972, discuss the early fortunes of the company and its formative productions of Pomerance's plays including, *The Elephant Man.*

ROLAND REES

NEW YORK 1965

In 1965, America, and New York in particular, was the place where major cultural and artistic upheavals were happening. Experiments in film, theatre, the visual arts, contemporary music and the fusion of these forms, the proliferation of new centres for their performance, the mushrooming underground presses, the organisations surrounding the Vietnam war demonstrations, the rent strikes, Black consciousness groups, the Feminist movement, and experiments in collective and personal life styles, all made a lasting impact during my two years in that city. The energy of New York taught me that you can step out of tradition, start your own and 'Go for it!' I did not need much nudging to give up my academic future and start work in theatre.

Researching in the Lennox Street library on 135th St, Harlem, that summer, I tried to get to grips with the significance of one of the most famous black heroes, Marcus Garvey. A State Studentship from the Department of Education and Science enabled me to complete a PhD on Garvey, for which purpose I was attached to the Columbia University History Department. It was one year after the riots. My passport to safety as a white Welsh man in the heart of Harlem was my strange accent which meant I was treated as the oddity I indeed was. Amidst black students in dashikis rediscovering their past history, I realised I was out of place and in the wrong time. I had studied American Civil War history at the University of Wales. Reading about Slavery in the American south led to my interest in Black history and experience.

Garvey was Jamaican, spent a lot of his time in the States and died in poverty in London in 1940. He was buried in Bethnal Green. He wanted to reverse the slavery triangle, Liverpool and Bristol, Gambia and the Gold Coast, the Caribbean and the southern states of America, and return black Americans back to Monrovia and Liberia in West Africa. He was both a business man and a charismatic leader. He started the United Negro Improvement Association and the Black Star Steamship Line. His emphasis on 'African Fundamentalism' influenced both Rastafarianism and the 'Black Power' and 'Consciousness' movements.

New York was the first large city I had lived in. It was like a shot of adrenalin. I discovered what an advantage three thousand miles of the Atlantic could be in learning how you have been moulded and what your real interests are. I needed this journey to unlock my past and point me to the future.

I lived on a Puerto Rican, Irish, Hungarian block off West 124th St, opposite a liquor store which was held up at gun point every Saturday night. The stolen liquor fuelled the weekend parties around the block. In the railcar-shaped neighbourhood bar, as the night shift workers stopped by, I heard every Central European language mingled with Spanish and Irish. Hundreds of dollars changed hands over the pool table. Harlem started one block away. I became deeply influenced by the city. But despite the excitement, the longer I stayed, I became more certain that I was a European. I kept saying to myself that even the language differences would not prevent me feeling more at home anywhere between Lisbon and Ankara than amongst these canyons of Manhattan. I didn't have to stay but the night workers did, to earn their 'fortune'.

The city also taught me to 'see' differently. At home I had not been encouraged to enjoy the visual arts. Like many UK students, I was ignorant of contemporary developments. The middle Sixties in New York was a flourishing time for experiment in painting, sculpture, happenings, installations, 'events'. Watching artists at first hand interact and respond to their city changed my ways of seeing. The Abstract Expressionist tradition, the massive use of colour, the sheer quantity of canvas, the destruction of the barriers between painting, sculpture and performance all gave me a visual education.

New York was also a major centre for Jazz. This was inspirational music for me. Naturally this was another track which led me to study Black history. I had listened to Miles Davis, Theolonius Monk and Sonny Rollins on vinyl but here they were playing in the flesh. Early on, I heard the kind of music which reached the record stores some years later. Among my best memories: Ornette Coleman rehearsing in a loft on the Lower East side, a club called 'Slugs' in the same neighbourhood, where the adventure of reaching the destination was as exciting as the music itself.

There was so much new theatre in Manhattan. An abundance of actors, writers and directors were drawn to the city who could not find work in the conventional areas of theatre. They *had* to find alternative means. It was thought Miller, Albee, Williams and O'Neill had had their say. Now it must be the turn of a new generation of writers, particularly those with ethnic, urban, gay and feminist interests.

It is impossible to forget the mentally retarded 'Baby Girl' in Ed Bullins' *Clara's Ole Man*, an awesome image of black urban experience, nor Jean-Claude van Italie's work with Joe Chaikin's Open Theatre including *America Hurrah* or Charles Ludlam's crazed pieces for The Playhouse of the Ridiculous for whom Bertolt Brecht's son, Stefan, then worked, and the plays of Rochelle Owens at La Mama. I saw the unknown Dustin Hoffman with an inimitable 'scouse' accent in Henry Livings' *EH!* at the Circle in the Square. But the greatest pleasure was provided by the vitality and variety of work produced by 'groups' or ensembles – physicalised productions at La Mama, environmental use of space by Schechner's The Performance Group, and the utopian visions of the Living Theatre. Watching their *Frankenstein*, with the actors seemingly swimming up and down the scaffolding of the set, and Julian Beck as the doctor at the centre of the frenzy, was a very powerful image. The Beck's thought America had created its own Frankenstein, a colonial empire, of which the war in South East Asia was a principal part.

The La Mama productions were theatrically exciting but too obsessed with form and often merely expressionistic. The Company which influenced me most was Joe Chaikin's Open Theatre. Less internationally renowned than The Living Theatre or La Mama, his approach was more subtle. A wonderful actor and director, like the Beck's, his work was political, but it did not attempt their anarchic super-visions and ultimatums which so suited the springtime of the Sixties. A memorable Chaikin performance was created for the 1966 Angry Arts week. He took a group of liberal New Yorkers exercising their guilt over their country's involvement in Vietnam, and intercut with scenes representing the war. Theatrically, it was presented as a film edit and re-edit as the company were cut, freeze-framed and run back from one scene to another. Whilst La Mama made experiment into a shibboleth, Chaikin used images but made the form match the content.

La Mama, however, showed me the way to combine music with theatre, plays with music which relied neither on the musical or opera tradition. The orchestra or musicians were not banished to the 'pit'. They were part of the show. Most of the plays I did on my return to London contained live music. I sought out actors who were also musicians so that text and music could be fully integrated. The manner and the image of many of the plays at La Mama were like Jazz. There was a sense of improvisation – an unscored response to a tune or theme. Jazz is an urban music, as those plays were.

The real spawning grounds of this new theatre were the naves of churches, basements and lofts, restaurants and clubs, the parks and streets of the city. Any place where actors could meet their audiences. So off-off Broadway was born in precincts all over Manhattan. New Yorkers, wanting to experience this theatre, had to reach parts of the city formerly they had feared to travel to. Nobody made any money – it was profit share.

My two years were up. My student visa would not let me stay longer. I had accomplished some professional work at the Riverside Church and at Barnard College directing Brecht, Max Frisch, T.S Eliot, James Saunders and a surrealist musical *Home Movies* by Rosalyn Drexler. I was to revisit New York a number of times in the next few years. But I knew as I left the dock on South Manhattan aboard the Queen Elizabeth that I was leaving behind a most formative period of my life. I was armed with a mass of plays and a certain vision in that summer of 1967. Many of my pre-occupations for theatre had been focussed – an interest in history, black theatre, music in theatre, a progressive and experimental approach to production, and above all new writing.

Returning to that other city, London, where I knew absolutely nobody in theatre, I would have to prowl around the outskirts of London's social and cultural life until I found my feet.

LONDON 1967-72

London was alive with the same excitement. But on a smaller scale. It was early days. New York had pioneered and London was to follow. As in New York, there was a burgeoning population keen to enter the performing arts. With a few audacious exceptions, mainstream theatre represented a fossilised tradition which did not reflect the reality many of us saw around us. It provided very few opportunities for a new breed of theatre makers who were cast or had cast themselves outside that tradition. It was a period when many who would ordinarily never have found their way into theatre chose it as a path of expression. Students from Arts Schools and with musical backgrounds, saw attractive opportunities in performance. Mainstream theatre was about specialisation of skills. The New theatre dusted down an older theatre tradition. It wanted performers to be able to offer mime, juggling, acrobatics and the ability to play musical instruments; the desire was to fuse the variety of a single performer's expertise within a show. This method is visible in the work of many of today's companies experimenting in new forms.

Theatre spaces and groups

As the variety and exuberance of work surged forward, new spaces for theatre – pubs, clubs, churches, warehouses, synagogues and cinemas – were pressed into service. The migrations of Ed Berman's Lunchtime Theatre were particularly representative of that period. His first season was held in the basement of the Ambiance restaurant on Queensway. From there it travelled to Norman Beaton's club, the Green Banana in Soho, then to the ICA Cinema and finally came to rest at the now defunct Almost Free theatre off Piccadilly Circus. Jim Haynes' Arts Laboratory at the top of Drury Lane was converted from a warehouse. The building on Alie St in Aldgate, which housed the original Half Moon theatre, was a synagogue. The People Show made their performances in the basement of Better Books, Charing Cross Rd. Ed Berman and Naftali Yavin's TOC [*The Other Company*] Troupe first performed at the Mercury Theatre, Notting Hill Gate, home of the Ballet Rambert. Here, Ed presented Jerome Savary's first London show. In such spaces, there was no division between performer and audience, the impulse being to invade and include, not separate.

The most adventurous occasions happened at the Arts Lab; including music by The Third Ear band and split-screen movies from Andy Warhol. There I saw a remarkable production of *Antigone* by Nancy Meckler's Freehold, with Stephen Rea and Dinah Stabb among the company's fine performers. I was fortunate when Nancy asked me to direct Brecht's early play *Drums in the Night* with the company. [*See interview with Stephen Rea*] Freehold had a particular style evolved by Meckler through exercises, popular with American companies, originating from the Polish director Grotowski. It was not language based, but deployed physical and non-naturalistc methods of exploring texts. An important company.

Grotowski's book, *Towards a Poor Theatre*, was very influential. Whilst I realise his use of the word 'poor' did not carry economic significance, the title infuriated me because I was desperate to get rid of our poverty of means. I saw Grotowski's *The Constant Prince* presented by Michael Kustow, in the Nicholas Hawksmoor church near the City. The audience stood looking down into a wooden cattle trough and watched the actor suffer some remarkable deprivations. It was intended as a metaphor of what it was like living in communist Poland.

One of the pioneers of ensemble theatre in the UK were The People Show, [*See interview Mark Long*] who I first saw performing at The Arts Lab. Their approach has remained unique and unswerving to this day. Some members of the group like Jeff Nuttall [*A founder of the group with Mark Long*] personified the impact Art Colleges made on the new theatre. Mark Long says they had no heroes or influences, a claim difficult to accept. Dada and Surrealism clearly made some impression on their work. Experiments with performance and installations, pioneered in the States, were already making an impact over here. Jazz has also been a frequent visitor to their shows. However, whatever the current fashionable influences were, the great attraction of The People Shows was their essentially European ambiance. Playwright, Bernard Pomerance, in his interview provides ample testimony to their influence on the work of others, especially writers.

The other pioneer group was Roland Muldoon's CAST which started in 1965. [*See Roland Muldoon interview*] They performed in the clubroom above the Royal Court, now the Theatre Upstairs. The energy of their performances shot off the stage. CAST stands for Cartoon Archetypical Slogan Theatre. Not since the San Francisco Mime Troupe had I seen anything approaching this kind of work. It was overtly political but tremendous fun. Muldoon had taken the 'commedia' tradition and called it 'archetypical'. CAST dealt in stock characterisations with enormous relish for comedy and style; the derivations of which came out of Charlie Chaplin, Lennie Bruce and English stand-up comics, plus physical movement borrowed from dance. The main character, 'Muggins', was a working class anti-hero who *pretended* he believed everything he was told. The plays were short and fast like rock and roll, to the political point and performable anywhere. This style influenced me considerably when I came to direct a second production of Brecht's *Drums in the Night* for the 1973 Edinburgh Festival and the Hampstead Theatre, also with Stephen Rea. [*See Stephen Rea interview*].

Muldoon teamed up with John Arden and Margaretta D'Arcy to present a play at Unity Theatre in Camden. He wanted to resuscitate Unity into a thriving theatre again. His usual company were augmented with other actors, of whom I was one. The main parts of 'Mr and Mrs Muggins' were played by the Ardens. Muldoon directed. Given the strong personalities involved, and the very different theatre backgrounds and practice, it was a recipe for disaster. But the show got on and provided Unity with a type of entertainment and audience that theatre had not experienced before. Muldoon made his point, but soon after the theatre burnt to the ground!

The two strands of the new theatre were exemplified by the work of Portable Theatre and the Pip Simmons Theatre Group. As with most of the groups, Pip Simmons improvised their shows around a theme. To these groups, the solitary and omnipotent position of the writer represented the 'old' theatre they were trying to displace. The Portable Theatre, started by David Hare in 1967 as a touring company, wanted to present new writing. Howard Brenton, whose play *Christie in Love* was produced by Portable: 'We were plugged into the new circuit but we were not liked. We were looked on with great suspicion by the Sixties lot.'' [*See Howard Brenton interview*]. Portable were pro-script, the others were anti- script. Portable hired their actors for each production, Pip Simmons relied on the input of his group of actors to make their shows, under his direction. Brenton: 'Ideologically we were similar but it was quite clear that the writers carried the banner into the difficult Seventies and Eighties.'

Popular music of that era was seen by the groups as an analogy for theatre. Popular music had radically changed since the Fifties. The new theatre companies adopted the term 'group' from the musical world. Both music and theatre groups saw themselves as operating outside the entertainment business, even if the bands appeared on television. Much of this music originated from fact or inspiration born in the States. Certainly Muldoon and *Cast* saw rock as an inspiration for their work. Simmonds saw his group in the same way, employing music in many of his shows. In *Do It!*, a show about the trial of the Chicago Seven, the main character was the rock band. This was the era of the great open air music Festivals and Vietnam demonstrations. Popular culture comingled with the new theatre, and touring theatre acquired the image of the rented truck with the roadie driving up the M1 to a 'gig'.

If much of the inspiration for the work was American, so were many of the actors, directors and writers. Whether it was for reasons of avoiding the draft or the atmosphere of America at the time of the war in South East Asia, or that the overflow from off-off Broadway came to London, or simply because it was cheaper then to make movies here, there were lots of American actors and directors in London. Some were key figures in the development of the new theatre in Sixties' Britain. Jim Haynes was instrumental in starting the Traverse Theatre in Edinburgh and The Arts Laboratory on Drury Lane. Ed Berman set up InterAction. Charles Marowitz, with Thelma Holt started The Open Space Theatre. Beth Porter and Nancy Meckler formed the Warehouse La Mama company until Meckler created Freehold. They did not exclusively present American plays, but their work drew attention to the new American writers.

Ed Berman and InterAction

A chance response to an advertisement set me on course to my first directing job. I met Ed Berman and Naftali Yavin at the Oval House one Sunday after a Vietnam demonstration in 1968. They wanted to start a new theatre and were looking for plays for their first season. Ed's big idea was to do lunchtime theatre and attract the commuters and office workers who disappeared back to the suburbs at night. A new audience! I knew Ed was keen to find plays fresh to London. Those I had brought from New York suited the fifty or sixty minute slot. I gave him one by black writer Ed Bullins, *The Electronic Nigger*, which Ed scheduled as the last play of the season after John Arden's *Squire Johnathan* and Ed's own play *Nudist Campers Grow and Grow*. I was very excited. Ed allowed his intuition to judge since there was no way he could have seen any of my work. I do not think that would have happened, if he had been English!

The Ambiance at Queensway was a coffee shop by day at street level. At night in the basement it became a club with steel band music. Its owner was Junior Telfer, a Trinidadian. Ed had a knack of making business contacts at no cost to himself. In return for being the host, Junior got some lunchtime business, usually his quiet hour. We rehearsed in the basement, which was the theatre space. The acting area was pocket-handkerchief sized. The audience were crammed in nose to nose with the action. *Electronic Nigger*, a title you wouldn't get away with now, was an acrid farce about a black creative writing teacher in a Californian Adult Education College. In the class, there is an irrepressible 'Electronic Nigger', a black would-be writer who spouts language like an Ivy League automaton. Clearly he wanted to be thought 'white'. Only in recent years would upward mobility and class assimilation of a black character have been possible to contrive in a British play. Deborah Norton, Sheila Scott-Wilkinson, Charlie Hyatt and Stefan Kalipha were in the cast. Ed Bullins came from New York to see the production. I was fearful lest his Black Panther associations would make him shoot the production to bits. Luckily, he was satisfied.

Ed Berman is a forceful and complex character. In the early Sixties he had been a Rhodes Scholar specialising in Educational Methodology, spending some time in Turkey studying their Educational system. During an anti-American demonstration in Istanbul, when Turkish feeling about Cyprus was running high, two demonstrators spotted Ed sitting on his patio. They climbed up and tried to club him to death. He suffered severe head injuries resulting in a blood clot on the brain. Doctors told him he had one year to live. The story he tells, by now apocryphal, is that, grateful for his survival, unable to read and pursue his studies, he underwent a Pauline conversion, determining to devote what little life he thought he had left to socially conscious projects. Hence InterAction. With a philosophy combining participatory group, educational and theatre work operating on the then uncharted area between school and the street. I am very glad to record that the doctor's diagnosis was wrong, Ed is alive and well and living in London.

The theatrical branch of InterAction was only one of its many activities. The heart of the organisation was based in Chalk Farm. However, I had no intention of joining the InterAction community, I was only interested in the theatre. Full-time members, many of whom lived and worked at InterAction, saw the theatre as a marketing operation to raise public awareness of the organisation's more important social activities. Each member had to take a turn at each InterAction job. When it was the time to be a stage manager, some were not pleased by a lot of actors 'poncing' around in rehearsal nor being ordered around by a 'power-hungry' director. There was meant to be a collective spirit! But two stood out for their interest and ability – Jim Hiley, now journalist and theatre reviewer, and Patrick Barlow, actor and Director of the National Theatre of Brent. Part of their job was to help Ed with his Barnum and Bailey act, barking on the pavement outside the Ambiance, persuading people to give up their lunch for a show.

Ed's philosophy for the theatre was hit-and-run. Do the work where you can as long as the work happens. His first office was opposite the Roundhouse in Chalk Farm. He used to rail at the bureaucracy, as he saw it, of Arnold Wesker's Centre 42 based at the Roundhouse. This was intended as an alternative to, but on the scale of, a National Arts organisation for the people of Camden. A North Bank to the South Bank. Ed thought it was a waste of time waiting for the funding and sponsorship and then completing the building before activity happened. He preferred the low cost, nomadic approach with immediate production of work.

Most of the shows I directed between 1968 and 1971 were for InterAction. All of them written by Americans including further plays by Ed Bullins. I was able to introduce the work of Rochelle Owens, Israel Horovitz and Bernard Pomerance at the Ambiance. In 1971, Charles Marowitz presented an American season at his Open Space Theatre, and there I directed plays by two more Americans Leonard Melfi, and Michael Weller. With the exception of the work I did later with Bernard Pomerance, this was the end of my absorption in new American plays. The meeting with Bernard Pomerance was of key importance. It led to a fruitful, creative relationship lasting a number of years and over six productions. He lived in London. [*See Interview with Bernard Pomerance and David Aukin*] *Hot Damn High in Vietnam*, his first play to be produced, which I directed at the Ambiance, did have an American theme as the title suggests. But his interests were international and the language of his plays could have only been realised in theatre. Both of these were highly attractive qualities. To produce his play *Foco Novo*, set in Brazil, we formed the Company Foco Novo in 1972. I directed the first production of his play, *The Elephant Man*, in 1977.

Black Theatre

In 1970, Ed Berman wanted to mount a 'Black and White Power Season' with the Ambiance, by now based at the ICA. He was talking of American plays again. I said we must produce an indigenous black writer or we risked failing our responsibilities to new British writing. Ed agreed: 'Okay but go and find that writer.' So I put feelers out through Stefan Kalipha and Horace Ové, the Film Maker. Eventually a Trinidadian turned up at InterAction with some scraps of yellow paper containing a number of short plays. He worked in a hospital and lived in Surbiton. It was Mustapha Matura. These plays became *Black Pieces*. They were a picture of life on 'the Grove'. The main piece *Party* was a vignette of whites looking for a 'smoke of weed' and cultural excitement, whilst the blacks partyied and sweet-talked the white women. In this production I used formal devices of overlapping time and place which I had learnt from watching Chaikin. Oscar James, Stefan Kalipha, Alfred Fagon and T-Bone Wilson were in the cast.

Black Pieces was an immediate success and led to a commission for Mustapha from the Producer Michael White. Success also took us to the Mickery Theatre in Holland, then situated just outside Amsterdam in Ritsaert ten Cate's farmhouse in Loenersloot, where we all stayed. The Mickery's own theatre company were rehearsing parachute drops in the garden and the contrast between the exuberance of the *Black Pieces* company and the silent practitioners of the European avant-garde could not have been more pronounced.

Amsterdam had become an outpost for London's alternative theatre, the patronage of Ritsaert being important for British groups like Pip Simmons. Howard Brenton remarked that it was there rather than in London that he saw The People Show for the first time. Dutch government subsidy to the arts was the envy of us all.

But there was a further and more far reaching success. A dam was broken for black writers in this country. Black actors were seen playing roles written by a Trinidadian writer in a play about the aspirations of a particular generation of migrants and in language specific and local to those characters. In Mustapha's early plays, his characters, or rather the male characters because few female characters appear, reveal the connection his generation had made with a particular part of English society – middle class and bohemian. Two black members of the cast, T-Bone Wilson and Alfred Fagon, were immediately spurred by this experience to start writing plays themselves.

The Almost Free was a beautiful, intimate theatre in the heart of the West End which disappeared as a result of the Piccadilly Circus development. There I directed Alfred Fagon's *11 Josephine House*. The venue was well suited to this family drama. Alfred came from a Jamaican family of six brothers and two sisters brought up in the rural heart of the island. He was the only one to come to this country, his other sisters and brothers migrating to the States. Alfred was a larger than life character. He was in the Army, claiming distinction as a boxer, worked on the railways and for a time as a night club singer. In St Paul's in Bristol, where he lived, he became interested in acting. A year after *11 Josephine House*, I directed his play *Death of A Blackman* at the Hampstead Theatre. The 'blackman' in question was the brilliantly gifted Jamaican musician, Joe Harriot, who died an early and untimely death. The title was a terrible premonition for Alfred's own life. In 1987, returning from his regular early morning jog, he collapsed outside his flat in Camberwell. He died, aged 49, before the ambulance reached the hospital.

11 Josephine House was Alfred's first play, a strong evocation of Jamaicans, living in St Pauls, Bristol, recreating the pattern of their island life as a protection against the alien world they now found themselves in. Oscar James, Mona Hammond, T-Bone Wilson and Alfred himself were in the cast. Matura viewed his characters with detachment through a beady, mercurial eye. His early plays were structured like Comedies of Manners. In comparison, *11 Josephine House* revealed a writer in search of a form from within his own culture, but muddled by the models from his inherited culture. Nevertheless, the play was sustained and powerful, portraying characters who were, by turn, passionate and melancholic, yet for all that stuffed with humour, and achieved in an entirely different way to Matura.

Matura's next play, *As Time Goes By*, was written courtesy of the Michael White commission. [*See Black Theatre Interview 1*]. It opened at the 1971 Edinburgh Festival and played in London at the Royal Court, winning Matura the John Whiting Award. Many of the same cast were in this production. Stefan Kalipha played Ram a 'swami' or 'smart man', who in return for a fee advises his black clients on their matrimonial, family and business matters. The play's structure relied on a stream of visitors with their various stories of woe and Ram's quick-witted supply of unlikely solutions to their problems. The play allowed an English audience to experience a world hidden from their view, and again provided an insight into that demi-monde where a vibrant black culture connected with an inquisitive white bohemian world. The play further substantiated Matura's reputation, though essentially the play remains an expression of its own time.

For a period I earned a living working as an assistant director for Michael White on two West End shows, both American imports – *The Dirtiest Show in Town* by Tom Eyen and a musical of *Two Gentlemen of Verona* with a book by John Guare and music by Galt McDermott of *Hair* fame. The American casts came over for the first six weeks and would then be replaced by English actors. My job was to look after the English casts once they were rehearsed in. *Dirtiest Show* followed on White's success with *Oh Calcutta*, proselytising sexual freedom. The cast had to appear naked and it was part of my job to audition a large number of the English hopefuls without their clothes, under the watchful gaze of the Equity representative. *Two Gentlemen* started its life in Joseph Papp's Shakespeare in Central Park season and drew its inspiration from New York's Black, Hispanic and Chinese communities.

This commercial experience provided a weekly stipend with which I could continue my work in unprofitable profit-share ventures. I could also observe the unromantic workings of commercial theatre. After the opening preview of *Two Gentlemen*, one of the young female leads was dumped. The argument went that, unless she went the show would flounder. The decision was largely made at the insistence of the theatre owners. It made me realise how crucial their position was in comparison to the more publicised relationships of producer and their employees.

Clive Goodwin was my agent. His introduction to Michael White led to the commission for *As Time Goes By* by Mustapha Matura. His sudden death in Los

Photo © John Haynes 1970

Left to Right. Robert Coleby and Stefan Kalipha in The Traverse Theatre/Royal Court 1970 production of Mustapha Matura's *As Time Goes By.*

Angeles, initially treated by the police as a case of drunkenness, rather than the brain haemorrhage it was, came as a great shock. His interests were wide, both culturally and politically – he was one of the founders with Tariq Ali of the radical newspaper *Black Dwarf* – and visits to his home and offices on Cromwell Road provoked discussions, rather than mere advice on a particular job. His introduction to Richard Neville led to one of the more bizarre incidents in my career. A good proportion of his clients were writing and directing for TV and film. Television in the Sixties was the hot medium for writers and directors with social intentions. Meeting playwright Trevor Griffiths, a Goodwin client, at that time, I remember being struck by the importance he placed on television exposure, in comparison to theatre, which was surprising for someone I considered a theatre writer first and foremost. Goodwin brought the producer and film director Tony Garnett down to the Ambiance. Garnett was bemused by theatre, not understanding why anyone wanted to work in that medium. The people he wanted to reach only watched television! But I never wanted to give up the possibility of making theatre accessible and exciting to any audiences, especially those who were addicts of TV.

The road to Oz

In 1971 I met Keith and Pam Gems through Clive Goodwin. I had been searching for a space to convert into a theatre in the Notting Hill area and elicited their interest. Keith ran a thriving business making wax models for Madame Tussauds and other museums. Pam had written a children's Christmas tale which they wanted to produce. I liked it and took It to David Aukin. *Betty's Wonderful Christmas*, Pam's first show, which I directed, was presented at the Cockpit Theatre. It challenged what was possible for a Christmas entertainment. The fairy tale was no *Babes in the Wood* or *Cinderella*. Betty, a thirteen year old, ventures into a wood one winter night and is raped. She is then transported for the rest of the show into an Alice situation, meeting many strange characters on her journey, including a Goth on a motorbike. The journey is a metaphor for her brutal gaining of adulthood and her ability to cope with the experience.

David Aukin devised a fortnight's Festival to accompany the show. The groups who appeared that Christmas of 1971 represent a microcosm of the English Fringe of that time – Pip Simmons with *Alice in Wonderland*, The People Show, Freehold with Roy Kift's *Genesis*, The Theatre Machine and Max Stafford Clark's Traverse Theatre Workshop with John Spurling's *In The Heart of the British Museum*.

It was at this point I met Richard Neville. The RSC had put on a reading called *The Trials of Oz*, an edited transcript of the court case in which the editors of the magazine *Oz*, one of whom was Neville, became the subjects of an obscenity trial as the result of a children's edition of the magazine. An American producer Van Woolf wanted to present the trial as a show in New York. Neville had an open mind about how it might be turned into an entertainment, and he liked my ideas for animating the cartoon elements of the magazine to extend the comic and anarchic possibilities. I proposed we use a rock band and get lyrics written. I had no way of knowing that these welcome ideas would lead to such contention. Neville was an instantly likeable person, an engaging conversationalist, curious about the most eclectic subjects – in short good fun.

Neville, Geoffrey Robertson, his Sydney friend and legal adviser, and I flew to New York. Suddenly it hit me. I was back. Travelling from Kennedy all the familiar sights came into view, particularly passing over the Triborough Bridge. The old feeling of excitement which the city used to generate in me returned. I had thought that I was purged, that I had exchanged my addiction to the speediness and energy of New York for the more measured and quieter tones of London.

Up to this point I had found out little about our producer Van Woolf. Richard kept saying: 'Wait till you meet him!' Eventually our limousine pulled up in the courtyard of the New York Hospital. Richard said this is our destination. We went to the ninth floor and were shown into a private room. Van Woolf was in bed. He greeted Richard with effusion, booming his welcome. He was a large man with a black beard and considerable energy. I was about to step forward and shake hands when an arm restrained me. I must not get too close since Van Woolf was undergoing heavy cobalt treatment! He 'ticked'. Indeed at the first opportunity, he gleefully showed us 'the thing' in his chest where the treatment occurred. He had terminal cancer and was subjecting himself to this potentially lethal treatment. The secret was out.

We sat at a reasonable distance in a semi-circle around the bed. Woolf told us to help ourselves to drinks in the bathroom. The bath was a floating alcohol cabinet, awash with ice. A nurse gave him his pills. After she left, he spat them out and reached in his drawer for his own brand of 'pills'. I got used to these occasions. They were called production meetings. They were bizarre, but then so was the whole project. We did not have a new script or lyrics and already I was looking at theatres and casting. But I grew to appreciate Woolf's amazing drive in the face of death.

I soon got back into the American swing of things, visiting old friends and haunts. But these hospital meetings became more and more bizarre, and we would be greeted by a party of Woolf's friends spread over the hospital room floor. They might include Jerry Garcia of the Grateful Dead – Woolf knew many of the West Coast bands, having made the film *Gimme Shelter* – or Allen Ginsberg singing mantras in a corner accompanied by his thumb bells. They had all come to pay their last respects. However the longueurs of not making any decisions began to grate. It became evident that Woolf would make every decision his own way. After all, it was his swansong. I should have taken the ride and enjoyed myself. but I found the process too self-indulgent. We disagreed on a number of issues. Matters came to a head when Woolf threatened to cut off my per diems. I visited the travel agent to book my return flight, knowing I was throwing away the chance of an off-Broadway opening. As the agent handed me the ticket, the phone rang – it was Woolf trying to cancel the ticket. I made haste for Kennedy.

I had fallen out of love with New York and the American way of doing things. Van Woolf held court, liked the naked power, and now personified the world whose appearance I had formerly found so exciting after the sleepiness of England. Now it was unacceptable. I no longer wanted this freelance life. Instead I wanted to form a company and control the means by which the work was achieved. It was an important decision for me.

When I returned to London, I heard Jim Sharman [*Director of* Hair] had taken over the direction of *The Trials of Oz*. It opened and closed. Van Woolf, I heard, died on the opening night. At least he had his swansong! But already I had forgotten America, busy in preparing the first show, *Foco Novo*, to inaugurate the company that was to be my life for the next sixteen years.

MARK LONG

Mark Long with Jeff Nuttall was one of the founder members of
The People Show in 1966. The Company is still flourishing,
emphasising visual, surreal and physical elements of theatre. The
People Show has become internationally famous, playing to audiences
in many countries. Long remains the central focus of this the earliest,
one of the most seminal and influential examples of Fringe and
Performance Art theatre.

REES: How does The People Show make shows, put things together? How different is your practice to mainstream theatre?

LONG: The first and major difference is that we do not have a script. Creative ideas are the starting point.

REES: Is there a leader? An artistic hierarchy?

LONG: No. We generally start with a theme, an idea. The idea might be the set, might be a picture, a piece of music, a prop or an action. But there would be a large parameter for one idea within which all other ideas could be sparked off. I only want to work with people who contribute to the original creative process, of creating the piece as opposed to being told what to do, what is required of them. Actors do tend to have a problem over this.

The other major difference is that narrative is not our primary concern. That the show makes sense is a primary concern. But narrative in terms of plot development would not be. That is very releasing. Generally a theme, not a plot, will emerge in a good People Show. A good People Show has a definite dynamic, theme and a feeling: 'Yes this does make sense!' The process was never a loose ragamuffin affair. And that still is very constant in our approach to work. One of the big differences now is that we don't have to waste so much time exploring and finding out. We have a much better idea of what will work or won't early on.

REES: How did you get into theatre?

LONG: In the early Sixties I went to Trent Park [*now the University of Middlesex*] and there were three Arts courses at that time – Music, Art and Drama. I did Drama, but worked very closely with people on the other courses. I think this connection was very instructive in the route The People Show has taken, the fact that we work with Art and Music and Dance and that's where it started.

REES: What was the first step that pulled you into professional theatre?

LONG: I worked with those at College very well. And then when we left, Jeff Nuttall came into our lives.

□ *Jeff Nuttall poet, painter, maker of Assemblages and Happenings, ex-Jazz trumpeter. His book* Bomb Culture, *published 1968, became an influential cult book.*

We all lived at the Abbey Arts Centre, where studios existed and artists could work. Very cheap. And Jeff came to live there. He asked us to do a show with Pink Floyd in Powys Gardens, Notting Hill Gate. And he wanted us to help him do this event. We are talking about the autumn of 1966.

☐ *Pink Floyd became one of the major bands of the Sixties and Seventies.*

Well we all enjoyed it. It went very well indeed and we thought we should do this again.

REES: What form did the show take with Pink Floyd?

LONG: It was not with Pink Floyd but on the same bill as the Floyd. It was in those days described as a Happening. I very much prefer the word 'Event'.

☐ *Happenings were events created/constructed by an artist with live performers*

Jeff was certainly more mature and better known on the scene than we were. What he knew about was 'performance', but we had a very minor pedigree of performance having studied drama. I think we were very like-minded in many ways, receptive to Jeff's madness and the fact that we were not dealing with theatre at all. So there was a definite sympathy. The show was very visual – a lot of props, a huge net that descended from the ceiling and covered the audience. It was to become very typical of the work of that time.

REES: How important was the connection with Pink Floyd and rock and roll bands?

LONG: It was important but tenuous. It was totally acceptable then to work that way in the Sixties. The Sixties did not start here until 1966. It was a concentrated explosion. Audiences were very receptive to happenings and music occurring in the same place, at the same time. Pop music started using theatre.

REES: This was the period of the introduction of light shows during music gigs and concerts which had already happened from the early Sixties in the States?

LONG: That's right. Mark Boyle was already working for Pink Floyd and then later the Soft Machine. So there were certainly light shows going on alright.

☐ *Mark Boyle, artist with mixed media, assemblages and happenings, created liquid light projections which became known as 'light shows'. The Soft Machine was a progressive rock band.*

That occasion led us to gather people who worked on that event into a more solid relationship. We then did a show called 'The People Show' in the basement of Better Books, Charing Cross Road. It was packed out. We did the next one about three weeks later and in that first year we did, I think, a new show every three weeks for eight months.

☐ *Better Books was one of the earliest alternative bookshops and performance spaces in London.*

31

REES: Who were the personnel then?

LONG: Me, Jeff, Laura Gilbert, Sid Palmer and John Darling plus others including The People Show band. Since that point, we have nearly always worked with live music. First a very free form of jazz. Now not so specific. We work with all kinds of music.

REES: Were there any particular influences on you? Any heroes?

LONG: No. I didn't have any at all. I didn't have any influence or any hero. I knew quite a bit about theatre and quite a bit about art and jazz but there were no heroes in my life. The People Show did not ever try to emulate one body of philosophy or person. That is very important. That is why the People Show have survived so long. It has always been artistically led by its members, as opposed to led by other influences or sociologically led.

REES: Heroes or influences need not necessarily come from one's own arena of work. In those days they were found across the whole cultural spectrum. In particular for those working in theatre, outside theatre.

LONG: We had a lot of influence coming from the art world, the happening world and the music world. In the general sense The People Show mixed all those things.

REES: At that time companies of performers were referred to as groups. You belonged to so-and-so group. This represented a particular way of working, a particular way of looking at relationships within work as opposed to a production company assembled to produce a single show.

LONG: In that sense The People Show bore a much closer relationship to music, to pop bands than to theatre. It was very important to recognise what was happening in music then. It gave us the feeling that we can do this – we don't need a stage, rows of seats, lighting, sound equipment and a director. You can go out on the road, find spaces and perform. Many, many new ones were opening up. That was not really known at that time in theatre in this country. Now it is taken for granted. Initially, we performed at Better Books, UFO, Middle Earth, a lot of Colleges and Universities and a lot of outdoor work, on the street.

□ *UFO and Middle Earth were the earliest underground music clubs with light shows and were situated in Covent Garden.*

That was when we started touring. We did not get grants in those days. Our main source of income were Colleges and Universities. Difficult to believe that now. When we went full-time that was our main source of income, our means of survival.

REES: Did the Colleges and other venues have theatres?

LONG: No, we performed in halls normally used for bands. We shared the circuits, a lot of the venues and a lot of the bills with bands. The only other theatre group at the very beginning was Roland Muldoon and CAST, who played on a different circuit. But the principles of their work were very similar. You did not have to perform in theatre spaces. You could find other spaces and new audiences.

☐ *CAST – Cartoon Archtetypal Slogan Theatre playing to the Labour Movement and left audiences .*

REES: Do you believe the practice of The People Show is different to that of groups which have emerged in the Eighties?

LONG: The practice is different. The first thing is – and lots of groups followed in our wake – whilst we use a structure and a scenario, we do not use a literary script. A group can create work not just through a script. There are other sources. I think a lot of groups originally followed into that gap which we created. Now there are very, very few groups working from that principle. Most groups now are writer-based. Not all. There are exceptions. A group like IOU for example. But the large majority are writer and theatre based, part of the mainstream of theatre.

☐ *IOU is a Performance Art group similar to The People Show in using a thematic approach in their work.*

REES: Surely there are a number of groups who would say they are not writer-based, are not literary. There has been a new generation of such groups to emerge since the Seventies.

LONG: Are there a lot saying that?

REES: For instance. Whether you would agree or not, Lumiere & Son are not just literary, they also derive their sources from the visual arts. Their work is not just text-based.

LONG: In a sense that is right. They are not primarily script-based. But writers do play a part in the origination of Lumiere's work. It is very interesting because it is so varied. Writers play a far larger part in their shows than writers do with The People Show. May I be clear here. This is not meant as disparagement. It is just a different way of working.

REES: What about practice in rehearsal? Would you employ an actor used to the methods of mainstream theatre in The People Show?

LONG: I don't think so. We have had actors work with us and it has been quite satisfactory, but actors on the whole ask different kinds of questions about

33

work and rehearsal. They need specific motivation in terms of character. An actor's question would probably be 'Why?' A more typical People Show question would be 'How?'

REES: Was there a greater lack of understanding of your work by those involved in mainstream theatre than there is now?

LONG: Definitely. In those days there was actually quite a lot of resentment extended towards groups like ourselves by those in theatre. They actually did not like us. They found us slightly frightening, thought we were trying to undermine them or were making some comment about the way they worked. They were entirely wrong. Now there is a whole generation of actors – of my peers – who actually come very much from the group background in theatre. In a way the groups have replaced Reps haven't they?

REES: The personnel who started work in your area in the Sixties, who are now around the age of fifty, and have now percolated into larger companies, national companies, TV and film, have they carried shared work methods and aspirations with them? Have they influenced and changed the practice in the areas they now work in?

LONG: Very much so. Theatre is far healthier as a result of this interaction between our tradition and mainstream theatre. The move and the mix is important. Our generation has brought a lot to mainstream theatre, and it has benefited enormously. We are not talking just about actors but also writers, directors and the designers. If you look at what was being produced in the mainstream in 1966, it looks like it was a hundred years ago. Mainstream theatre has made enormous strides for the better in the last twenty five years. That is because of the growth of our movement and the work of people with our kind of background and influence.

REES: You see yourself as an artist, rather than a commodity to compete in a market place. There in the market place, you would neither be offered the work you yourself have pioneered or be able to achieve it in the manner you want to see it done?

LONG: Yes, I do see myself as an artist who requires and needs the structure of a small group as a means to achieve the work. But I would like it to be a larger group. It is small because of the finances. Quite often I would like to be working with a lot more people than I do.

REES: Stephen Rea said that in the days of Freehold they would rehearse until they had something to show the public. Now he has to work in the situation where the rehearsal period is financially proscribed, the design and the concept defined before the actors assemble for rehearsal. Stephen said of Peter Brook that if you can afford a great length of rehearsal, anyone can become a genius!

LONG: The People Show has never had limitless rehearsal. We have always had deadlines. Financial survival has always been part of our work. In the Eighties the use of the creative imagination has become more limited than it was in the past. And not only has it been more limited, but also audiences have not wanted to see creative imagination as much in the Eighties as they have in the past. Subsequently during the Eighties and the Nineties, The People Show have been going through a difficult period. The audiences are also not as receptive to our work as they were in the past. So it is not just the fact that actors have intentionally limited their imaginations or played a mainstream designer sort of game. It is what audiences have required and wanted from theatre and theatre does subconsciously respond to what people want, whatever people say. You saw far more imaginative theatre of The People Show kind in Europe during the Eighties than here in the UK. Especially from countries like Spain, eg *Els Commediants*, and from some of the Central European countries, where there has been an enormous political release. This in turn has generated a cultural explosion, and that explosion of work is comparable with what happened here in the Sixties.

REES: Perhaps these kind of cultural upsurges need such a political and social moment to bring them to the surface. Are the important issues to influence the development of theatre now to be found outside the UK, and even outside Europe?

LONG: That is something which this country has allowed to happen. Financial and artistic constraints in the Eighties have affected our ability to respond to that process and to broaden and change our direction. The risk of artistic failure is far greater now.

REES: When you talked about your time at College, you emphasised the importance of bringing different elements together, their equal fusion within a show. In the future what kind of different theatre will emerge?

LONG: We are talking about an art form – theatre – that is a magpie of all the arts, that can involve dance, music, the visual arts in a manner where language is not the dominant force, where theatre can be a collection of the aural and visual senses. I think that is where the future in international theatre lies now.

REES: But that type of theatre, which is now far more common, can, if those involved are not careful, lack a kick, a bite, the specifics of meaning, and may become about the abstraction of performance.

LONG: But that could be said of a scripted show.

REES: It can be easy to hide behind the kind of work you are describing.

LONG: That could be a criticism of The People Show.

REES: I don't think so. I have always understood your shows, known what's going on emotionally.

LONG: In our area of work, the danger of intellectual pretension is enormous. To be able to hide behind what is seemingly an abstraction is very easily done. To camouflage a paucity of ideas. I have seen many people fall into that trap.

REES: Being in a new Spain, a new Eastern Europe, is very specific. It is a fresh political situation conditioned by an emergence from a particular past. Internationality, as an approach to work, in comparison could lose sight of its earth, its origins, the specifics of why it exists.

LONG: I understand what you are saying. But the adventure of being able to work with artists of other countries and the cross-fertilisation of ideas between artists is very exciting. I am sure that is going to happen. Already it is happening more than ever before. In terms of the application of light and sound to production, The People Show has blown out a lot of boundaries within its financial constraints. We want to use technology. When you see the Canadian, Robert Lepage, it is wonderful to see a man working with large budgets, using large casts, really pushing technology further and further, and using it theatrically. I love watching all that. He uses different languages, he employs French and English and many different nationalities in his productions. In Edinburgh, he used Scottish performers and then came to the National with *Tectonic Plates*. Brilliant to see the Cottlesloe used as it should be and not as a one-ended theatre.

REES: People came into theatre in the Sixties, art students and musicians, because culturally that was where the energy was. But now that kind of person would not be attracted, not find that kind of opening in theatre?

LONG: People came from very different backgrounds into theatre. Before, there was a feeling that if you want to be an actor, you have to go to drama school. If you want to be a director you have to come out of university. In the Sixties, it was stated you did not have to. We opened it right out. A lot more people then thought this is something accessible, this is something I can do!

STEPHEN REA

Stephen Rea founded with Brian Friel, in 1980, the Field Day Theatre Company, acting in nearly all the company's productions. He has appeared in many Royal National Theatre productions such as *The Shaughraun*. His films include Neil Jordan's *Angel* and *Company of Wolves*. He played Kragler in Foco Novo's 1972 production of Brecht's *Drums In The Night*.

REES: When you started working in the theatre in the Sixties, did you think the work you did was breaking with the past?

REA: Initially, I didn't really break with the past. I started work in Dublin with the Abbey – what you would obviously describe as the most traditional area of Irish theatre – and like everything else you start where you can. Because it was the Irish National Theatre and all that aspect of nationality, to me it was interesting. When I came to London in 1967, and looked around at what there was there, what was available to me there, it became clear that in order to work, pragmatically, I had to break with emotions, with Ireland, and maybe do plays with the Royal Court, or the RSC or do *Z Cars* and it also became apparent that there was all that kind of energy around in London, like in the Arts Lab.

□ *The Arts Lab, a former warehouse in Drury Lane which the American, Jim Haynes, converted into a performance space, gallery and cinema in 1967. For a few years, the Arts Lab became London's first and perhaps only experimental and underground Arts Centre.*

REES: Did people in London who worked in the new theatre come from very varied backgrounds in comparison to those you came across at the Abbey?

REA: That was the wonderful thing about Freehold's production of *Antigone*, which we did at the Arts Lab. The whole question of being an Irish actor – 'Would you have to be an English actor to get work?' – was raised and answered by that production. Freehold had all kinds, from all backgrounds working together. Americans, English, and Irish. That was the point. Doing the play as best as possible. No question of what class you came from, or if you would have a socially homogenous company. It was international. That was the flavour of the Sixties.

REES: What drew you to working with Freehold?

REA: The aim certainly was to explore theatre in a physical non-naturalistic way, to find means of exploring texts not dependent on language-based practices. I don't know if you can do this. But we did it in a sense. I don't know if people do it anymore. It's kind of trying to blow open texts and, of course, what happened with the *Antigone* production, was that it worked enormously well because the physicality of it was what made it immediate and powerful. That was the American influence. No doubt about it.

REES: There was a lot of American influence on London theatre in the Sixties. Apart from Jim Haynes' Arts Lab. There was Marowitz's Open Space. Ed Berman's InterAction. All Americans.

REA: The main influence. And the influx of people who had worked with Ellen Stewart's Cafe La Mama Theatre in New York – Nancy Meckler and Beth

38

Porter. Freehold started as Warehouse La Mama. Nancy had to change the name because the original belonged to Beth. No question that it was an American movement and that was interesting, that was good. It happened in the situation in which the English actors respect for texts, a confidence in texts, was the background most actors had. But the Abbey School had very sporadic classes. I regarded my really serious training as the time with Nancy and Freehold. I do regard that as training. When I came to London, Jacky McGowran gave me a job, and he had been to mime school in Paris with LeCoq, which was his training, and he urged me to go and join Freehold. So he wrote me a letter of introduction. At that time, the Fringe was beginning to happen and I was doing Jacky's production at the Mermaid of O'Casey's *Shadow of a Gunman.*

REES: You used methods and techniques in rehearsal and performance with Freehold, which conventionally experienced actors would have baulked at?

REA: No question. They would have found it unnecessary and an intrusion upon their personal process of work. Instead, a certain group of actors, who were more radically minded, who were not thought technically equipped to be at the RSC, and so were not immediately employable in these areas, found their way into what was called the Fringe! And why not experiment in that situation? Throw things up in the air? The groups I worked with, apart from The People Show, were interested in doing plays, doing drama.

REES: Did this mean that people who would not perhaps ordinarily have been attracted to theatre, joined companies like Freehold?

REA: Very much in The People Show case. We did have people in Freehold – Hughie Portnow – who vanished from theatre after. But the nucleus of the company went onto mainstream theatre [*For example – Dinah Stabb, and the late Maurice Colbourne*]. Maybe Pip Simmons had people whose only theatre experience was working with his group.

REES: How did Freehold rehearsal methods differ in practice to those in mainstream theatre?

REA: For a start, young actors now are keen to do a physical and vocal limber up that actors in regular theatre in the Sixties would have dropped down dead at the thought of. As a result of our work, in the Seventies and after, it had become acceptable to do that. There was no philosophy of work in the Sixties at the Abbey. It used to have one, but it was lost. It had a colourful tradition but it was dying. I would imagine that was the case in most English theatre then.

REES: So you found a great difference between the mainstream and the Fringe in the Sixties? It was difficult to travel between the two?

REA: You couldn't. When I actually got a job at the Royal Court with Peter Gill and I was packing in work with Freehold and things, I was regarded as a kind of traitor. The journey between the Fringe and the Royal Court was quite a big journey. There was a big gulf. Now there is no gulf at all.

REES: So the Fringe developed into a preparatory school, training actors for work in the larger companies, TV and films?

REA: Yes. Now the Fringe is not a way of working. The Fringe now is a series of buildings above pubs and small theatre buildings. When we were working then, we were involved in a way of working. Freehold I would say, was the most vigorous of all the companies in that way.

REES: For instance, you used 'The Cat' exercise.

REA: The Cat came from Grotowski originally. We never took it as seriously as he did. It was a way of preparing the body, based on the movements of the cat, and a way of preparing concentration. Very physical. Americans took it very seriously but Europeans, especially Irish Europeans, were not as entirely po-faced about it as perhaps the Poles were! You know how serious Americans are about 'getting into character' and all that stuff. At their worst, Americans really distort the 'Method' because they take it so seriously. So I could never regard the Cat and our rehearsal methods in Freehold as a religious experience. I would not get so far into the Cat that it would immerse me, so that I did not know who I was. That was certainly one of the things we did. All the time, Nancy was bringing people in, like Emile Wolk, back from Paris, having studied mime there. He was doing workshops with us. Trying to expand our physical vocabulary. It was astonishing work and it was all down to Nancy, who had the vision to see that this way of working was new and different.

REES: How long did Freehold last?

REA: It was all gone by '71. A couple of years. Nancy went to have a baby and so the central figure was gone. We had done *Antigone*, perfectly suited to the way we worked. It was a play that could be expressed through physical methods. The political feeling of the time also ignited the play – Vietnam and Northern Ireland. We never found a play again that was as powerful and amenable to the way we worked.

REES: What were your influences then? Who were your heroes?

REA: I was naive. There was a German girl, Zeila Roks, who came into our company then and I remember her saying to me, you know because I was the outsider in England: 'You have come to London to find the new theatre?' And, of course, I hadn't. I had just come to work, having exhausted the possibilities that I saw in Dublin. The next step was London and if I exhausted London, there was America. So I don't know about heroes. For me I was just very involved in acting. My heroes would have been great writers and actors. One's heroes change all the time.

REES: Our heroes at that time were not always people associated with theatre?

REA: People were attracted by the way of life as well. Travelling around was attractive. It was not like an ordinary theatre group on the road. It was more hippy than that. There was a sense of personal style. You had long hair whether your character needed it or not. In that era, political figures were talking of liberation. It was a theatre movement in the sense that people were interested in current ideas, rather than achieving personal success.

REES: So the way people worked in theatre then was strongly connected with the way they wanted to live. One was intended to be an expression of the other. That attitude seems to have changed.

REA: Yes. But Field Day does express for me things about Ireland. I feel my work with Field Day has come full circle with that attitude to theatre.

REES: Foco Novo produced *Drums In The Night* by Bertolt Brecht in a new version of C. P. Taylor. I had directed this play for Freehold in the previous year. I was very keen to do it again to bring out the humour and to sharpen the political references with an adaptation, rather than a translation. This time, you played the main protagonist, Kragler. We produced it at the 1973 Edinburgh Festival and then at Hampstead. This was Foco Novo's second production.

It is a very early play of Brecht's. The second full length play he wrote after *Baal*. The political ideas we associate with him were not yet part of his dramaturgy. Did there seem good reason to produce Brecht in 1973? Or was it just another part, another play to you?

REA: Brecht was one of those writers talked about a lot but never performed. The reason I did it the second time was because I wanted to play the main part, Kragler, because I thought there was a way into it that had not happened the first time when we did it with Freehold. There was a way of being more clownish. Your Freehold production was surreal. Lots of effects. In the nightclub scene people were in strange groupings. It was like dance. No scenery. Just chairs and tables. The theatre of poverty.

☐ *The term 'Theatre of Poverty', much used at the time, was coined by the Polish director Grotowski. He provided the theoretical basis for much of the physical work so popular amongst American ensemble companies. Use your body physically and theatrically was the motto, instead of relying upon verbal means of communication.*

41

REES: Both productions attempted a surrealism but in different ways. After all, the period in which Brecht wrote *Drums*, at the end of World War I, was in Berlin the era of Surrealism and Dada. And I wished to bring that feeling into the productions.

REA: But the second one – the Foco Novo production – was more successful. There was a lusciousness about it. Colourful blinds that came down with paintings on them based on George Grosz cartoons. That was much more in keeping with how it should be done. The characters were very sharply drawn. Very comedic. You cast it from the market place of actors so you had more chance of success.

REES: The comedy had a lot to do with the inimitable touch of C. P. Taylor's writing. Had you seen Brecht productions before?

REA: No. I had read Brecht and found it difficult. I would still love to do Brecht again. I was interested in the politics, but *Drums* was not regarded as one of his political plays.

REES: At one point he excluded it from his canon of work for that reason.

   □ Drums in the Night *was about Kragler, a soldier, returning to post-war Berlin from Africa. There is revolution in the air. But he wants his girl. She is celebrating her engagement that very night with her new fiancee. Ejected by the father, from the celebrations, Kragler finds his way to the bars of the worker's districts. With schnapps inside him, he joins the march to the barricades. But at the last moment, his girl turns up and he has to make a choice. He chooses her.*

REA: I always thought *Drums* was quite political anyway. Kragler was so fucked, he could not make a political decision. The system had so destroyed him. Although it was meant to be a pre-political play, I thought what was important to Kragler was that he was mind-blown by the war, by the capitalist bourgeois system, to such an extent that he was not capable of making a decision. I thought that was quite political. It was an implicit theme of the play. Not an explicit message.

REES: You mention the 'lusciousness' of the Foco Novo production of *Drums*. Is the British approach to producing Brecht usually more austere and puritanical, say, than the German approach?

REA: I think so. The English approach is to miss the point really. That potential for lushness, which *Drums* had. I thought English National Opera's *Seven Deadly Sins* with the music, the family singing in four part harmony, was very sensuous. It was thrilling. Maybe everyone says English productions of Brecht are like that but I don't think so. It mostly does not work here. It is the wrong combination.

REES: Companies, such as Freehold consisted of permanent members. The play had to fit their needs, whereas with *Drums* I cast as required. In the Sixties and the Seventies, groups had a definite outlook to their work but this was also strongly formed by the composition of their personnel. The material needed to take account of who was in the company – age, sex, background. Age was confined to the 20's and early 30's. Companies exist now, touring companies, but you can barely think of one which keeps the same personnel from show to show.

REA: And are of the same age as you say. Part of that is commitment to a way of life and to each other. You would never have got older people travelling with us or Pip Simmons. I remember travelling to the Edinburgh Festival in the back of a transit van, on top of the luggage all the way from London to Edinburgh, and that is a long way by road. You did it.

REES: Pip Simmons used to think of his group like a rock 'n' roll band.

REA: Yes, they were very self-consciously that. We all identified with that. We were part of that musical era. That was the difference, the big, big difference really. I find a lot of the kids now in theatre can play a musical instrument. Previously actors over a certain age, they could just act. All kids now learn instruments because they know they have to do a lot of things. Much more interesting. I can still only mime an instrument!

REES: Foco Novo was a touring theatre company. Field Day is also. You must think bringing theatre to those who normally do not see live theatre, on their doorstep, an enormously important function for theatre to perform?

REA: The prime function. When you go into someone's town and set up in their local hall or theatre, that situation is completely different to what happens when they get into a car and drive to Dublin or Belfast. The fact that they have to make a journey, makes that audience look at the performance in a different way. It is not part of them. They do not see the questions raised in the show as being as relevant. All I know is that the chemistry is very different when you go, with the kind of show we bring, to their town.

I remember sitting with an actor, working with Field Day, in a no-horse town, in County Derry and that actor said: 'What are we doing here? What is the point?' And when the show was over, he knew, because the audience was hanging from the rafters. Their response was intense. That does not happen in the same way in mainstream theatre. Pre-conditioning happens every time, they, the audience get in a car and drive. Something is gone, their taste buds are dead, blunted.

For me touring theatre is the sharp edge of theatre. I've been doing it for ten years with Field Day – I know that's what you must do. Ian McKellen agrees with that. If you go to some ivory tower downtown, what does it mean? But if somebody 'comes to a local town and the set doesn't fit properly and all that, there is a spirit to what you are doing, and they know you have come because you want to make contact with them.

REES: What kind of administrative structure does Field Day have? Foco Novo had a Board of Directors, many of whom had worked for the company in different capacities, particularly writers – Howard Brenton, Tunde Ikoli, Nigel Williams, Mustapha Matura. There was a full-time artistic Director and Administrator. All the other people – writer, actors, designer, stage management, were hired for the specific show.

REA: That is more or less the structure we have. Our Board is made up of poets, people like that. Up to the last couple of years, the work was done by me and Brian Friel. Tom Kilroy has joined the Board in the last two years. He is now very actively involved. That's the way it happens and I think the right way. I would love to have a permanent company but the best way ideally is to cast each play. It's getting harder and harder. People are less inclined to tour. Money is getting tight. They can earn more money with less expenditure in big companies.

REES: The theatre which started in the Sixties, which we helped create, made a definite impact by emphasising the importance of new work and new plays. The personnel, who were influential in developing this work, are now reaching the age of fifty. Some have gravitated to the most influential positions in UK theatre. Have in any way these original aspirations travelled with them?

REA: They do not exist in a vacuum. Those people, who you have not named, their situations, which they have to administer, have demands and those demands might not be compatible with such aspirations. They do not have time to spend experimenting with a text and then deciding how they will design it. If you are working at the National Theatre, you arrive with a completed set of designs. The concept of the thing has happened. In the director's and designer's head. Freehold was about making it happen in the group. The demands of a large theatre make it impossible for those aspirations to travel.

REES: For instance, we wanted to change the conception of hierarchy in the rehearsal room. People did have their specialisations, such as being the director, actors had their parts, maybe a small part, but there was an attitude and openness to receiving opinions whatever position you held. Have people been able to take with them, some of this attitude to work when they are in larger companies? Or has that experience been lost in the past?

REA: I don't know if it has all gone with them but something has filtered through. Like I say, the kids all do physical warm-ups before rehearsal.

REES: Do you find in Field Day, when you are in rehearsal, that actors can accept different opinions about their role in a text or do they remain in the old ways of –'You must not talk about that. That is someone else's part'?

REA: You still have to create that atmosphere. It has to be worked at. It is not just there, as a given. Discussion has to be opened up. There is still that defensiveness. I still find there is a defensiveness in a lot of actors, where there should not be, because they have no direct experience of working like that. They have not been touched by it. My feeling is that it only remains with the people who experienced it. They find it for themselves, not from us.

I have been working with the mainstream for fourteen years. Whatever Field Day's attitude is, we operate in a mainstream way. Although this year, we did not design the show until the end of the first week of rehearsal. That was wonderful. Brinkmanship. Basically, the demands of a five week rehearsal process make you make decisions early. We worked for no money in the Sixties. We did not do anything until we had something to show. There was less pressure. That was an incredible luxury, which we paid for ourselves. I don't think anyone is doing that anymore. That's what I regard as a terrible indictment. I would like to see more of that, more of the workshop periods.

REES: You don't mean people doing new plays above pubs, as you mentioned earlier, hoping for a split of the box office at the end?

REA: That is a showcase, to move on for career purposes. Like New York, they had showcase theatre and then someone said, there is a whole way of working to be had out of that. So Cafe La Mama started. It happened the other way round here. We started with experiment and now it has degenerated into showcase theatre on top of pubs. An animated version of Spotlight.'Go along and pick them!' It is not about an approach to work. When we, in the Sixties, worked, it was only about that, otherwise we would all have gone and made money somewhere else. I got drawn into that almost by accident. But it became what I was there for. I think that's gone, that attitude. Obviously Brook does it.

REES: With unlimited resources.

REA: I actually think that if you can rehearse for 9 months anyone can be a genius. If we could have taken Heaney's text of *Philoctetes*, reached a certain point in rehearsal and said that's pretty good and then said we are not going to do it that way, we are going to do a different production. We are going to throw our first version away and do something else. If you are able to put a play through several processes, you would be bound to come up with something astonishing, something unrecognisable from what you started with. But if you go on after four weeks, you have to cut short discussion and say about an individual's input: 'That is all very interesting, but we are going to do it this way.' I am not being disparaging of Brook, but we cannot afford long rehearsals. If the business of being able to have long and endless rehearsals is happening in the UK, tell me. But I don't think it is.

REES: We have not mentioned the policy adopted by companies of paying each company member, regardless of their part or age, the same wage. It was a feature of this kind of work. This principle is different to subsidised building based companies and it is, of course, antipathetic to commercial management.

REA: Absolutely. Take Field Day. Because we cast from a wide range of actors and cast older actors, I always feel an actor with three children deserves more money than a twenty year old actor. By any standards, they deserve more money. Not paying everyone the same wage, not observing the equality of democracy, that is not the real sufferer. It is the approach to the work that suffers.

It is the fact that you have to define the work before you start rehearsal. That is crippling beyond belief. I don't actually like spending months in a workshop situation. I find it very frustrating, and I was difficult with Nancy in Freehold about this, because I wanted to get on and perform. But I also know we are cutting ourselves off from the real world by not being able to afford enough time to prepare and rehearse.

DAVID AUKIN
BERNARD POMERANCE

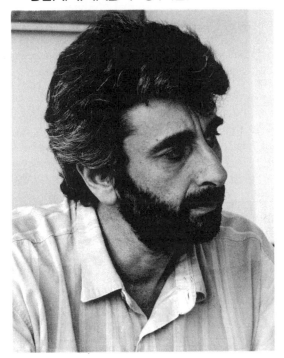

David Aukin

David Aukin and Bernard Pomerance, along with Roland Rees, founded the Foco Novo company in 1972, initially to produce Pomerance's play, *Foco Novo*.

David Aukin was Director of the Hampstead Theatre Club and the Haymarket Theatre, Leicester. A former Executive Director of the Royal National National Theatre, he was appointed Head of Drama for Channel 4 in 1990.

Bernard Pomerance, poet and playwright, is the author of *The Elephant Man*, first produced and directed by Roland Rees for Foco Novo and, subsequently, for the Royal National Theatre. The play was also produced on Broadway. Pomerance's play, *Melons*, was presented by the Royal Shakespeare Company.

47

REES: What first made a serious impact on you in theatre?

POMERANCE: O'Neill. I saw the original production of *Long Day's Journey into Night* in New York in the Fifties. In the Sixties I saw the production of *The Iceman Cometh*, also at the Circle in the Square Theatre, Greenwich Village. But the production which knocked me out was the New York production of John Arden's *Sergeant Musgrave's Dance*.

AUKIN: The first serious impact on me were two performances, which I saw on successive nights at the Old Vic in 1956 – the Berliner Ensemble doing *Arturo Ui* and *Coriolanus* by Bertolt Brecht. To this day I cannot believe that Ekkehard Schall played both lead parts. The whole thing was extraordinary. That was the sort of theatre I was so lucky to be exposed to. It was not that it was intellectual, it was so exciting.

REES: What was your first *professional* contact? Did you do much theatre at Oxford, for example?

AUKIN: A lot of acting with OUDS [*Oxford University Dramatic Society*]. I played Malvolio and so on.

REES: You came to the University College of Wales, Aberystwyth in 1961 where I was a student, for a Drama Festival with a show about the American West.

AUKIN: It was the only time I directed. A role reversal. All the directors of OUDS acted in that production, and I was chosen to direct it as an actor. That's where I learnt I did not want to be a director. A more boring job I could not imagine existed! When I left Oxford, I had an offer to go to the RSC, or finish my legal qualifications. Those were the days when you could go straight from University to be a spear carrier at Stratford. I had to make the decision. I succumbed to parental pressure and finished my articles. I qualified, and practised as a lawyer and, when my father retired, I did too. I was 25.

REES: Bernard, you came to the UK in 1968 and it was here that your first play was professionally produced.

POMERANCE: Sally [*Sally Belfrage, writer*], to whom I was then married, met Veronica Rudman at a children's playgroup. It was suggested I show my play to Michael Rudman. It was my first play. That was 1969. Michael read it, and said he wanted to show it to 'my producer friend, David Aukin.' He told me David was married to 'a director who runs a Fringe group, Freehold.' The play sat on David's desk and, one day, his wife Nancy

Meckler, looked down at the title page and said: 'There cannot be two Bernard Pomerances. I think it *must* be the one I went to High School with!' Then David directed me towards you at InterAction, if you call five pounds a week an introduction!

☐ *InterAction: A social and cultural community organisation based in Chalk Farm, created by Ed Berman, of which the Ambiance Lunchtime Theatre seasons were a successful part.*

REES: David, at that time you had a connection with a number of Fringe groups acting as Administrator or Producer. Mark Long of The People Show says you were known as the 'King of the Fringe' after you brought together so many of the original groups for the *Christmas at the Cockpit* Fringe season in 1970. [*The Cockpit Theatre off Lisson Grove, NW8*]. The original inspiration for the season was a play for older children by Pam Gems, *Betty's Wonderful Christmas,* which I wanted to direct, and which her husband, Keith, was prepared to invest in. I came to you with the project, and suddenly a whole fortnight of exciting new theatre was spawned, including Pam Gems's first play. What groups and what relationships?

AUKIN: I couldn't name them all now. My degree of involvement with each group varied. The house where we lived in St. John's wood had this basement which I used as an office. If I was going to look after one group, I could look after many, since I was only peripherally involved with some. Others more intimately, where I was involved in the development of their artistics policy, as well as the booking of their tours. It was groups like Nancy Meckler's Freehold. Foco Novo, of course, later, Pip Simmons, Berkoff and, in particular, The People Show. Then I got involved in bringing over Jerome Savary's Grand Magic Circus from France [*a surreal and magical pantomime and circus show*] and Joe Chaikin's Open Theatre from New York [*leading American experimental theatre group*] to play at the Roundhouse.

☐ *The Roundhouse: Formerly a British Rail engine shed in Chalk Farm which became a home for contemporary music, theatre, happenings and events of all kinds in the Seventies. Including the Living Theatre's London appearances, Jim Morrison's last concert, Ariane Mnouchkine's Theatre du Soleil.*

REES: Bernard, your first play to be produced was *Hot Damn, High in Vietnam,* which I directed for InterAction at the Almost Free Theatre.

☐ *Almost Free Theatre: One of the earliest London Fringe venues which has now disappeared amidst the massive redevelopment around Piccadilly Circus. In its time it was one of the best small theatres in London. It belonged to the International Language Centre.*

The play was composed of three short pieces lasting an hour, perfect for a lunchtime season. Two GI's, Hunk and Stamper, are guarding an ammo dump somewhere in Vietnam. Happily stoned, they help two Vietcong to work their bazooka and blow up the dump. The latter play saw our GI's at home with Hunk's parents celebrating Thanksgiving. Now turned freelance explosives experts for urban guerilla groups, they were on their way in 1968 on a mission to Detroit. After they depart, we learn that Hunk's parents have been complicit with the police in monitoring their son's activities.

POMERANCE: I remember the plays very clearly and how they got on. I had never been in a rehearsal process before, and I was very taken with Richard Pendrey, an American actor. He was extraordinary. Then he got lost to the theatre.

☐ *Pendrey studied at RADA and, the story goes, one day left his girlfriend's house in Fulham for a packet of cigarettes, never to return. Some years later Pomerance got into a cab in New York and saw that the cabbie was Pendrey. He had left the business. It was a great loss.*

The plays were about what was happening in America then. There was a generational division of such murderous nature, and also I felt the soldiers in Vietnam were kids who were always being seen as monsters, but they weren't. They were just trying to get out alive.

REES: This was a time when there were a lot of Americans in London, and many worked in and influenced theatre here. You came in 1968. Did you come for similar reasons to other Americans? Many came to avoid the Vietnam war and its domestic repercussions.

POMERANCE: I realised there was a point where we found it real tough going in New York. We thought we would try six months in London. My wife's parent's were natives of the UK. When we reached here it was so congenial and relaxed in comparison to the US. In comparison to a growing fraudulence and hysteria going on in America. So we stayed.

REES: David, was this kind of theatre of the late Sixties and early Seventies – its aspirations, its work methods and forms of production – particular to that era, and different to what happened before and what followed?

AUKIN: Yes. There was a real feeling that there was a West End, and I include the National and the RSC in that. There there was this alternative, and it was completely different. Nothing like you would see in the conventional theatre. All of the Fringe was run by Americans.

POMERANCE: There was also a sense of a lot of talent around. People did talk about each other's work. There was a genuine colleagiality of feeling.

AUKIN: There was a lot of energy. There is always an energy that wanders around and hits different art forms at different times. At times it hits dance and at times it alights on alternative comedy – and lasts for three months! That time it hit theatre. The other absolutely crucial element was *Time Out*. It was the cement that connected us together and told us what was going on.

REES: Much of this was down to the pioneering work of the then Theatre Editor of *Time Out*, John Ashford. [*Now Director of The Place Theatre, London. See also separate interview with John Ashford*]

AUKIN: The magazine had a definite policy. It was not a critical magazine. That was not its function. Its function was to network, what was happening where, and describe what the work was about. Never with value judgements. We are talking of thirty people turning up for a performance, and that was a full house! The buzz was terrific.

POMERANCE: Another factor. There was no movie industry to skim off talent after it emerged. So it was recycled into theatre. You got a compost effect. You did get a thickening of things. You did get years available for a certain amount of development, because people were not disappearing into TV and films.

AUKIN: The other important factor was the lack of serious subsidy.

POMERANCE: Nobody was doing it for money.

AUKIN: People did it because they wanted to do it. They lived on the dole and that's how they survived. There were no Arts Council cheques coming in. It was the development of the Arts Council that destroyed all this!!

REES: What particular characteristics emerged from that theatre? Could you pinpoint these for people who have not experienced those times.

POMERANCE: It was fun. A sense of fun and skill coming together. Originality. What's gone today for sure is the fun. Nobody, even people with money available for production, appears to be having the spirited time we were having.

REES: Is that your age talking?

AUKIN: 'course it is.

POMERANCE: No, I don't think so. I'm only 85 anyway!

AUKIN: We forget how circumscribed our lives had been prior to 1968. All sorts of things we now quite readily take for granted.

REES: You mean the Censor?

AUKIN: Not just officially, but in morals and all sorts of things. I watch films now that were not allowed to be shown twenty years ago, and you cannot work out why – why they were banned. You can no longer understand the reason. That generation, that period made an enormous breakthrough in what is permissable, and what is not permissable in our society. Today we take all that for granted. And that was very exciting.

REES: There was an emphasis on new approaches to work and new writing. Neither had been emphasised so clearly before. Also a *style* of work. Productions took place that were more physical, and in spaces not known previously as theatre performing areas. Like Welfare State in the open, Freehold at the Arts Lab, and Foco Novo in a garage in Gospel Oak. Playwrights, if there was a playwright, got rid of the play set in a room. They got us outside onto the street and into public places, and they ripped the usual dramaturgy apart. Bernard, earlier you mentioned two productions of plays by O'Neill which influenced you. But didn't they come from a very different tradition?

AUKIN: The long boring tradition!

POMERANCE: When I think of the single high point of that period, I think of The People Show. If I had to pick out a single person who was a genius, I would pick out Mark Long. The People Show pioneered forms of communication, theatrical forms, that were absolutely extraordinary and which no writer could duplicate, and yet which many writers learnt from.

   □ *In the interview with Mark Long, the approach of The People Show is discussed. Long refers to the fusion of music, dance and the visual arts that became a hallmark of The People Show productions.*

REES: David, do you think the practitioners of that time, who moved into more mainstream areas, maintained the aspirations and energy of which you talked? Did they influence the mainstream with their new methods and the kind of work they chose to produce?

AUKIN: Of course it had an impact. Clearly, directors like Trevor Nunn were very influenced by that work and went on and used those techniques. Productions of Shakespeare changed. Dear old Peter Brook, probably a greater genius than any of the people we have been talking about in terms of putting on a show – his work continues to contribute to this tradition. That special sort of energy did leave the theatre. It will come back again. That's why I find theatre slightly boring these days. There used to be a sense of danger. You were not quite sure what would happen.

POMERANCE: There was no pre-selection of subject matter by audience taste. You could see a play about almost anything. In fact, you usually did. There was incredible liberation of acting and directing techniques, and important external influences, such as the Open Theatre, Grotowski, Brook. There was the kind of energy released from a total overhaul of what theatre might do, might be. I reckon that, in retrospect, a lot was mistaken in its formulations at that time. Yet, what is undeniable is that energy *was* released in the Sixties. Freehold, InterAction, The People Show, Portable Theatre.

AUKIN: Joint Stock.

POMERANCE: They didn't ask first what the audience might enjoy. If they decided to do the story of what the Chinese Revolution [Fanshen *by David Hare*] meant in a rural village, they went ahead and did it.

AUKIN: All art forms play with the form itself. Theatre had been hidebound within the proscenium arch for, it seemed, forever, and this was the first attempt to break away from it.

POMERANCE: One thing begins to feed off another. You go to see something and say: 'I would like to use that in my next work.'

AUKIN: I have gone full circle. I now feel the proscenium arch is the best form of theatre. It's what goes on inside it I object to!

REES: Foco Novo produced shows for audiences who had never seen this sort of work before, and who were nothing to do with theatre. Now, those types of shows are done for the theatregoing community. Bernard, your play, *Foco Novo*, which we produced in 1972, gave the company its name. At InterAction, actors were on a profit share and we determined, with this our first production, to take a different course.

POMERANCE: We determined to pay Equity minimum. We were committed to that.

AUKIN: That was our first mistake!

REES: The minimum weekly wage had just gone up from twelve pounds a week to twenty pounds. Paying people meant we had to employ people.

AUKIN: We just got some notepaper.

POMERANCE: There was a bursary from the Arts Council for the production of the play.

REES: For you, the writer.

☐ *Royalty Supplement Guarantee, intended to make up the shortfall on authors' royalties, due to expected small box office takings. It was common practice, with the author's co-operation, to treat the grant as part of the production budget when no other funds were available.*

POMERANCE: Well, it seems to have gone into the production. In any event, it required us to form a company to receive and dispense the money. We were playing at the Roxy.

☐ *The Roxy: A large garage in Kingsford Street, NW5, converted into a theatre performing space, favoured by groups at that time. It became for a while the Headquarters of Bubble Theatre.*

My sharpest memory of *Foco Novo* is when the lighting board broke down. Nigel Morris, the percussionist, said he had an electrician friend called Jock – naturally, a Scot – who could rig it up in an emergency. It was just before opening. Jock came in and rigged it up, and I sat next to him during the performance. I watched him intently. I reckon he was in his thirties. The play was concerned with the converging destinies of an American adviser, based on Dan Mitrione, who was killed in Uruguay by the Tupameros, and Carlos Lamarca, a Brazilian army captain, who led an urban guerilla group against the dictatorship of Brazil, and who was killed in 1971. The play was about the meaning of sacrifice under the conditions of the kind of colonialism which the American presence in Brazil represented.

☐ *The film*, State of Siege, *was made by Costas Gavras a few years later, based on the Mitrione story.*

Jock sat watching all this intently. Afterwards, while we were having a few drinks, he came up to me and said: 'Did you write it? I've got to tell you my life story. You have got to write it. You are the only one who can write it – understand it.' I could not imagine what he had to do with Brazil, with torturers, multi-nationals and international banks meddling in Third World politics. I couldn't imagine! Of course, there was nothing *to* imagine because that was not what he saw. He saw something about *his* life in this curve of sacrifice, defeat and rebirth. That taught me something about theatre which I had never experienced before at first hand. It was not as if it was a wonderfully crafted play. It was swift, with a lot crudity to it.

REES: Crudity can be a very engaging quality. It was part of the aesthetic at that time. That's why we chose to perform the play away from a theatre in a large garage and forecourt. Perhaps that rawness also attracted Jock?

POMERANCE: We performed the play both inside and outside the Roxy. Outdoors represented certain scenes – the public ones, like the police searches, for which we used the corrugated roofs above the audience – and inside, with the doors closed, for the scenes set within an interior – the torture scenes, for instance. Roughly speaking, it was an epic structure. We had a hell of a time casting it. Tom Kempinski, who was to play the lead – Lamarca, the guerilla leader – left us a few days before we started rehearsal.

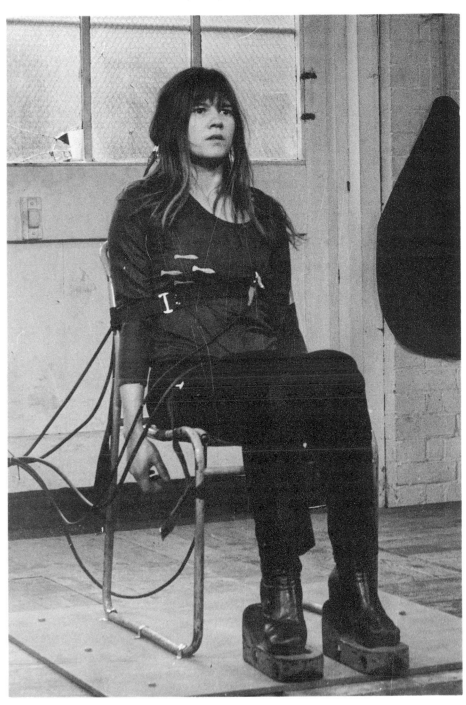

Judy Monahan in Foco Novo's 1972 production of Bernard Pomerance's *Foco Novo*.

REES: We cast both black and white actors.

POMERANCE: It was the first open casting, I believe – 1972 – with Mona Hammond and Oscar James. The title, *Foco Novo*, is derived from Foco, a theory of Guerilla warfare, long since discredited, but current at the time, of really vaccinating a situation with a cadre of fighters who gathered support locally as they fought, and so expanded their sphere of influence. It was based on the Cuban model – Che Guevara. Novo just means 'new.'

REES: It's Portuguese – the story taking place in Brazil, the only Portuguese speaking South American country. The title means a new starting point, a new focus, which seemed to me an excellent title for the kind of plays the Foco Noco Company should produce.

David, you were a Board member until the early Eighties, and you, Bernard, until 1977. The Company first worked from the basement of David's house, and later from an office at Nugent Terrace, St. John's Wood. We debated whether it would remain as it was – a production company – or whether it would become a collective – whether we should keep a permanent company of actors, or cast to the needs of each play. The kind of discussion common to many theatre companies at that time.

AUKIN: Sure, I remember them, but I don't know how important they were. In fact, I think they were unimportant. They were a smokescreen for the most important issue of what the focus of the Company should be. It was searching for another focus. And that's not a bad thing. It had to evolve, and it was searching. If you, Roland, had come in and said, 'this is what I am going to do next,' we would all have gone along with it. They were like the discussions that went on at the Comedie Francaise in 1968.

☐ *Paris, 1968: The Comedie Francaise was occupied and became a centre of discussion about art and politics.*

I'm not belittling those times. They were important then. But they disguised the fact that we were changing direction. I have always felt about Fringe companies generally that they do not know when to stop. That there is a certain energy which lasts for a certain time, and without any loss of face they should stop. When the next energy happens you move along with that. Somewhere, Foco Novo got cautious and worried about the impact of what closing down might mean.

REES: We did not talk of closing down. On the contrary, we had started Foco Novo in 1972. These discussions too place in 1975/76, not long after we had started. Considering that only two shows could be produced each year, we were only eight shows old. Indeed, we had only just received our first Arts Council subsidy. Funny to think of closing down at such a time! Some of us wondered then whether some large institutional theatres might not have had *their* day and should close down.

AUKIN: We didn't talk of closing down, but perhaps we should have. That was the agenda which was not being discussed.

REES: I'm glad it wasn't, since we continued producing plays for another twelve years until 1988. And the period covering the production of *The Elephant Man* by Bernard, and *The Seventh Man* by Adrian Mitchell [*based on the John Berger book of the same title*] up to 1988, with our last production, *Savannah Bay*, by Marguerite Duras, was the most productive period in the Company's existence. By this time there were a number of different Board members.

POMERANCE: It was a very instinctual company in the beginning. Then ideas came to be dominant at a certain point and things changed. Of course, the meetings had to deal with the question: 'Which ideas do we want to be dealing with?' As the composition of the Board changed, so the company changed. You, Roland, had a visceral reaction in the beginning to anything you did – Mustapha Matura's plays, my plays, the Ed Bullins plays. It was a gut reaction. You always put your feelings on the line. Once a certain level of self-consciousness entered into the work, which went along with the Arts Council funding, the instinctual quality – I'm not going to say it disappeared completely – got downgraded. Particularly, I am thinking of the shows with the two Johns.

☐ *John Chadwick and John Hoyland who wrote two shows specially for touring mining areas in 1975/76* – Nine Days and Saltley Gates *and* Tighten Your Belt. *See* Politics and Experiment.

REES: The plays we toured through the Labour Movement promoted the discussions. The company responded to questions raised by the work but, at the end of the day, we decided to remain as we had started – a production company with an Artistic Director, commissioning work along lines that interested us. As with yourself, Bernard, with your version of Brecht's *Man is Man,* and with the plays the two Johns wrote for the Labour Movement. We remained as we had begun. As a company, we were funded to produce new work and to tour to new audiences who would not normally expect to see this kind of work. That was another important debate we had – to which audiences should we tour? Arts Centre audiences, Labour Movement audiences, theatre audiences? Was the same sort of show appropriate for each audience?

POMERANCE: The touring issue became very important. This was marginal at first, but it began to occupy more and more the centre of attention. It also decreased the instinctual aspects within the company which represented their best work.

AUKIN: That's why I believe the Arts Council destroyed this type of work. They imposed a sort of bureaucracy on it!

REES: We were funded for specific objectives – new work and touring. That was the bargain. But you are right. If we had just been funded without the condition of touring, we might have taken a different course. But then many audiences around the country would never have seen, for instance, *The Elephant Man.* That kind of touring is a special kind of work and reached people who in other circumstances, in Wales, Scotland, Manchester, or wherever, would never have experienced it. Touring is, as Stephen Rea says: 'The cutting edge of theatre.' [*See interview with Stephen Rea*]

Anyway, Bernard, it was these discussions that led you in 1977 to resign from the Foco Novo Board with that one note, which I still possess: 'We cannot go on meeting like this.'

To turn to other plays of yours, produced by Foco Novo, your version of Brecht's *Man is Man.*

POMERANCE: With *Man is Man* it was like demolishing a house, except for the facade. I completely rebuilt the inside. I thought the original dated, and to do any work on the cavortings of a Western army in Asia, you had to come to terms with what we knew now about such things – Vietnam.

☐ *The story centres on the English Army in India. A local porter, Galy Gay, is co-opted onto a machine gun unit and given a new name. Attracted by his new position and unable to say 'no', Galy becomes a British 'Tommy' and departs by train with the Army, bound for the Tibetan frontier.*

Brecht was writing about a colonial situation, using a background for it which in 1975 had to be treated on an equal basis with the theme of malleability of the individual. You could not ignore that. The theme you proposed was one which had characterised both *Foco Novo* and *Hot Damn, High in Vietnam,* the story of a soldier turning against the order he has sworn to uphold, and so breaks it – although the meaning of it in *Man is Man* is not so much tragic as affirmative – turning Brecht on his head. The individual is so definitely malleable that he might reach the point of changing himself in ways that were not predictable, and in the process would also inevitably destroy his origins.

REES: Talking of origins, we again used a Black actor, Stefan Kalipha, for the part of Galy Gay. Indeed, we cast him before you started work on your version, and it was with him in mind you wrote the part. This was Foco Novo's second Brecht adaptation, coming after C. P. Taylor's version of *Drums in the Night.* In hindsight, did this idea of adapting Brecht's early plays make sense at that time?

Photo © John Haynes 1975

Left to Right. Alan Hulse, Terry Jackson, Peter Marinker and John Salthouse in Foco Novo's 1975 production of Bernard Pomerance's adaptation of Bertolt Brecht's *A Man's a Man*.

POMERANCE: Adaptation is a basic theatre tradition. Dramatists have always been doing it, from the Greeks onward. Brecht was a mountain you had to climb, at least to see what the view looked like. I don't think Brecht was ultimately as useful as people, myself included, thought he was. In fact, he became a succubus for certain writers and destroyed their natural talent. But it was like a college you went to, where you studied approaches which had not been tried out in English-speaking theatre.

REES: Turning to *The Elephant Man*. It was first produced by Foco Novo, and directed by myself, in 1977 on tour and then at Hampstead. As a result of this production it was produced on Broadway, becoming the longest running straight play Broadway has known. Then it was remounted here at the National Theatre in 1980, again directed by myself and with some of the original cast, including David Schofield playing Merrick and Jenny Stoller playing Mrs Kendal. The film had nothing whatsoever to do with your play despite the fact that it claimed it was: 'The true history of The Elephant Man.'. By 1977 you had left the Company and had offered the play to number of people before I read it. How did Foco Novo come to do the play? What were the problems other directors and theatres had encountered that they did not originally produce it?

POMERANCE: This was a case where the instinctual quality of Foco Novo's work came back. It was a play which you were passionate about when you read it.

REES: I read the play on a 159 bus travelling from Piccadilly Circus to St John's Wood and made the decision on that bus.

POMERANCE: That's what I mean by the instinctual quality. You went right for it. At that point I felt certain things had happened in theatre. One: the focus of Fringe Theatre had moved away from the areas I still wanted to work in. Two: no longer was international subject matter of much interest. The focus was increasingly British. And also the touring format and funding problems were debilitating. I felt I should try and work in another way, elsewhere. I offered it first to Neil Johnston, who had been in the play *Foco Novo*, and to Nancy Meckler. Neil was unable to find a theatre which would take it. Dusty Hughes at the Bush [*Playwright, and at that time Artistic Director of the Bush Theatre*] said: 'We have put it eighth on our list of seven plays for the next season. So if one falls out....' The resistance was stupendous. I first called the play *Deformed*. A title designed to keep people away in droves!

REES: When Foco Novo first started selling the play that title still remained. One theatre had already gone into print and so it played as *Deformed* in Derby! Nigel Stannard at the Gulbenkian Theatre, University of Sussex, said that over his dead body would we come into his theatre with a play called *Deformed*. The natural title became *The Elephant Man*.

POMERANCE: There was a lot of natural fear that it would be exploitative, manipulative of audience impulses. It was only when Foco Novo took it up that somebody could say, yes, we would like to take the production.

REES: What were the dramaturgical problems that caused people to wonder if the play could be performed?

POMERANCE: Basically my original commitment was to see the play done without make-up for Merrick's deformations.

□ *Merrick suffered not only from considerable osseous deformities, in particular the large size of his head, but his body was covered with growths likened to cauliflower and he stank terribly from neglect..*

I had in my mind an abstraction, that the actor should represent Merrick with slight bits of changes of voice and body. I had no idea what this might mean. I was as knocked out as anyone else when I saw what you had evolved in rehearsals with David Schofield. I was away in Portugal until the final run through. The translation into reality was absolutely extraordinary.

AUKIN: To put the record straight when Michael Rudman [*Then Artistic Director, Hampstead Theatre*] read the play, he did not hesitate to take Foco Novo and offer a co-production.

POMERANCE: In 1975, when I talked to Michael about the idea, he said: 'I'm not having that freak in my theatre.' When he read the play in 1977, he did not hesitate.

AUKIN: You and Roland were the two most obstinate people we ever worked with at Hampstead. Absolutely resistant. Apart from the odd cut here and there. The two things we insisted on was an interval and the change of title. It felt to you both like a compromise. You were artists and were dragged screaming and kicking into a realm of commercial theatre. It is no surprise that the play ended up on Broadway. Extraordinary. After that Hampstead run, I sent the play to every theatre and producer in the US, with the wonderful notices from London. I barely got replies, let alone rejections. I would meet people years later to whom I said: 'Do you remember me sending you the script?' And they would absolutely deny I had sent them it!

REES: Then why did Richmond Crinkley, the eventual New York producer of the play, bite?

AUKIN: It was a vanity production!

POMERANCE: Philip Anglim, who played Merrick on Broadway first, before Bowie, apparently came to see the play at Hampstead.

REES: A number of times?

POMERANCE: I only know about the once. He had gone, to ANTA [*American National Theatre Association*] to raise the money for a New York production, as a result of seeing the Foco Novo production. That's why Richmond Crinkley took an option. Otherwise nobody would have touched it.

REES: When I saw the show in New York, it contained a number of production values similar to the Foco Novo production, including elements of David Schofield's performance.

POMERANCE: If the point you are making is that Philip Anglim took David Schofield's performance as a model, I think it is fair comment. But, over the course of the time Anglim was in the play, he made it his own. And of course that seminal performance has been all over the world now.

REES: I was also meaning the transformation scene during Treves' lecture. In which Merrick alters from a strong male, body beautiful into an imaginative indication of the deformed physique, we have observed from the slides, illustrating the lecture, taken of the real Merrick in the 1880's. How to achieve this transformation was not indicated in the original script. We were going into uncharted territory. Now that moment – the transformation – as you just said, has become part of productions throughout the world.

☐ *Treves was the surgeon who took pity on Merrick and placed him in the care of the London Hospital.*

The slides of Merrick, which took patient months of wheedling out of the very reluctant Curator of the London Hospital museum, became available for every production. The use of the Cello playing Bach – your choice of music because you had been listening to Bach whilst writing the play. So elements we created transferred across the Atlantic and became part of subsequent *Elephant Man* productions.

AUKIN: That's the very nature of theatre. The first production in many ways defines the play. One wonders what Wesker's plays were like before Dexter got his hands on them. It was the chemistry between Dexter and Wesker which created those very successful plays. One thing I would vouch for is how I felt the play was different in New York because of the response of the American audience. It startled me to realise what an 'American' play *The Elephant Man* really is.

POMERANCE: Do you think so? I never thought of it like that.

REES: It was a more naturalistic production on Broadway in design, detail etc. Things got included that we excluded since to us the text did not require them.

POMERANCE: You have to work with actors in America whose essential direction in life is towards film and towards naturalistic acting.

AUKIN: It was being performed in a huge theatre in New York in comparison to a small theatre in Hampstead. The scale was different. Clearly that imposes conditions.

POMERANCE: There was a big fight over who should direct the play in New York. I felt you should direct and had this written into my contract. They just stonewalled to the point where there would be no production for reasons that never made sense.

AUKIN: I never understood. It was very cruel why they should have vetoed Roland.

POMERANCE: There became an increasing desire to deny the origin of the play. The folk wisdom of the time said no English director can make a British production work for New York.

AUKIN: *Amadeus* somewhat disproved that, and a number of other shows.

REES: In 1980/81, the play went to the National with three of the original cast of seven, although the cast for the Lyttleton was twenty plus, and with the same original designer and director. Was it different? Did the fleshing out make a difference?

POMERANCE: I think the requirements of the Lyttleton detracted from the focus that the original production had. I also think the notoriety of the play had detracted from the freshness we had in 1977, where people had the most extraordinary reactions. On the other hand, during the last performance, watching David Schofield and Nicky Henson, I thought they were like great musicians playing together. Extraordinary.

REES: Have the companies which emerged in the Eighties followed a different route to those which started in the Sixties and Seventies or have they followed on the tradition which was already in place?

AUKIN: They would not be doing what they are without what happened before. But I am surprised at what they picked up on. I think the way people like Declan Donnellan, Nicholas Hytner, and Deborah Warner work is very clearly a hand on the tradition of the Seventies but they picked on slightly different things.

POMERANCE: It is more about enhancing theatre than it is about enhancing life. The quality of the early Seventies was that the theatrical enterprise was a valuable addition to life.

AUKIN: I don't think so. When you take Donnellan's production of *Fuente Ovejuna*, in a new translation by Adrian Mitchell which was supremely successful, that enhances my life to have seen that production.

POMERANCE: I'm not saying it cannot happen as a by-product. I'm saying, that's not the general thing going on in theatre now.

REES: One of the outstanding differences surely is that it is not, now, new work which is being done, it's work on re-interpreting texts. In the Sixties and Seventies it was work brand new and hot from the press.

AUKIN: Yes. I am not sure how profound a difference it is though. It may be more superficial than you or I like to believe. Donellan's re-interpretation of *Fuente Ovejuna* for our times was just a great piece of theatre on every level, so I am not going to feel superior about what we did.

REES: I am not wanting to do that. I was trying to understand the difference.....

AUKIN: Clearly that is the difference. The work of the Eighties is interested in rediscovering the work of the past rather than in encouraging new writers.

REES: Shakespeare is now produced across the gamut of theatre, from the largest companies to the smallest.

AUKIN: I know. That is a sort of crime. John Mortimer made this wonderful speech at the National, reminding everyone that one of the most exciting things ever to exist in London had its site 400 yards down the road at the Globe. We forget Shakespeare had his world premières once, in a theatre that only did new plays. Where are the theatres today only doing new plays? And that is ghastly because there are hardly any.

REES: There are a few, usually small, theatres like The Bush, Hampstead, Theatre Upstairs committed to and only producing brand new writing. There are very few touring companies with the courage to present first-time new writers.

AUKIN: If there are not more theatres doing new plays, theatre will finally die, you're right, or become sidelined, marginal.

REES: Is theatre going through one of its many interminable crises or do even more serious times lie ahead? Will more small touring companies – the ones who break the mould for others to follow – continue to disappear and only the large institutions remain?

AUKIN: To go to theatre, you have to have a reason, the urge to leave home and pay money. All the problems of going out – the travel, taking a bus in London is expensive, forget parking a car. You have to be really highly motivated to go to theatre. What motivates is when you see something wonderful. I think people do hanker after the live experience. But now dance and music are the draw more than theatre. I get worried that the audience for theatre is going. What has happened to theatre is that awful thing when an art form separates itself from popular culture and becomes a high art form. Theatre will become like opera, more and more expensive, which fewer and fewer can afford. It will cease to be a popular art.

POMERANCE: In a certain sense that is reflected by the condition that the most adventurous talent is heading towards one form of film or another, because they feel they can reach a wider audience. The narrative structure of film is something that has changed what is in the audience's head. I've always felt that was one of the secret reasons for the success of *The Elephant Man*. There was something about the play and its structure which matched an inner structure within the brains of people who watch a lot of TV. I had not intended that. A montage on film now changes faster and faster – rock videos and advertising. The attention span is affected.

AUKIN: The irony is, of course, that the great writer, who still writes like that, is Shakespeare. His plays still work on the basis you are talking of. O'Neill does feel stodgy, dated and heavy.

POMERANCE: It is also because writers and theatre people in general have not come to terms with the fact that you have to slow down the opening of a play for the audience's mental processes. You have to bring them into harmony with what theatre does.

REES: And film does not?

POMERANCE: If you fail to take them out of the mentality of video quickness without boring them, you are in trouble.

REES: Do you find there is greater vitality in theatre outside Europe? Are the reasons for making exciting theatre and the content that forms its basis, there, more urgently, outside the English-speaking world?

AUKIN: The energy is now in films. And partly I am sad since I love theatre. The money is there in England to make a living in theatre, potentially. You can still earn more money from a very successful play than a film. What Bernard earned from *The Elephant Man*, people don't earn from movies. Economically, the power, the potential, is still there. People are not interested because the public have lost interest. People who go to theatre are not the people who writers want to engage with. Those people go to the movies or watch videos.

POMERANCE: There are people who say: 'I have a very urgent story, which you have not heard before, and it is important for me to tell you.' You see it in African films, in Yugoslavian films. The early great films had urgency. Here it is an industrial product to some extent and the description 'very good' tends to mean 'another' film. It does not have urgency, the sense that there is an important story to tell and you'd better listen. I think it is a morbidity in the culture. I don't say it will last for ever.

POLITICS AND EXPERIMENT

Roland Muldoon's CAST was, with The People Show, the earliest of the groups creating their own touring circuits. They played Political Theatre to students, political organisations and the Labour Movement. Their iconoclasm and anarchy was like a 'trip' in comparison to the 'right on' approach of agit-prop groups like Red Ladder, General Will and Broadside. I worked as an actor with CAST in *How Muggins Was a Martyr* by John Arden and Margaretta D'Arcy at Unity Theatre in 1968.

Four playwrights, who worked with Foco Novo at separate periods, Jon Chadwick and John Hoyland in the mid-Seventies, Nigel Gearing and John Constable in the early Eighties, describe the different contributions they made to the company.

Foco Novo produced two shows in the years 1976/77 by Jon Chadwick and John Hoyland, which toured under the auspices of the National Union of Mineworkers, at a time when both the Labour Movement and the NUM had the cash and the desire to promote cultural activities. By 1992, the position of the Labour Movement and, in particular, the NUM had, over the last decade or more, been so weakened that this type of touring was neither possible nor appropriate.

Nigel Gearing and John Constable wrote plays in an entirely different vein. *Snap* and *Black Mas* respectively, toured through the Arts Council-supported small scale touring circuit and fulfilled another policy plank of the company with the production of a first play by a new playwright.

John Hoyland refers to this change of direction in Foco Novo's work between the mid-Seventies and the early Eighties. It was, he says, not only a 'break' for Jon Chadwick and himself, it was also a marker in the company's development, just as it was more widely a reflection of what was going on in British culture. It is summed up in the phrase 'politics versus experiment'. We wanted to do both.

The influence of Bertolt Brecht raises its head in these discussions, as it does elsewhere in the book. Bernard Pomerance remarks:

66

'Brecht was a mountain you had to climb, at least to see what the view looked like.' Nowadays, he is thrown in the dustbin as passé. I contend this is fashion. We live in an historical moment where the political and cultural agenda of the left is somewhat discredited, particularly because of the events in the former Soviet Union and Central Europe.

Howard Brenton and Joshua Sobol attest to the clarity Brecht brought to the production process. This is a commodity we desperately need in these times. Whatever the final verdict on his plays, the effect that Brecht has had on production values, is, of course, enormous. Sobol speaks of the way Brecht got rid of 'ornamentalistic overweight' from production. That ornamentalism has, as an expression of our own times, first of all crept and then finally rushed back onto the stages of contemporary productions.

Brecht gathered a variety of political and artistic tendencies and cohered them into a philosophy and aesthetic. In the juxtaposition of image against image, the singular use of objects, and the emphasis he placed on the inter-disciplinary and collaborative nature of theatre, he continues to be a covert influence on many of the most adventurous in contemporary theatre, even though they themselves would often dismiss him as an irrelevance.

ROLAND MULDOON

Founder member and driving force of CAST [Cartoon Archetypical Slogan Theatre]. THE PEOPLE SHOW and CAST were the original Sixties groups, touring the new circuits which they created. CAST played to Labour Movement and student audiences throughout the Seventies. Muldoon won an American 'Obie' in 1980 for his one man show *Confessions of a Socialist*. The creation of *New Variety* followed in the middle Eighties, touring new cabaret to pubs and clubs around London. In 1986, he became the Artistic Director of The Hackney Empire.

Roland Rees acted in CAST's production, directed by Roland Muldoon, of John Arden and Margaretta D'Arcy's *How Muggins Was A Martyr* at Unity Theatre in 1968.

REES: In 1967, having just returned from the States, I saw CAST performing in the clubroom above the Royal Court, now The Theatre Upstairs.

MULDOON: In 1967 it would have been *John D. Muggins*, one of our classic *Muggins* shows.

REES: I was struck by the raw, physical energy of the performance, the acting style you had developed, its beat and jazzy feel, and a language, full of slogans and argument. It was a wonderful buzz. A real ensemble approach in which everyone backed up the others. I thought this is the way to do British Brecht. When was CAST formed and how did you choose the title Cartoon Archetypal Slogan Theatre?

MULDOON: In 1965. It's Archetypical. Archetype is Jungian. 'Cartoon', that was the style. 'Archetypical' was our philosophy, We were influenced by the archetypicality of Laurel and Hardy, Charlie Chaplin, and the characters in the movie *Les Enfants Du Paradis*. But we were looking for a British theatrical style that was not Commedia dell'Arte or Brechtian. We wanted a style that would make our plays come across like rock and roll. Our great heroes were the guitarists and the saxophonists who won the appreciation of our generation. We believed that there were archetypical characters and Jazz and Rock did that more than anything.

So we wanted to invent a physical language for characters, who would be individual, recognisable people in their essence but, archetypical of theatrical gesture, in that they were generalised to embody all their contradictions. No one Muggins character in any of our plays was the same, but there were identifiable Muggins traits.

'Slogan' because we made the language of the plays out of this sort of imagery. 'Theatre' because we made theatre. And CAST because that made us anonymous. For years we pretended we did not have anyone in the group called Roland Muldoon or Red Saunders. [*Early member of the group who was a professional photographer*]. Naming the cast would be bourgeois individualism! If you are into archetypicality, you don't need to know the name of the actors! Of course that was stupid.

REES: What about the derivation of the acting style and the movement you had in the show?

MULDOON: There were a number of influences. Ray Levene injected the New York style of dance and Claire Muldoon, [*Roland's wife, also in* CAST] used to mould the movement and blocking of our shows. Red Saunders and Pete Bruno were Mod in physical attitude. I was more the Teddy Boy!

69

A lot of CAST's style was about reaching an audience in halls or clubs unconducive to performance, and making it entertaining and dynamic. Our big advance was when we bought two speakers and a PA. This allowed us to do stand-up comedy. The buggers had to listen then!

REES: You borrowed a lot from stand-up comics?

MULDOON: I lived on a council estate in Surrey, and I was a good show-off, so I kept saying: 'I'm an actor.' But nobody thought I had the education. So I used my technical training at the Bristol Old Vic and became a technician for a year and saw the great problem theatre had. It would never reach my council estate in Weybridge because it was not dynamic. It could not walk up to someone on the estate and say: 'Bang,! Wallop! Watch *This!* Don't watch telly.' Rock 'n roll can do that, telly can, cinema can, theatre couldn't. That intrigued me. If I was going to be in theatre with the idea that it must be popular culture and have the attraction of rock 'n' roll, then I had to invent a style for that theatre. Twenty, twenty five minutes long, totally compressed, totally dynamic, cut, cut, cut, speed. So much so, that we would move faster than you could think, like a flicking page we used to say – you flicked so fast, you told a story.

So 'Popular' Theatre *would* look for inspiration from a stand-up comic, playing off an audience. We used to watch the Old Time Music Hall evenings at Unity Theatre. We could see how you walked out and gained the audience's attention. We learnt from these enthusiasts the simple lessons of traditional music hall. And we learnt the elements of melodrama.

REES: You mentioned you had musical heroes. Were there others?

MULDOON: Lenny Bruce [*The seminal American comic satirist*] became a hero very early on for us because we met Andrew Loog Oldham, [*Producer of the early Rolling Stones albums*] who had some tapes of Bruce. We liked his use of streams of consciousness, so we made use of that. We got from him the idea that you could change the script to fit the mood of the audience. So Lenny Bruce was an inspiration.

REES: The Theatre Upstairs clubroom, I imagine, was an unusual audience. Who were your usual audiences?

MULDOON: But that clubroom was part of the underground. I sometimes forget how important the existence of the Lord Chamberlain was. Pre-'68, the office had not been abolished, so the very idea that a theatre group was going to perform a play, that they had not told anybody they had written, meant there were not many places we could perform. In the mid-Sixties, folk clubs were often run by the Communist Party or other left organisations. They heard about us. We became incredibly fashionable.

After '68 students began to book us. There was a famous time at Warwick University, where Ken Livingstone was then a student. They rang us and said: 'Look we want to book you and we want to occupy our College at the same time! So tell us when you're available!'

REES: Quite a lot of your gigs, I remember, in '67/'68/'69 were for specific political organisations?

MULDOON: IS [*International Socialists*] was a classic. We did a lot of shows for them. IMG too. [*International Marxist Group whose public face was Tariq Ali*] But we played for anyone who would book us.

REES: Built into your acting style and your approach to performance and politics was a great sense of anarchy and iconoclasm.

MULDOON: The Labour Movement always accused us of being anarchists. We never thought we were.

REES: I acted in *How Muggins Was a Martyr* which CAST and John Arden and Margueretta D'Arcy decided to produce in 1968 at the Unity Theatre.

   □ *Unity was owned by a Trust which had strong affiliations with the Communist Party and lay on the Camden Town, Kings Cross borders. It was burnt down in the middle Seventies and never rebuilt.*

MULDOON: CAST started at Unity. I was a stage manager there. I love proscenium arch theatres and Unity at Kings Cross was a fine example. It had flies, a raked stage and an auditorium with an almost perfect view wherever you sat. We saw it as a tragedy that the old CP Management Committee had run out of ideas and choked its development. We thought our new, free-wheeling idea of modern variety for the theatre would turn it around and bring the audiences back in!

REES: How did the partnership of the Ardens and CAST come about?

MULDOON: The idea was that CAST and the Ardens would create the play by improvisation as we went along. But then when we got an almost complete script from the Ardens, we heaved a sigh of relief!

REES: You were the director. The Ardens were also acting in it, as were quite a few people who were not CAST regulars, like myself.

MULDOON: Critics and Theatre historians have put that production in the category of: 'Most important cultural event in the twentieth century sort of/almost crap!' Because it happened to be 1968, happened to have people like you on its cast list and Richard Seyd, one of the founder members of Red Ladder, who in New York recently I noticed was directing a production

71

of Molière on Broadway. It became one of the mythical rolls of honour of the Sixties with the Ardens and Muldoons inscribed on it. Then there was the stripping scene.

REES: John Arden was playing Muggins and his wife, Margaretta D'Arcy, Mrs Muggins. They were the owners of a broken-down cafe ie Britain. In the stripping scene, another character, a prostitute, stripped in front of them in a purely functional manner and Muggins says when she's finished: 'Is that all there is to it?'

MULDOON: I didn't like the scene at all, but my main resistance to it was that it was an additional scene in an already over-long show, put in by the Ardens late in rehearsal. The controversy continues to run and run and run! For example, only recently this academic from Lancaster University sends me a draft of his book on modern British theatre in which he seemed to be saying, looking back over all these years, that the scene represented an ideological crunch point between the 'proto punks' of CAST and our view of sex, and a strain of feminism represented by the Ardens!

But the Ardens got their way and broke ranks stylistically with the production by presenting the scene ultra-realistically. Whereas CAST would have preferred a throw-away, hinted at version. But it happened. And when I unsuccessfully resisted, the Ardens said I was more arrogant than Sir Larry!

REES: On the face of it, the combination of CAST and the Ardens was potentially combustible. I remember the parlous nature of the rehearsals!

MULDOON: It was a difficult thing the meeting of us and the Ardens. They didn't want to do it at Unity. They wanted to do the play in the All Saints Hall, off the Portobello Road, with a San Francisco-style meets-the-people kind of protest show. We wanted a Labour Movement audience at the Unity. They hated me for that.

Into this situation, the Ardens invited John Fox from The Welfare State and Albert Hunt, with the students from Bradford College of Art, to make an environment in the Unity Theatre forecourt. They were committed to getting the neighbourhood in. Unity did not want this because they had been censored in the Forties and Fifties for being a left wing theatre, and had preserved themselves by having a license from the Lord Chamberlain on the basis of allowing in members only. So the public could not walk in. The old Stalinists were cringing when the Ardens said: 'Let's get everybody in and have a community '68 summer Festival!' So there was a complete clash of cultures.

REES: I remember the opening was quite a star-studded occasion of the Left.

MULDOON: Yes they all came – Tariq Ali, Wolf Mankowitz and Geoffrey Reeves, who was the big name working with Peter Brook at the time. They all lined up afterwards to give me a wigging! Nobody dared tell the Ardens off. I lay in bed on Sunday morning and there was a review by Harold Hobson in the Sunday Times. He said what a load of old crap this was, and why should such a great playwright as John Arden mess about with this bunch of hysterical anarchists?

But it wasn't a happy thing. We were far more rock and roll than the Ardens were. There was nothing wrong with them, don't get me wrong, I think they were absolute living wonders of British theatre. They inspired us. But it was difficult because we had expected to do a different show to the one they wrote.

REES: You received subsidy in 1975/76?

MULDOON: Mike Leigh helped get it for us. He was on the Arts Council Drama Panel. We got fourteen grand. It had been very hard for us. After 1971/72, when the group broke up, we had lost the very best people who made the company a real company. We got some friends around and slowly tried to build the style back again.

REES: You performed under the name CAST until?

MULDOON: Until we were cut in 1985. These were our golden years really. CAST was always more left field than anyone. We saw our job as holding the critical mirror up to those who were saying this is the way forward in the class struggle as well as to those who wouldn't mind something happening but wouldn't follow those who said they knew the way. That was the dichotomy which our Muggins character personified and which I often played.

During the 1984-85 miner's strike, we met many people in the middle of their struggle. Performing for them, we realised how real our characters were. Our plays were not based on a myth. Our heroes had long hair when it was fashionable, smoked dope and still went down the mines. They weren't this working class stereotype with a cloth hat that a lot of the Agit-Prop theatre groups portrayed in the Seventies. We did not have heroic workers in our shows.

Our classic play was *Confessions of a Socialist*. It became very controversial because the critique it made of the socialist male in the play did not satisfy certain feminists. I did it as a one person show in New York and San Francisco in 1980, for which it won an 'Obie' [*The highly valued Village Voice Drama Award*].

We tried to build up a circuit of our own from the middle Seventies. You had all ended up playing in Arts Centres with large grants. We never got a large grant. We were about cost effectiveness and touring to pubs, where we would always play end-on as if it was a pros arch theatre! We could see the trend was to cramp the new theatre by pushing it into smaller and smaller Arts Centres, where there was nice coffee and salads, but no beer or community feel like in the pub. So we would find someone in a town who would book a pub, put up our posters and the audience would come.

When Thatcher came to power at the end of the Seventies, Gavin Richards of Belt & Braces, John McGrath of 7:84 and I met to discuss the way forward. Gavin said he was going to get out of touring, McGrath said he was retreating north of the border and we said the answer was Cabaret, working through the circuit we had created with CAST. So the seed for 'New Variety' was formed.

In 1981, Belt & Braces were filling a West End theatre with over six hundred seats, performing Dario Fo's *Accidental Death of an Anarchist,* so they were disqualified from receiving the rest of their grant. This was like being struck down on the road to Damascus. What? A left wing play could be on in the West End and people would flock! Flock to see it! It became totally fashionable. Lucky for us, Belt & Braces gave us the last three months of their Arts Council grant!

We knew Thatcher was going to get rid of us. So we deliberately became more controversial. We did a play in which I smoked a joint, gave it to the audience and said: 'It's a rebate from the Arts Council!' The Arts Council issued us an instruction that we must not go on stage and offer illegal substances to audiences in the name of the Arts Council! Our friends on the Drama Panel said: 'Boy, you're on the hit list!' In years to come, you will find in the Cabinet minutes a note saying: 'Get rid of that lot!'

By 1982 we had started the New Variety project, as a means of recruiting the new comedy talent – the New Cabaret – who similarly played out front in the way we had been doing since the Sixties. We did a very successful panto *Reds Under The Bed.* This coincided with a lot of GLC money becoming available. At one point, we ran eight pub venues in London. We had two circuits with two vans rotating the shows. We used our old approach of touring nationally, but this time the shows were directed to playing in London pubs.

We did a prototype of New Variety in the Sixties. This was with Adrian Mitchell, the poet, Ram John Holder, the actor and singer, [*Featured in* Desmonds *on TV*] a light show from Tim and Janet Street-Porter, [*Now a BBC Producer*] and CAST doing two twenty minute plays. We called the show *AgitPop.* Cost two and sixpence entrance!

REES: Political Theatre is a much bandied phrase. I am interested what you think it means, how broad a church it encompasses. Is Community Theatre, Political Theatre?

MULDOON: We hated the word community. People tried to hoist us on that petard. We always asked what community? Interestingly, the Poll Tax is called the Community Charge. Lord Bedford pays the same as the woman who lives round the corner. Community Theatre we weren't. Nor were we Agit-Prop. We were Political Theatre.

It became fashionable to be political. You got a grant for it. And the fear was that you could be climbing on a band wagon and would lose your edge of danger. It became a debased word.

In comparison to General Will, Red Ladder and Broadside, CAST were like a psychedelic trip. We never told people what to do in our plays. We were part of the culture to whom we played our theatre.

The one thing about CAST was that it was seriously avant-garde. If you accepted that we were not a kosher theatre company like Foco Novo but were an ensemble company then nobody could touch us in England.

REES: The San Francisco Mime Troupe effected a similar ensemble approach?

MULDOON: Under Ronnie Davis, [*Founder of the Mime Troupe*] they were very much Commedia dell'Arte. After he left the group, he complained to me that now the new Troupe were doing American musicals! I thought that was much better than Commedia, because they'd found what was truly American!

REES: How did New Variety become the Hackney Empire?

MULDOON: We decided to make the big jump.

The Arts Council cut us for, I believe, being too dangerous. We had to be stopped because of the ideology of the Conservatives. What they didn't know was that the GLC would take us on. That was the only time we were generously funded, so we determined to achieve things.

When they finally got rid of the GLC, we were supported by local Borough Councils. We used that energy, money and the support of those cabaret artists, who had previously worked for us, to promote our new genre, New Variety. We became like a mini Arts Council booking artists such as Brian Hibberd of the Flying Pickets, poets John Hegley and Benjamin Zephaniah, comedians like Julian Clary, Harry Enfield, Paul Merton, Ben Elton, French & Saunders, in pubs from Stratford East to the White Horse in Brixton, from Slough to Cricklewood. It reads like a *Who's Who* of contemporary popular entertainment. Now, we don't do this because all those places do their own independent promotion of cabaret and comedy. In the Eighties, the artists carried the dissent against Thatcher into the pubs and clubs of Britain.

Then we found the Hackney Empire was for sale. I came down here and I quivered. I drove past five times before I dared go in. Eventually, I took a look from the back of the auditorium and saw the sight lines of this theatre. They were a dream. All I ever loved. I thought it must have anthrax! Why would anyone set us up to get it? I jumped at it. We calculated we would pull it off. We had twelve grand within the company. We pushed our way in on November 2nd 1986 with Mecca's tacit agreement, yet they did not sign the deal till six months later. Our theory was sneak up, open the theatre, put the fly posters up all over London and say: 'Look it's on!'

REES: What was the last time it was used?

MULDOON: After the decline of variety in the Fifties, it had been used as a TV Studio. And now and again, as a theatre. It became a Bingo Hall in the Seventies.

REES: What funding do you receive at the moment?

MULDOON: £250,000 odd. Our turnover is now a million and a half. We hope next year to get £600,000 funding from the LBGS [*London Borough Grants Board*], Hackney Council and LAB [*London Arts Board*]. In 1990 I opened the financial year, April 1st, with £40,000 and knew I could not get to June. But we reached July then August and then we rang up the funding bodies and convinced them we needed realistic subsidy. If we can get £7$^1/_2$ million by 2001 to do up the theatre, we will be a very important regional theatre based in London.

What gives me the energy to carry on in the morning is that the young people of Hackney think it is dead normal to come here as part of their social calendar. They come in, buy a beer, walk around, see a show and they are very comfortable.

REES: Your basic diet for the Empire is your New Variety genre?

MULDOON: Comedy meets dexterity, meets music but you would expect to hear something of content, rather than bland TV comedy.

Look at our programme over the last year – 291 Club, Comedy and New Variety on Saturday, Billy Bragg on New Years Eve, *Dick Whittington* with Linda Robson and Pauline Quirk from *Birds of a Feather*. We hosted *The Moscow Clown Company*, *The National Theatre* and Oliver Samuels, the Jamaican farceur.

Even the youngest comedian walking onto the Empire's stage knows that they must reach the upper circle first. They know how to fill the big stage. My question is, will theatre learn to fill our big stage? We have 1200 seats. Can we make Molière and Restoration Drama work on our big stage? Can popular and contentious theatre fill 1200 seats? That is my question. It is the development I want to happen at the Empire. I hope I see the answer in the next ten years!

76

FOUR PLAYWRIGHTS
JON CHADWICK
JOHN CONSTABLE
NIGEL GEARING
JOHN HOYLAND

Left to Right: Jon Chadwick, John Hoyland, John Constable and Nigel Gearing.

John Hoyland and Jon Chadwick together were commissioned by Foco Novo to write two shows for the Labour Movement, *Nine Days and Saltley Gates* and *Tighten Your Belt*, 1976/77. Nigel Gearing's play *Snap*, 1981, was about the self-styled founder of the Motion Picture, Eadweard Muybridge from Kingston-Upon-Thames, and John Constable's *Black Mas*, 1984, was about a female singer from London visiting the Trinidad Carnival for fresh inspiration.

REES: In the late Fifties, it was the Europeans who were performed at the Student Drama Festivals – Frisch, Dürrenmatt, Ionesco, Arrabal, Beckett and Brecht. Somehow the Osbornes and Weskers were only just beginning to filter through. I remember a strong reaction, by students of my generation, to the English Theatre tradition of the Thirties, Forties and early Fifties. We resisted a preoccupation with our own country. Our horizons were European in literature and international in politics.

  The next stage of influence was again exterior, from America. Catching sight of companies like The Living Theatre, La Mama, Bread And Puppet, Joe Chaikin's Open Theatre was very exciting. This influence was further fortified for me by a two year stay in New York during the middle Sixties.

  The third stage was about creating an English version of the new theatre and this took many forms. We wanted to challenge not only the institutional theatre of the West End and the mainstream subsidised theatres but also the new 'orthodoxy' of social realism being created by The English Stage Company and the 'popular' formulas of Stratford East, important as they were. We, those of us involved in the new theatre, saw ourselves creating a parallel but separate tradition. English mixed with European and American. We now seem to have come full circle again with the renewed popularity of European plays and design.

  When each of you made contact with theatre, what were the characteristics which attracted you?

HOYLAND: My history is a little different from you others. You have located yourselves in a theatrical tradition. I was a political journalist and came to theatre from a very anti-institutional angle. One which, at that stage, we wanted to get rid of. But, nevertheless, I was intensely interested in theatre. For instance, my connection with Bath Arts Workshop, a performance based group. They clowned around and disrupted the notion of community. It was interventionist. That attracted me. And my involvement with Foco Novo was motivated by that notion – challenge and intervention through theatre. Theatre involves a coming together of people, actors and audience, and so seems supremely able to fulfil that function.

CONSTABLE: Although I loved some writers – Pinter, Beckett – that kind of theatre did not draw me into theatre. In Cambridge, I liked the rawness and physicality of European plays – Arrabal. Then, in the early Seventies, I got involved with the work of David Medalla, an outrageous, flamboyant, Maoist, Philippino performance artist. He had this Artists for Democracy organisation and gave over his squat, on Whitfield Street, off Tottenham Court Road, one day each week to an event. Very off the wall! Sheer Madness, the street theatre group I worked with as an actor, was poor and we used that as a virtue. In the same way that an unpretentious rock band could generate raw excitement, the roughness and the vitality of our approach was part of the show. Whether we played on the street or in a theatre, we tried to keep that raw style of the street, for the theatre.

I wrote my first play, *Black Mas*, to be produced by Foco Novo, whilst still living in Amsterdam. I was a member of a Company called Kaktus. As a writer, actor and stage manager, I was totally involved in keeping it going. That is what excited me. That is my root connection with theatre. In a sense the institutional theatre, or whatever you call it, was not my scene. I have always felt uneasy about the big institutions like the National, the RSC. The kind of theatre I worked in was characterised by being in continuous contact with all the people involved in producing that work.

GEARING: I have been most attracted by those whose work has tried to square the endeavour between progressive formal developments and progressive political content.

On the one hand, I would not have wanted to join The Living Theatre, [whom I saw and admired] because their work – although challenging and experimental – seemed too unfocussed in its political address. On the other hand, although admiring of writers of the Left who criticised social and political structures, I was not drawn then or indeed now, to writers such as Trevor Griffiths, who is very accomplished, because he works within a format I am uneasy with – inherited Ibsenesque.

This is why I am drawn to Brecht and Godard. In their work, they seem to combine progressiveness, both formally and politically. I have found this quality more in evidence outside of England. This approach was taken for granted in France, where I went to study film after leaving Cambridge.

I wrote a show on George Orwell [Down and Out in London and Paris, *performed at the Riverside Studios by Paines Plough*] and I was conscious of an extreme orthodoxy of representational modes, of ways of speaking and talking, for me to choose from, here in the UK. That orthodoxy remains, regardless of how radical or challenging the political content of the work is.

CHADWICK: I was drawn towards theatre that was an event, that – as John Hoyland described – reorganised the audience's consciousness of the world. There was an aspiration to do something new and at that time 'new' had a good reputation. You could feel that things were moving. You felt you were on the edge of the transformation of political, personal, social and economic relations and you wanted the theatre to be part of that transformation. You wanted your art to figure in that movement. And so you were attracted towards any formation which encouraged that movement forward.

I couldn't wait to get out of my job, as an Assistant Director at the Royal Court, and to create, as I felt then, something that was part of the real world, because the theatre at the Court was part of the habitual, where thought and behaviour had become dead. So you wanted to find a new audience, new plays. All of these things made the time of the late Sixties/early Seventies very exciting.

CONSTABLE: It is hard to make a general statement, but the one thing that characterised a lot of new work then, was to do with the quality of acting. It was not just the writing and, therefore, how one wrote for an actor. What the smaller companies could achieve, was the commitment to the physicality of performance – I don't mean to Physical Theatre as the term is now used. Nigel, you referred to English Ibsenesque writing, and I think similarly one of the qualities of straight English acting is acting from the neck upwards. There isn't a physical sense of theatre which there is in Europe. In the last five or six years, this approach has begun to make inroads into the productions of institutional theatre, eg. *The Mysteries*, which showed the National doing a play on a big scale, in the form that poor street theatre did on a small scale ten years ago. And Berkoff.

REES: You were all at university. Who were your heroes then?

CONSTABLE: My mind scattered over a whole range as you asked that question. Marx, Marcuse, Wittgenstein, Bob Dylan, Eldridge Cleaver, Brecht, Julian Beck, Freud, Reich, countless others.

HOYLAND: I would name the same pantheon. At university, William Blake. I visited the Berliner Ensemble in 1961 to see *Arturo Ui*. That influenced me enormously. The Living Theatre and Bread and Puppet Theatre were very influential. *Hair*.

CONSTABLE: I agree with the list. Lindsay Kemp's *Flowers*, Peter Brook, Theatre du Soleil. Blake and Jung at university. Burroughs had more influence on me as a writer than any playwright. During the Sixties I was still at school, but despite our age differences there seems to be no generational gap amongst us.

HOYLAND: I travelled around South America in the early and mid-Sixties making a living out of talks on the 'Angry Young Men'. In the Fifties, when I was seventeen, Osborne, Pinter and Wesker were influential, and that dialogue between the Angry Young Men and the Absurdists was very powerful. In the early Sixties, the cultural vitality was in the theatre.

CHADWICK: Genet, Meyerhold and Artaud should be added.

REES: Did that era, the late Sixties, attract people to work in theatre, who might, in other circumstances and times, have not been attracted to theatre?

HOYLAND: It did. Theatre then was one of the exciting things to do. It was not out of a love of theatre historically but because theatre then allowed other things to occur. Theatre activity at that time was very diverse, ranging from obscure Performance Arts to heavy Marxist-Leninist groups. But a common denominator was a stretching of what theatre could do, both formally and in reaching new audiences. And so many got into theatre, perhaps for the wrong reasons, and then left.

CONSTABLE: There was also retrospectively a naive optimism. A real belief that a transformation was taking place at all levels of society and theatre was potentially a transformational event. What that movement of theatre lacked was the wide appeal of rock music.

REES: Pip Simmons saw his group as a Rock n' Roll band.

CONSTABLE: Before Rock went self-consciously theatrical, a dirty-arsed band on stage with a few guitars and a drum kit could be a very theatrical event. What we are all talking about is that popular culture was flowing together and therefore there was not the feeling that entering the theatre would represent the same academic quality it had in the Forties.

CHADWICK: We are dealing with social history. The movement at the end of the Sixties was accumulated into the movement of the working class against the Heath government, 1970/74, and the great upsurge of militancy then – the Pentonville Five, the struggle against the Industrial Relations Act, and the fact that the working class through the Labour Movement was seen as the repository of the transforming force of society. That had implications for the kind of productions we did at the time with Foco Novo. My own experience was in Derry in 1971, being on that march when people were shot dead by British soldiers – Bloody Sunday. That came home to me extremely forcibly. I was a member of the Berwick Street Film Collective making a film about these people's struggle. Going back to the hotel after the march and being among journalists and newsmen, I had the sense that I must make my art as real as what I had seen that day and what they would report.

HOYLAND: I am glad we have come to Foco Novo. An important feature of the work we did with the Company was the involvement it had in the Labour Movement.

REES: First I want to put one more general question to set the stage. Do you think that the aspirations you have been describing have or have not continued into the Eighties and now the Nineties?

GEARING: I came into theatre in 1981 and I am conscious that already there was a whittling down to specific skills, ambitions and aims within theatre practice. I suspect this happened in a short space of time. Politics in the

Seventies had a general feeling, an overall outlook. But by the Eighties, everything on the left was issue-based. You could argue that, in theatre, the same thing happened. By the Eighties, someone would say that they were into one kind of theatre and not into another, ie Theatre de Complicité or Red Ladder.

CONSTABLE: The commitment was there but were the skills there to match? That era exhibited an explosion of raw energy which was often unstructured but was very exciting. When something happens, a revolution, times are exciting but after that feeling dissipates, a slow process of disillusion sets in. The initial act is the exciting thing. Now every Tory Minister pays lip service to the ozone layer. In the Sixties and early Seventies that was an underground thing. Bob Crumb cartoons were dealing with that. In the process of being assimilated into daily political commentary, the issue inevitably becomes sanitised.

CHADWICK: We cannot say something big happened in the Seventies, then it finished and we all went home. That was when I was young and so it seemed like that. As far as I am concerned, we carry on doing our theatre work as best we can. What you always go for is vitality, meaning, interaction and fun.

REES: John Chadwick, tell us about the Ad Hoc Collective group, which met in the early Seventies and which eventually became the Community Theatre. It was funded by the ACGB to produce a play called *The Motor Show* which was performed, 1971, near the Ford plant in Dagenham.

CHADWICK: We met above a garage in Chalk Farm in 1970/71 – The Roxy it was called – which some groups like Freehold used for performance and where Foco Novo produced its first production *Foco Novo* by Bernard Pomerance. The group consisted of Rob Walker, Ron Daniels, Steve Gooch, Michael Wearing, Di Seymour, Paul Thompson, Pam Scotcher, Pam Gems, you and me.

We wanted to start a theatre that was part of the Labour Movement. We chose Dagenham because it was a large working class area with a prime industry based there. We thought the group, and there were others like it, should be called Community Theatre. We wanted to seek out a new audience. And now there are courses in the subject!

REES: It was an on-going Sunday afternoon talkshop over some eighteen months.

CHADWICK: We advertised in *Time Out* and more people joined.

REES: At these sessions, we debated what community theatre should be. Should this kind of theatre be directed at the whole community or should it be directed towards a geographical area that was predominantly working class?

We were against the idea that this theatre so often became like a hit-and-run job. There, in one place, for an evening and then on to another part of the country.

I remember Philip Hedley *(Now Artistic Director of Theatre Royal, Stratford East)* at the meeting, advertised in *Time Out,* saying to us that you want to do the same thing as Joan Littlewood, except you want to do it as a collective. We were suspicious of this idea, because we felt that popular as Stratford East was, it was popularist rather than committed and did not function within the Labour Movement and in the democratic way we cherished.

☐ The Motor Show *was a play for the people of Dagenham and the workers at Fords and was written by Steve Gooch and Paul Thompson, directed by Ron Daniels and designed by Di Seymour.*

REES: In 1975, Foco Novo presented *The Arthur Horner Show* by Phil Woods. Jon Chadwick, you were the Administrator for the show. The impetus for this play was a pantomime, written by Phil Woods, we did for the Sherman Theatre Company in Cardiff in 1973. *Aladdin* was performed with all the traditional panto roles intact but we transposed the story to one about the miners' overtime ban recently in progress. So Aladdin became the Rhondda miner, Abanazer the Coal Owner, Wishy-Washy a left intellectual, and so on. We also performed the show in miners' clubs in the valleys, and this contact Phil and I made, with the Welsh NUM and Dai Francis, the Union's Secretary, gave rise to the *Horner* show. Dai Francis was nearing retirement and brought up in the traditions of the Thirties when great emphasis was placed on education and the cherishing of mining traditions and working class culture. He, it was who suggested the subject of Horner, a previous incumbent of the same post that Dai now held.

Horner was from Merthyr, in the heart of the Rhondda, and was three times imprisoned for his beliefs and political activity. He was instrumental in forming all the separate, regional coalfields into one single national union – the NUM. And the battles he fought, in the Thirties and Forties, seemed to have a great resonance for 1975 and the renewed struggles the miners were engaged in.

CHADWICK: It was that contact with Dai Francis which was crucial for Foco Novo's next shows. We toured *Horner* all over the UK but in Wales, through the auspices of the NUM, we played in miners' welfare halls. This show led to *Nine Days and Saltley Gates* and *Tighten Your Belt* which were written for, and directed at, exactly the same circuit.

REES: This period of time coincided with Foco Novo receiving its first annual subsidy. *Horner*, like our previous shows, was produced on Project grants.

In 1975 we received £16,500 from the Arts Council to produce two shows in a year. We seemed to have come of age.

HOYLAND: *Nine Days* was about the 1926 General Strike, the key role the miners played in it, and the terrible defeat they suffered. But it also recreated the extraordinary mobilisation of the British working class into what were virtually Soviets based on the Trades Councils and which became called Councils of Action. The play also portrayed the 1972 picketing of the Saltley Coal Depot which contributed to the fall of the Heath government and hence the reason for the play's title.

CHADWICK: We recognised that 1976 was the 50th Anniversary of 1926 and so there seemed an important pretext for the show.

HOYLAND: There was a total strike throughout Britain in 1926 and the Councils of Action decided what should and should not happen in the economic life of each community and for a while there was dual power. Government continued to govern but in effect a lot of the Councils ran the localities.

I vividly remember the meeting with Dai Francis in the NUM offices in Pontypridd, where we addressed the entire executive of the South Wales NUM – granite men – and put to them our idea for the play and a plea that they encourage the National Executive of the NUM to put it on throughout all the coalfields. After Jon Chadwick had addressed them, there was a silence and then Dai said: 'You want to put on a play about the General Strike? But that was a great defeat!' Many others agreed. Dai turned them around by suggesting that a victory should be celebrated and so the idea of including the picketing of Saltley Gates was born. To our astonishment, eleven voted in favour of supporting the tour and three abstained. Dai said: 'See you boys later.' Afterwards, his executive mask dropped and he talked about the importance of culture, his involvement in the Paul Robeson concerts *(Robeson's voice was carried live by telephone into the miners' halls of the Rhondda with fraternal greetings and song)* and how the younger miners coming up were hot on the business of the executive but failed often to recognise the importance of wider issues.

REES: After that meeting, some younger miners on the Executive said to me: 'Why don't you put plays on about how so and so on the Exec. gets a car and I don't and I'm on the Exec. too!' They wanted bread and butter issues debated. It was Dai Francis who saw the overarc of things and wanted the history of his community enacted out for the younger people in the coalfields. But the younger miners were more immediately conscious of what was coming, what their future would be. Indeed, not even their worst fears could have forseen the speed with which the most productive coalfields have disappeared or how the communities dependent on them would be decimated.

HOYLAND: Some months later we met Dai at the County Hotel in Holborn, near to the then NUM Headquarters on Euston Road. He told us that he had arranged for us to meet with key people from the Derbyshire and Yorkshire coalfields – Peter Heathfield and Peter Tate – and from Scotland – Bill Owen. Peter Tate subsequently became a computer freak with Poptel, a network connecting Labour Movement organisations around the world.

Dai Francis gave me a letter of introduction to take from pit to pit, lodge to lodge in each coalfield. Although I was co-writing the play with Jon Chadwick, I was also organising the dates of the tour. As I booked a fortnight's performances in Yorkshire and then Scotland and so on, this experience came to fertilise what we would write about. My conversations in the coalfields fed into the play.

One of the features of that time, 1975/76, was that the Labour Movement felt very bullish. It felt that it could have a major influence on what was happening in society. It also had money. It believed it was a repository that contained the seeds of the future and that this involved a cultural obligation. The Labour Movement at that time was willing to financially help the production of *Nine Days*.

REES: The mining industry was more singular than most. Bar two or three small unions representing managers and clerical people officiating the running of the mine, there was one single union, the NUM, with a membership who shared a similar job wherever mines were located. Miners were highly motivated and very proud. They felt that they were responsible for providing energy which ran the ships during two world wars and which generated wealth for industry. That was the attraction of the miners rather than an industry with a variety of skills and therefore representation. The mining communities were also singular, having been created around the very mines where the people worked.

HOYLAND: The Labour Movement felt they must provide culture for their members. So they found the venues and promoted our show which was providing a history of their movement with 1926 and 1972 as milestones and with lessons to be drawn from those events.

The Labour Movement does not now have those resources. It used to be a powerful part of society and able to support that kind of activity. I remember Jack Taylor of the Yorkshire NUM addressing a packed hall of 300 at Leeds who had come to see our show, and saying that: 'We have seen here to-night an example of working class culture.'

REES: In 1987 we did James Pettifer's *Needles of Light*, about South Wales Miners going to the Spanish Civil War. We approached our contacts in the NUM to support the show. There was no way, after the miners' defeat of 84/85, that they were in any position to do that. It was survival time again.

HOYLAND: That's right. It's a major change over twenty years. And we believed at that time that this kind of touring was more important than appearing at the Royal Court.

REES: Do you remember the cast sizes in those days?

CHADWICK: Seven or eight.

REES: Ten plus one or two stage management.

HOYLAND: They were, by touring standards, large shows.

REES: In 1976/77 *Nine Days, Tighten Your Belt*, which followed, both touring through the Labour movement, and *A Seventh Man* by Adrian Mitchell, based on John Berger's book about migrant workers, touring through the small scale circuit, all had casts of ten. We said that it was imperative to catch the whole cross-section of a society. An epic not a voyeur's picture. Ten years later a maximum of four actors became the norm. In our last year, we scrabbled around for two handers.

HOYLAND: They were big shows, lasting two and half hours and we had audiences of up to 300/400 often sitting around tables, drinking beer and enjoying the show. The experience was thrilling, wonderful. One of the most exciting experiences of my life. At that moment, it all jelled.

GEARING: Can you pin down why it was so exciting? Obviously the work had to have quality. But was it a moment where what you were offering and what the Labour Movement wanted jelled?

HOYLAND: You are talking about the isolated role of the writer/intellectual suddenly becoming tremendously social. This is what happened then. And particularly because we were dealing with new audiences and not traditional audiences.

I shall never forget the first night of *Nine Days and Saltley Gates* at Abertillery in the Valleys. They have a theatre there. A very beautiful old building with sloping floors. It was lovely. However we said to Dai Francis that we wanted to open the show in a miners' club. His booming voice proclaimed: 'No'. He said this show is culture and culture happens in theatres and it must have that stamp on it. So that's why we opened in Abertillery. They had a theatre. I remember 1976 was a fantastically cruel winter. Very, very cold. The icy streets of the town sloped down the side of the valley. You fell over as you walked around. Here was this beautiful hall waiting for an audience, in what seemed to us Londoners a foreign part of the world. The hall was empty. The show was ready to go up at 7.30pm. At 7.10pm nobody was there 7.15pm still nobody. Would anyone come on such a night? Suddenly they all started tramping through the icy streets and filled the hall and it was a magical evening.

Photo © John Haynes 1976

Left to Right. Robin Summers, Stewart Preston, Aviva Goldkorn, Terry Jackson, Alan Hulse, Gareth Williams, Stuart Golland and Ian Heywood in Foco Novo's 1976 production of Jon Chadwick's and John Hoyland's *The Nine Days And Saltley Gates*.

GEARING: That is a very engaging paradox. You lot saying: 'Take the play to the miners' clubs!' And the miners saying: 'Put it in a theatre!' That is a very rich cross-over.

HOYLAND: After South Wales, we toured the Yorkshire, Scottish and West Midlands coalfields, the Liverpool and Leeds Trades Councils and then London.

REES: This is a special kind of touring. One touring week in the West Midlands gives a good indication. We played Bold Miners Club, The Brightmet Labour Club, The Longbridge Hayes Community Centre, The Pirrie Ward Labour Club, The Gala Restaurant, West Bromwich, the Mid-Cannock Sports Centre and finally the Saltley Action Centre. This last date so enraged a Tory Manchester Magistrate that he demanded to know why, via the *Daily Telegraph*, arts funding was being used for such a purpose?

In Wales and Scotland, the general lack of public places of entertainment amidst semi-rural communities, created around a group of mines, meant that we played exclusively miners' clubs.

This list also throws light on the kind of touring involved. One night stands. After the performance, strike the set and load the van, find and sleep in that night's B&B, travel next day in the transit to the new venue – the one stage manager drives the set, costumes and props in a three-ton truck – everyone unloads the truck and erects the set between 11.00am and 5.00pm, a quick bite to eat and then do the full two hour performance. Then strike and load and off to the digs and let's hope the landlady is up and so on during the six day week and this goes on for two months. You have to be fit, youngish and committed.

HOYLAND: In London we played a fortnight at the Oval House Theatre and, on the strength of that, Mike Laye booked us at the ICA for a month. *Nine Days* was an incredibly successful play, both in clubs as well as theatres. It worked a treat. It was right for its time.

CHADWICK: By 1977, when we toured the second Labour Movement play, *Tighten Your Belt*, on a more contemporary theme – hospital closures, use of labour power, redundant teachers, social resources being cut – already within that time, one year, the climate had changed.

GEARING: If anyone said to me to name two years in your life when you got the impression that the forces of political change could happen, 1974 and 1975 was it. I was so aware of the extreme forces of political activism then.

HOYLAND: *Nine Days* had celebrated something which had finished. *Tighten Your Belt*, which again started its tour in Wales at Islwyn, contained a darker theme. The Sixties revolutionism had run out of steam. The context had changed. There was a recession and there were cuts and the Labour Party were making them. This was the bedrock of the play. It described a process of the fragmentation of working class communities. In this the play was very percipient of what was increasingly going to happen, particularly after 1979.

REES: In the light of Nigel's comments that progressive theatre must be as much to do with form as with content, how would you describe the two plays you wrote?

HOYLAND: The trick that made *Nine Days* work was borrowed from Red Ladder. The key moments, drama of the play, centred around the Councils of Action. They were composed of people we had chosen to represent different trades and crafts and who held different opinions about the action. And we wanted to include women on the Council. In this sense the play was schematic.

Audiences adored the way that we made these meetings come alive. The actors placed themselves around the auditorium, amongst the audience, and argued at each other from many vantage points. The audience loved being part of the meeting.

REES: This technique has an honourable pedigree and was employed by Clifford Odet's in his play *Waiting for Lefty*, which was also about a strike, that of cab drivers in the States during the Thirties.

GEARING: If you saw Bill Bryden's *Ship* at Glasgow, you get a few dramatised moments, here in the workshop, there in the home, the Company sing songs together which represent the community – I am not knocking this – and the play moves from individual incident to the wider political community. Was it like that? I have not quite got a handle on the dramatic form you used.

CHADWICK: The meetings of The Council of Action punctuated the play. These provided the wider context within which individual scenes such as the Sports Day, the arrival of a motor bike messenger with urgent news, others in homes etc, were played out.

REES: By Bryden's standards we had a laughable budget. Nevertheless, our commitment was to do a play and not agit-prop.

CHADWICK: That was very important. To create a whole world and that was very much what the miners wanted. We did not put on a cabaret. We wanted to put on something that militated against the usual forms of entertainment found in clubs.

HOYLAND: With good actors, stage management, recognisable characters, musicians. It was a play. We purposely did not wish to use the popular political theatre form of the seventies – Agit-prop.

□ *Agit-prop: Agitational Propaganda theatre, whose purpose is primarily to spread information and argument in support of a cause. Originated and deployed in a creative way during the early days of the Russian Revolution and subsequently employed during the depression of the 1930's, particularly in America and Britain.*

REES: One of our heroes was Brecht. Yet these plays seemed to display a very different practice?

CHADWICK: There was a lot of Brecht in the writing.

GEARING: Brecht's *Fear and Misery in the Third Reich* is composed of many short scenes, interludes of music, naturalistic writing within scenes.

REES: I thought that the dramatic means employed by the play were more familiarly English and rightfully so to make a real connection with our audiences.

CHADWICK: The way the songs were used, the play's structure, a lot of the aesthetics Brecht used were employed in the writing. Indeed, the way the screens of the set revolved, moving us to and from 1926 and 1972, was very reminiscent of his techniques. You could not have done these plays without Brecht.

89

REES: I thought the two plays were more influenced by British Theatre traditions – working class realistic drama for 1926, and some spicing with front of curtain, stand-up comic scenes for 1972 – than by Brecht. The Council of Action scenes opened it out to the audience but this is a familiar music hall or pantomime form. There were many short scenes but so are there in TV plays. I thought your plays relied on British dramaturgical forms and were all the stronger for that.

CHADWICK: The point is you want to speak as directly as you can.

REES: Nicholas Fairbairn, the Scottish Tory MP, reported very negatively about the play in the press. Apparently the Home Office, as a result, monitored the tour. Certainly the top echelons of the Arts Council from Director-General Roy Shaw downwards filled the Oval House one night to see what they were funding.

CHADWICK: There was a ruffle in the state machinery. Questions were raised in the House. Should arts spending go on left wing propaganda?

REES: We sent many letters requesting the Council to spell out that the company was not compromised in any way by these events. It took some time in coming but eventually they assured us that nothing was amiss. 'Judgement is made,' they said, 'on artistic grounds.'

  You were both Board members of Foco Novo at the time. A debate arose as to whether we should continue to present Labour Movement shows at the same time that we were presenting shows to theatre audiences. Could the same piece of theatre suit both types of audience? Bernard Pomerance was convinced it could, saying he knew Moliere was presented very successfully to workers in Chile. But you both said that you cannot play 'art' shows in miners' clubs. You even proposed that we consider changing the name of the company because Labour Movement officials found it a mouthful to pronounce, resulting in some unfortunate variations!

  ☐ *Ironically, ten years later, when we were approaching potential sponsors, we were advised to do the same thing – change our name – since they considered it an unsuitable title for their 'product' to be associated with!*

  A debate also arose about turning ourselves into a collective based on a permanent company.

HOYLAND: Whatever work we did, we wanted it to mirror in its organisation, the intentions for which we made the work. Such shows were bound to throw up heated discussions about the nature of the company. In 1980, the same kind of discussions happened at *Time Out* and eventually there was a strike, no compromise was reached and a break-away happened, *City Limits* was formed.

GEARING: A lot of people came into the theatre at that time to articulate a chosen practice of political/sexual/aesthetic beliefs and, therefore, not to make your work mirror how that belief was formalised, was a denial of the reason you had chosen to do theatre.

HOYLAND: We argued that Labour Movement audiences required Labour Movement shows – different to the kind of shows for theatre audiences. We argued that we were more interested in reaching the former than audiences who went to Arts Centres. At that time, the composition of both audiences was different. No question. And we argued that the content of the plays we were producing would be better communicated to Labour Movement audiences and, finally, to do that required a different approach to how you organised the process of production. It was inconsistent, we said, to produce plays for such audiences, working through a producing company whose organisation did not incorporate those values. That's what we were arguing at the time.

REES: Nigel, when Foco Novo produced your play *Snap* in 1981, an event which persuaded you to return from Paris and settle in London, the company was firmly a production company primarily touring Arts Council subsidised small scale venues.

GEARING: I was aware that Foco Novo was a company which addressed itself often to political subjects but not exclusively so, and had at the same time been formally inventive. *Snap* was the least overtly political of anything I had written. It was about the early English photographer Eadweard Muybridge, from Kingston-upon-Thames, who claimed he was one of the founders of the motion picture. He won a bet for a millionaire in California, where he worked, by proving that all four feet of a horse are off the ground when it is at full gallop. In the play Muybridge's wife, a model for his experiments, has an affair with one of his male models. He pursues him to Napa County, northern California, and shoots him. In the trial the all-male jury acquitted him on the basis of justifiable homicide – Muybridge having pleaded Crime Passionel.

The story and form of the play to some extent mirrors the content and form of motion pictures. And so I felt confident in a company which did new work, and also had a political background. But not the background of old English social realism. I thought of Foco Novo doing more than 'political' theatre. As with *Snap*, you can take a subject which is not political, but the manner in which you approach it will benefit from, say, the director and the company having, as Foco Novo had, produced a lot of Brecht.

REES: In 1984, Foco Novo produced your play *Black Mas*, John Constable, on tour and like Nigel's play at the New End Theatre in London. How did that come about?

CONSTABLE: Like a number of other of my plays, *Black Mas* grew out of my experience of being an Englishman abroad.

REES: A very honourable tradition!

CONSTABLE: In 1982, I spent six weeks in Trinidad, including the period of the carnival. It was probably one of the most intense periods of my life. From the moment I arrived to the moment I left, I was continually being stimulated and challenged. At the height of carnival, there is a period of four days when nobody sleeps and everybody is fuelled up on dope, drink and non-stop music. There is no escape. You have to go with it. In *Black Mas*, I wanted to capture that energy and intensity. It is one of the most theatrical events I have ever seen. The entire streets of Port-of-Spain are filled with people enacting myths and dramas.

I also had to find a way of dealing with race that was not predictable. In Trinidad, I was continually confronted with people challenging me with racial history. It was confrontational but, if you responded, it opened the way to friendship. That excited me. Whereas I find that in London there is a desire to sweep race under the carpet. In the few plays written by white writers on racial subjects, it is rare to see positive images of whites in plays – they are either fascists or wishy-washy liberals.

I set two white Londoners on holiday in Trinidad and made them the embodiment of the street-wise and hip. The comedy of the play exposes racial myths and preconceptions, and shows the white couple 'going black' under the influence of the anarchic, chaotic energy of the Carnival.

I am very interested in the intrusion of magical and mythical elements into real situations without the play disappearing into fantasy. Carnival is full of dressing up and so is a natural outlet for that. But being my first play, it was undisciplined and you, Roland, pushed me to clarify the text and obtain that balance.

REES: John has described a visceral experience that motivated him. Nigel what was your inspiration for *Snap*?

GEARING: A friend told me the story of Muybridge. He captured 'reality' by putting his still pictures in a 'zoopraxiscope' and, as a result of revolving its mechanism, a person seemed to be 'in motion'. At the same time, he was famous in his own lifetime for the court case. Soon after that, he gave up photography and his wife, the model 'in motion', fell ill and became paralysed – an extraordinary paradox.

The parallel of and, perhaps, the disparity between, the personal and the professional life, interests me. Muybridge was anxious to capture 'reality' but did not see the reality going on around him. In my adaptation of George Orwell's *Down and Out in London and Paris*, the same thing interested me.

Orwell descended into the underworld of London and Paris but he came from a public school background. That reconciliation of apparent disparities interests me.

CHADWICK: Have you ever written anything dramatically which you yourself have experienced?

GEARING: A radio play, *The Distinguished Thing*, was based on my reaction to the suicide of a girl I was living with. That was very personal.

A lot of people kindly, well-wishingly and correctly, have said to me over the years, why do you hide behind a political or social metaphor? Maybe you should address your own life.

CONSTABLE: However personal a theme you pick, it is never a piece of autobiography.

HOYLAND: I want to ask Roland why he abandoned the kind of theatre we have been talking about earlier? The Labour Movement circuit? After 1977? Why the company changed course? Why did we never get to do the show about Grunwick?

GEARING: That is a valid question because I never thought the company was wedded to single issues or interest groups. So was there a break?

HOYLAND: That moment was a break for both Jon Chadwick and myself as well as yourself, Roland. But it is an interesting moment in Foco Novo's history and more widely a reflection of British culture.

REES: I was running a touring company. We did two shows in a year. The company was front-led. A building based company has the opportunity to create a varied programme. I felt strongly at that time that the way forward for Foco Novo lay equally with formal/artistic experiment as it did with plays produced for the Labour Movement. Prior to 1975, we had produced six theatre shows. After 1977 we returned to that formula. I was dedicated to finding a way of combining my interest in playing to the popular audiences the company desired to play to, and at the same time to continue to experiment formally with the work we produced. Both of these commitments have been a deep and abiding drive in everything I have done in theatre. But I have found it difficult in this country to combine these elements. So often pigeon-holing goes on in the minds of the subsidy providers, the producers and the theatres so that the audiences end up thinking the same way.

If you cannot afford this style of work, it is difficult combining your desire to experiment with the desire to play your work to new audiences. If you pioneer new ground, it invariably will not be cost effective and if you want to play to new audiences, it will be doubly not so.

After the Labour Movement shows, we produced *A Seventh Man* by Adrian Mitchell, based on John Berger's book of that title, about migrant workers travelling from countries bounding the Mediterranean littoral – Turkey, Greece, Southern Italy, Morocco, Yugoslavia – to France and Germany during the Sixties and Seventies to become 'guest workers'. Berger's book, written in conjunction with the photographer Jean Mohr, allowed the form, equally composed of words and photos, to express the content in a vivid and unique way. As with all Berger's books, it made you look and see differently. A new focus is also a key factor in Drama. So the theme greatly attracted me. I wanted to find a way of making a play that paralleled the formula of the book but which would be entirely theatrical.

Again we used a mixed cast. Responding to Adrian Mitchell's poetic version of the book with its many songs, we made prolific use of music by Dave Brown. This ranged from the use of Turkish instruments like the oud, announcing the start of the migrant's journey from their village in Anatolia, to dissonant electronic sounds heralding the strange glass castles which the migrants, arriving in Frankfurt or wherever, stood in awe before. We had some wonderful designs by Ralph Steadman.

You might have said that this was a show ideally aimed at the Labour Movement with our experience of that circuit. But as Jon Chadwick pointed out at the time, it was not. The theme was universal – migration. It was not sufficiently about local British issues. The manner in which we intended to express the production was, returning to an earlier theme, I believe much closer to Brecht than the theatre traditions which we tapped for our Labour Movement shows and which I believe were correctly, for the circuit we played, drawing upon British models.

I was cut down the middle. This show could be popular, but our experience was telling us that it could not play the Labour Movement circuit. If such a play with such a theme was unsuitable for the Labour Movement, then this insularity was circumscribing the work I wished to do. So I would have to achieve the work by playing it to other audiences.

This was an important moment. At that time there was no winner. I accepted there was a contradiction of purpose. But in the long run, I would not accept that this would always be so. If the Labour Movement had continued to be an important power base, and had been able to continue to promote cultural activities, who knows what sort of theatre might have eventually been able to flourish on that circuit?

The course I took after that meant a policy of presenting new plays through the small scale touring circuit – Arts Centres, Colleges and Studio Theatres on campuses and within Repertory complexes. *Snap* by Nigel was one of my favourite productions of that period, 1981. It stretched the company's resources to the limit, particularly because so many of the venues we visited were ill-equipped and even more poorly staffed. The companies which started in the Eighties have benefited from the building up of that circuit over the years. I remember Michael Kustow inviting many of us on the Fringe for a tour around the new National Theatre and telling us, in words to the effect, that this was our theatre too. Well, we, as Foco Novo, did not play there. But now some of the more recently formed companies do.

So I begin to wonder where my real interests lie. As a student in the late Fifties, European plays were our fascination. In the Sixties, the American influence arrived, then in the Seventies our own brand of theatre, contra the mainstream, flourished. Now, ironically, in the late Eighties and into the Nineties, we have turned back to Europe for our inspiration and I suppose the international avant-garde has become the benchmark by which creativity is measured.

My horizons reach beyond this Eurocentric view. Theatre which is exchanged internationally and is produced by and with people from all backgrounds is like World Music. In reality, this 'international' phenomenon is European or Western, by virtue of the fact that it is marketed for the west. And increasingly the product is produced in English whatever the nationality of the performers.

The content for the next stage of theatre will be found outside of these parameters. My recent experience directing theatre workshops in Kenya and Zambia has taught me of such possibilities. There theatre is at a formative stage in comparison to our practice. But, in time, such traditions could digest the lessons of European theatre without losing their originality and so create a fresh theatrical tradition. It could give a new lease of life to the art of narrative theatre.

GEARING: The interesting thing about Foco Novo was that it had a strong political bent but it was never interested in agit-prop or, on the other hand, social realism. That is why you had a commitment to Brecht and understood him better than any other British company. You were interested in formal inventiveness and a desire to challenge.

BLACK THEATRE

My interest in black writing has remained constant. Recently a puzzled acquaintance asked why? In the Sixties, the question would not have been necessary. By the Nineties, it has become suspect to pursue channels which do not directly contribute to your self-interest.

What started as a fascination with American and English colonial history, a passion for Jazz, a distant absorption in the Civil Rights movement of the Sixties turned into a hands-on desire to see plays produced about the accumulated experience of migrants who now constitute an essential part of British contemporary life. Standing on the shores of Manhattan in 1965 I became convinced, that to make sense of my experience, I needed to view English life through another's eyes. To look outside-in. The outsiders perspective continues to haunt me.

But the original question was posed and needed an answer. My reply did not convince. The young questioner required an answer that made sense within a world committed to values alien to the Sixties. At that time we crossed barriers instead of raising them. Liberation was viewed as personal, political and international. Apartheid in South Africa, a burning question now as it had been in the Fifties, was, to my questioner, a problem at some distance in comparison to ones nearer home.

I pointed out that since it took such a long struggle to get working people centre stage, in dramas that reflected their own experience, how much more difficult it is to move the Black character from the periphery to centre stage? The Sixties nurtured a desire to see the 'alternative' become its own distinct force within mainstream culture. One of the planks of this vision was Third World/Black Theatre.

Black Theatre, like others proposing a particular identity – Feminist Theatre, Gay Theatre, Theatre for the Disabled – was targeted by the funding bodies. The support of ethnic culture became a priority. This is a considerable achievement. However, for Black Theatre to survive, because it *is* targeted, is rather like providing Task Forces to solve the problems of the inner city – good PR, but dubious practice. It was necessary originally for Black Theatre to label itself to survive, to strengthen cultural identity. By the end of the Eighties, Black Theatre had gained a high profile. But without the aid of targeting, could Black Theatre maintain its development or would it be sidelined? The long term question is: will it be able to penetrate and share the domain of mainstream theatre and preserve its own identity?

The following conversations raise these issues and answer them in different ways. Mustapha Matura and six cast-members of his play *The Coup* at the Royal National Theatre, discuss the Caribbean tradition of playwriting and acting. Tunde Ikoli and actors, Brian Bovell and Trevor Laird, talk about black British playwriting and acting. Claire Benedict and Pauline Black look to expanding the horizons of Black theatre.

96

BLACK THEATRE I

From Left to Right. Mustapha Matura, Norman Beaton, Stefan Kalipha, T-Bone Wilson, Roland Rees, Oscar James, Gordon Case and Malcolm Fredericks.

NORMAN BEATON
GORDON CASE
MALCOLM FREDFRICKS
OSCAR JAMES
STEFAN KALIPHA
MUSTAPHA MATURA
T-BONE WILSON

This conversation took place in Rehearsal Room 3 of The Royal National Theatre with some members of the cast rehearsing Mustapha Matura's *The Coup*, 1991, who had previously worked with Foco Novo and Roland Rees. Taking part were the playwright, Mustapha Matura, actors Stefan Kalipha and Oscar James, all from Trinidad, and Norman Beaton, T-Bone Wilson and Gordon Case from Guyana. Trinidadian Malcolm Fredericks, former Artistic Director of Black Co-operative, who has worked with Foco Novo, also took part.

REES: Stefan, not only were you the lead in my first UK production, but also, during my career, you are the actor I have worked with most. I first met you when I was casting a play for Ed Berman's inaugural InterAction lunchtime season of plays at the Ambiance restaurant on Queensway. These lunchtime seasons became so popular that copies soon sprouted up all over London. Casting was at InterAction's first headquarters on Chalk Farm Road opposite the Roundhouse.

   The play was by Ed Bullins, an American Black Panther, whose work had so excited me when I saw it in New York that I brought his plays back with me on my return to London in 1967. Lunchtime shows needed to be no longer than one hour and the fifty minutes of *The Electronic Nigger* fitted the bill perfectly, opening in July 1968. Bullins came over from New York for the opening. Subsequently we did two more of his plays at the Ambiance. So, Stefan, tell me about the start of everything.

KALIPHA: Trinidad is a small island and so many of us wanted to see the world. Travelling on a boat was a way of doing that. We could visit North and South America, Africa. I signed on in 1959, working in the engine room. It was a kind of university with lots of discussion and reading.

   I had a British passport so I stopped off in London. Eventually I went to the E15 Acting School in 1961. I did *The Hostage* by Brendan Behan at Stratford East Theatre. That was the first time I got reviews. And I did the same play with Edward Fox at a Rep. The next thing I did was the series of Ed Bullins' plays with you, Roland, at the Ambiance.

MATURA: I came over in 1961. I got into professional theatre writing during the early Sixties – who knows when something begins? It was through hanging out with Stefan and Horace Ové, who I knew from Trinidad, the whole kind of West Hampstead life. [*Ové, a cousin of Stefan, is the West Indian Film maker*]. Everyone I knew was very creative, very active. The political consciousness of black people was raised then. It was an energising time and opportunities for people to do their own thing seemed much easier.

   I happened to write some short pieces which were subsequently produced by InterAction and directed by you, Roland, as *Black Pieces*. I wrote these plays, you know unconsciously in a way . . . reflecting the changes going on and the attitudes of the time, with little idea of having my plays produced or taking them any further. I just showed them to Stefan and to Horace. I didn't think it would be possible to have plays like that produced because they were about West Indians. As far as I was concerned nobody in theatre was interested in West Indians, how we talk and t'ing, because it was not a conventional English play. Then you, Roland, read them and encouraged

98

me. You opened the doors through Ed Berman and the Ambiance and then it became possible.

BEATON: I got into theatre primarily as a composer/songwriter. I wrote a play *Jack of Spades*, which was produced at the Liverpool Everyman and directed by Terry Hands. I then joined the Bristol Old Vic Company to write the music for Frank Marcus's *Cleo* and I was asked to play the Narrator in the production. In 1968 I got my first starring role at the Connaught Theatre, Worthing. I have been an actor ever since.

WILSON: I came over from Guyana in 1962 to become an engineering student. I was meeting black people from other parts of the Caribbean – Trinidad and Jamaica – and from Africa for the very first time. I was excited about this and my horizons opened. I used to go to work and try to figure out things about the theatre instead of doing my work. During that time I was writing poetry and stuff like that. Then I thought I can do something else. So I went to the Mountview Theatre School. At the end of the course I thought I was ready to become an actor or writer. I was not sure how I would go about it, how the theatre worked. I was at home a good six to nine months, not finding a job. And suddenly one night I got this call from a friend, Ray Blair, who said to me: 'There is a gentleman by the name of Roland Rees who is doing a play.' I said: 'Yeah, what play? Who has written it?' 'Mustapha . . . Mustapha Matura from Trinidad. Don't waste time, come down and meet him and then you can start doing what you want to do.' So, Roland, you gave me my first job, in Mustapha's *Black Pieces*.

JAMES: I came here when I was about 15. And I couldn't get any work or anything. I had lied to the Immigration Office, saying I had parents here, which I hadn't.

KALIPHA: Stowaway!

FREDERICKS: Refugee!!

JAMES: To get here, I worked on a ship as a galley boy. HMS Verde. We landed at Liverpool and I came down to London with the intention of studying engineering and then returning home. I came from a poor family and I wanted to do something for them. However I got marooned here in this country.

FREDERICKS: Good word. [*'Maroon' was the Caribbean name for a fugitive slave*].

JAMES: I started working in factories, washing dishes in order to survive. One day I was walking down Oxford Street and I saw this girl and started chatting her up. I spoke a bit of Spanish and French and tried to impress her. She said: 'What do you do?' I said: 'I'm an actor.' Because I had seen

Johnny Sekka on TV! [*A Senegalese actor who came to the UK in the Fifties. Subsequently went to work in the States*]. She said: 'My boy friend's father is an agent.' And I said: 'Really! I'd like to meet him.' From that I met the guy and he got me some walk-ons in films and thing like that. And I did get to meet Johnny Sekka! I stood in for him on a film [*lining up the shot*] and I watched all the things he did. This inspired me to study drama with Doreen Cannon.

One night I was singing in a club – the Emerald Beach – and a director came up: 'I like your singing. Can you act?' I said, 'What do you thing I was doing up there?' They put me in film called *The Comedians*.

Then I was in a stage play at the Mermaid with Rudolph Walker and you too, Stefan. Robert Lowell's *Benito Cereno*, directed by Johnathan Miller. I was in the crowd – one of the slaves. With Miller's help, I learnt the part of King Lear, and used it as a successful audition piece for the RSC. After I left the RSC, I thought: 'Yeah! Things will happen to me now.' I came out, swell up, looking for work and I almost nearly starved until you, Roland, came up with *Black Pieces*. Because for years, parts for black actors were few and far between. That play gave me back my dignity and my strength.

CASE: I came to Britain when I was twelve years old. I got interested in theatre at school when I was thirteen. I was lucky that I had a genuine drama teacher – later he became the Principle of Rose Bruford Drama School – because he generated my interest in theatre. When I left school, I kept looking for a place to act, express myself in theatre. I knew a lady by the name of Martha Gonzales who I always fancied, carrying on from Oscar's comments! I actually chased the girl all around the place! So finally to put me out of my misery, she said: 'Okay, I go to this amateur dramatic group in Kensington. Come along.' So I went down there. It was in a room in South Ken, no bigger that your ordinary kitchen. There would be fifteen or twenty of us at the weekends. Subsequently I went to the E15 Acting School, 1972 to 1975, and my first professional job was with the Japanese Red Buddha Company. I did some TV, and then I met up with you, Roland, for Alfred Fagon's *Four Hundred Pounds*.

FREDERICKS: I started acting when I was eight in Trinidad. As a kid, I was part of the Trinidad Theatre Workshop. When I came to England at thirteen, I met these guys on the street, sitting on the wall outside my house. My dad told them to go away, but they came back and took me to a workshop called the Caribbean Showboat, upstairs at a hairdressing shop in Tooting. Two guys called Aubrey Miller and George Lascelles ran it. On Sundays I used to watch these professional guys – including Gordon Case – go through their paces. After that some person called Norman Beaton came and took away half of our members to found the Black Theatre of Brixton. They did a coup!!

One night I met Alton Kumalo [*Founder of Temba Theatre Company*] in a club and he said: 'Why don't you come down and meet Mustapha Matura, who is doing a play?' Charlie Hanson, who was directing, gave me the job. I did three plays by Mustapha, one after the other. And that's when I met you. I dropped out of *Welcome Home Jacko* [*which eventually transferred to off-Broadway*] to join Foco Novo to do Mustapha's *Independence* in 1979. That's how I got my Equity card!

REES: In 1956 Errol John's *Moon on a Rainbow Shawl* [*John was from Trinidad*] won the *Observer* play competition and subsequently played at the Royal Court in 1958 with Johnny Sekka in the cast. Wole Soyinka, the Nigerian playwright, had *The Invention* produced at the Royal court in 1958. Barry Reckord, from Jamaica, had three plays produced at the Court: *Flesh to a Tiger* 1958, *You In Your Small Corner* 1960 and *Skyvers* 1963. After these plays I am not aware of any by black playwrights that were produced in the UK until we did the three Ed Bullin's plays and subsequently your's Mustapha, with InterAction in the late Sixties. It seems an historical moment.

BEATON: I cannot remember one. As a matter of fact when I started running the Green Banana Club in Soho, in 1968/69, I was astonished to discover there was a black playwright in England and that was Mustapha. It was an absolute miracle. A wonder!

REES: Barry Reckord's *Skyvers* was produced with an all white cast because, as Barry said, the Royal Court could not find any black actors. By the late Sixties, we were doing InterAction's seasons and Mustapha's plays with black casts. What happened? What had changed? Did this seem to you the start of something new?

JAMES: Listen, maybe the Royal Court and Barry did not look far enough! We were always there. You were the person, Roland, who went out and looked and found a cast for those InterAction plays. No black actors! That's an old excuse, which has been going on for ages.

MATURA: If we are talking about change, that is the change. Where you, Roland, wanted to find black actors because you had some vision of truth or realism that had been introduced into the culture of the times. You determined to find West Indian actors, and the Royal Court and Barry Reckord were not interested.

REES: When I saw Bullins' plays in New York, I was totally struck by the raw and real quality of black American urban life they portrayed. His work was full of humour but also anger. I felt that mainstream London theatres would not be in tune with what they would regard as extreme attitudes. So when Ed Berman talked of starting a new theatre, I took Bullins' plays to him thinking he would, as an American, want to promote black American writing. My faith was vindicated.

KALIPHA: That was the first time I did black American plays, as far as I am concerned. The first set of black plays I knew about.

REES: They became very popular. The Theatre was in the basement of the Ambiance restaurant at the top of Queensway run by Junior Telfer, a Trinidadian entrepreneur. It crammed in an audience of thirty or forty, and we presented the plays, starting at 1.15pm, environmentally. The audience's noses were stuck in the action.

A couple of years later Ed moved on to settle the Ambiance temporarily at the ICA on the Mall, where he wanted to present a season of 'Black and White Power' plays.

In America, black politics and culture had moved on from Martin Luther King. The activities of the Black Panthers, the proselytising of Stokeley Carmichael, Rap Brown, Eldridge Cleaver and the Black Muslims and Malcolm X, described a world that was separatist. Integration was not on the agenda at the moment. So the genesis for a season of plays with such a title arose from this background. Ed wanted to catch a whiff of this. And naturally all the plays were American. These attitudes were only just beginning to reach the shores of the UK. The emergence of a home-grown black power consciousness was yet to surface here. Michael X, self-styled black leader, who had once collected rents for Rachman from black tenants in Notting Hill, and who was to be subsequently indicted for murder in Trinidad, did not carry the intellectual weight of the American Black Muslim Malcolm X.

I said to Ed, we must find an indigenous black writer to represent this side of the Atlantic in the season. Otherwise we will not encourage new writing or reflect the different world over here. We must find someone who writes and lives here. He said: 'Okay, go and find them.' That is how I met Mustapha. Through Stefan and Horace Ove. I remember vividly to this day, Mustapha turning up at InterAction, then on Malden Road in Gospel Oak, with yellow scraps of typed paper.

MATURA: Beautifully typed!

REES: You had written a number of short plays. We used three, playing them under the title *Black Pieces*. They were included in the ICA lunchtime season and were an hour long with a cast of eleven. We stitched the plays together with Ray 'Charles' Blair's music and preceded them with *White Poem* by David Mercer.

MATURA: I remember it like it was yesterday. I did not attend rehearsals since I did not know writers could go to rehearsals and disrupt them – I only learned that later on in life! My first wife had booked a holiday in Cornwall. After about two days there, I said: 'What's the date?' She said it was the 18th, and I said: 'The 18th!! My play was supposed to open yesterday and it might be reviewed!' 'So let's go and get a newspaper,' she said. I said: 'No, forget about it. They won't review it.' She persisted and we went and got the *Daily Telegraph*, and there was a review. It talked about this girl in a tight mini-skirt, her legs and vulgarity and t'ings and I went: 'Wow! I've upset the *Telegraph*! This is great!' And that was it. I came back to London, and what may or may not be interesting for future scholars of drama was that, you, Roland, had misspelt my name in the programme. You had left out the 'h' in Mathura. And I thought it doesn't matter, it's the Sixties, cool man, go with the flow. Leave it at that. And that's how I got the spelling of my name, now – Matura!

FREDERICKS: Roland gave you your name!

REES: The reviews were very good. Lots of people came and the ICA Cinema sat more audience than the basement of the Ambiance. Oscar, do you remember where we rehearsed? You were always late, because you were driving your taxi! [*Oscar has been known to take actors home from rehearsal and put the meter on!*]

JAMES: Why I was late is because I was getting into character! And my character is still hanging on after all these years. It was the best play I have ever done and the best character.

REES: We rehearsed in an old Fire Station InterAction had use of, and it was dripping with water. There were puddles everywhere.

MATURA: The first play was called *Dialogue*. It was the first I ever wrote. It was about three guys watching TV. They were called A, B and C. I didn't learn to name characters yet and they were using the images on the TV screen in order to raid each other's consciousness. It reflected the politicisation going on among black people during the Sixties. The second one was called *Indian*. It was about a guy bringing home a nice, white 'chick' to their room and then they had nothing to eat so one went out to 'thief' a chicken. They all lusted after this girl and it ended up with someone 'thiefing' the chicken and hiding it under the bed! The last one was called *Party*. It was the most stylised and political, reflecting the contemporary, middle class, trendy, lefty society going on in London at the time. Black guys in parties mau-mauing all these white chicks in a corner saying 'your place or mine?'

☐ White Poem *by David Mercer preceded* Black Pieces. *It was a ten minute monologue of a Rhodesian farmer sitting on his verandah at dusk, gun in hand, voicing his determination to stay and prevent Independence. It ends with a hail of automatic weapon fire directed at the farmer, in this case from amongst the audience in the form of Oscar as a Zimbabwe Freedom Fighter.*

JAMES: It was the time of the Rhodesian problem and I remembered that was what sparked me up. The Rhodesian war, and taking up the gun, and I thought, I would shoot the whole lot up because I was so angry at the time!

☐ *This was still a time when you could hire from Bapty's, very real, imitation automatic weapons and fire blanks off amongst the audience! Within a year, IRA activities made the police very nervous and soon it became impossible to hire such weapons. Oscar made good use of the opportunity, releasing large amounts of ammunition every performance. The empty cases rattled across the floor of the ICA Cinema!*

For me that was what gave me strength. Because it was going on at the time and Mercer wrote about it.

MATURA: It was a very, very heavy time. Black people were discovering a lot of things, the history of their past and the way they had been brain washed. That was coming out, so fast and everywhere.

JAMES: I remember Ed Berman getting so excited by the success of the play, because people were coming from all over, that he ripped the phone from its socket at the ICA. He was so furious that they couldn't take the bookings fast enough. It was the first time London had a black play so successful!

REES: It very much caught the time.

MATURA: It did. It did. It raised a lot of questions.

JAMES: A lot of people argued in the audience – black and white.

MATURA: As a result of this, I was commissioned to write another play by Michael White, the impresario and then progressive supporter of minority tastes. Gratefully and hopefully, I wrote *As Time Goes By* within two months which is unheard of these days for me, especially now my prices have gone up! It was really a wonderful opportunity to write my first full length play.

REES: Norman, although you were not in the cast of any of the Ambiance plays, you did play host to them at the Green Banana in Soho.

BEATON: What gave me the idea of lunchtime theatre was Junior Telfer opening the Ambiance. So knowing he knew how to proceed, I contacted Ed Berman and said: 'Would he like to use my club?' And Ed said: 'Yes. As long as it does not cost me anything!' The idea was that, if I could get people in, I could sell food and wine and so on, because there was no lunchtime trade for a basement space in the middle of Soho. That's how I got involved in presenting theatre, an impresario so to speak.

REES: In 1970, we did *As Time Goes By* at the Traverse Theatre, during the Edinburgh Festival, and then at the Royal Court.

KALIPHA: I played a character called Ram based loosely on my cousin Valman, who lived in London then. In the Sixties black people were conscious of black power on the one hand and also Eastern religions. Valman used to portray himself as a sort of guru. Mustapha wrote the play about this character, Ram, living in a small flat, where people came to see him. He offered advice and would go into trances and speak in different tongues, things like that. His wife, Batee, played by Mona Hammond, was pretty fed up with all this because hardly any money came out of it. Ram put her in the kitchen, with the children, while he 'met' his clients. She said she would go on 'strike' and so on. It was great, full of humour and very enjoyable to do.

JAMES: I played the bus conductor! For me, looking back at the play, Ram was like Robin Hood because living in this country at that period was very tough for black people. It was as if Ram brought the whole community together. The play took the theme of the family coming over here from the West Indies to discover there was no family life. So when you lived with a woman, you tried to secure the whole situation, hence the poverty, the economical situation where there were so many blacks in the least paid jobs – on the buses and tubes. So you had these two characters, me and my brother, one on the buses and one on the tubes, competing with each other: 'Well I get more fresh air!' They had a conflict over a woman. Because one brother worked at night, the other during the day, there became a tug of war. They went separately to Ram to tell him their troubles and he showed them how it was part of black people's history. To understand this history, we visited people like Ram.

And the other thing I want to say is that if it wasn't for you, I wouldn't have made it in theatre. I am really grateful to you and for all the time you put into those plays because, as far as black theatre goes, nobody cared until you came along and got in there and did it.

REES: 'Bringing the whole community together,' included the regular visits of a white, bohemian, Notting Hill couple, who came to catch up on the Grove 'scene', smoke Ram's 'weed' and in return play him their latest 'sounds'.

WILSON: I was playing a brief part briefly. I was the middle man for the guru. He was doing his guru business and I was the light hands in town. I knew a lot about obeah and things and could also find people to take to the guru. For which Ram would give me a small commission.

REES: Alfred Fagon was in the play.

☐ *Alfred Fagon, playwright and actor, returning from jogging one day, collapsed of a heart attack outside the entrance to his flat in Camberwell, in*

1986. He was taken to hospital and declared dead on arrival. He was put in the morgue and finally cremated in the South London crematorium at the hospital's expense because the Police claimed no friends or relatives could be found, despite much evidence to the contrary in his flat. He was 49. His death only came to the notice of friends and family as a result of his absence from rehearsal for a new BBC series. Alfred's presence was indefatigable in these plays and his loss is great, both as actor and writer.

When I first met Alfred during the casting of *Black Pieces*, he was living in the Sheen house of three solicitors. He looked at the script and said: 'I cannot read this.' I said: 'Why?' He said: 'I dare not read it.' Alfred explained he had never seen anything written down in the way he spoke. [*In patois*] 'I cannot believe it. I don't think I should say these words.' To him it was a momentous occasion. And indeed these early plays by Mustapha broke that ground.

MATURA: They did. But as you said, looking at what had gone before, it was kind of academic black theatre. *Black Pieces* and *As Time Goes By* was the first time, as the reviews said, that working class black people had been written about. About people arriving here in London and laying down the roots of some kind of West India community in London. And I wrote it in the language they spoke and that was the major difference. That was easy for me and easy for the actors to get hold of the dialogue and make it live. In those plays there was a coming together of material and actors. I think before with Soyinka and Reckord there was not that closeness. That was the major difference.

REES: The fact that it played high profile places like the Edinburgh Festival, the Royal Court, and that you won the John Whiting Award, the George Devine Award, the *Evening Standard* Award, came to place your writing, in particular, firmly in the public's eye and at the same time began to create a tradition of black theatre.

MATURA: Yes, yes. It was the turn of the wheel, the turn of the corner that Caribbean plays could be written in the Caribbean language about Caribbean people, ordinary Caribbean people, without there being a big hullabaloo about it.

JAMES: Most of the black actors doing a West Indian part or an English play tried to be English. Whereas with these plays you no longer needed to put on an accent. Now the younger actors can naturally do this and the English audiences accept it. Mustapha opened this up. This really brought the West Indian idiom out and so it could be passed onto the younger generation.

Photo © John Haynes 1983

Malcolm Fredericks (left) and Stafan Kalipha in Foco Novo's 1983 production of Mustapha Matura's *Independence*

MATURA: This was, you know, a conscious political act on my part. With English people, if you were angry and you talked West Indian, they would say: 'Sorry, you must speak more slowly, I don't understand.' I took this on board and said: 'This is rubbish, you can understand what I am saying.' Maybe they don't like what the West Indian language is saying to them. But they do understand. So this was a conscious decision on my part to have West Indians talking West Indian. Anyway, I could not have written my plays in English. Impossible! But as soon as I did this, it was like stepping into a large room. Let us not forget the sociology of the time. There was a very, very strong motto or rap going on at the time – 'Tell it like it is!' And that is what I thought I was doing.

CASE: I remember seeing, in 1968, the Negro Ensemble from New York, at the Aldwych, part of the World Theatre season. This was the first time I had seen blacks on stage. I was in amateur dramatics at the time. It was tremendous but I could not identify with it beyond there being black people on stage. Then I saw *As Time Goes By* and that was something I could identify with.

JAMES: I want to know one thing, Roland. Out of all the directors I have worked with, you have helped the most. But I think you backed out in a way later

107

on. You could have kept a nice group going and the papers said you were the only 'ethnic director' and I think at that point you backed out because they started calling you that. You were the only theatre director directing black people in the late Sixties, taking those chances and standing up and doing that and challenging. As soon as they called you 'ethnic', you ran away. Why? I hope you write this down. After that you did not use black actors. I know you had to eat!

MATURA: He give him fatigue!

REES: That was true for a certain period. But later Foco Novo did many black plays. More in fact. Two by Alfred Fagon and six by Tunde Ikoli in the late Seventies and during the Eighties. With a new generation of actors. And remember, Foco Novo was employing mixed casting before the phrase was invented. You, Oscar, and Mona Hammond were in Bernard Pomerance's *Foco Novo* in 1972 and Stefan was in Brecht's *A Man's a Man* in 1974 and Stefan with Joan-Ann Maynard were in *A Seventh Man* by Adrian Mitchell in 1977.

But there were other reasons. Many people in the early Seventies said to me: 'Why don't you start a black theatre company?' I thought that wrong then and still do so now. Remember I had been living in New York for two years. I had been studying Marcus Garvey and Black Power movements. This movement was about doing it for yourself and not relying on the majority society for survival. I was very aware of the feelings which could exist towards me, whatever my credentials. I thought it necessary for black people to run their own theatres. In New York it would have been impossible for me to do the work I did here in the late Sixties and early Seventies. The climate of opinion would not have permitted it. But because that climate of black consciousness had not fully reached here, certainly not in the form it took in the States, I was able to achieve the work we did. It was revealing in the first place that I was accepted by Ed Bullins, an American Black Panther, to direct one of his plays here in London.

But there were further reasons. The Royal Court after Mustapha's early success took him up. His next play was done there and I was not asked to direct it. So I went off in other directions. In the end, you hope that the theatre will take up a successful combination and that the playwright will stand by you. The same thing had happened to me in 1968 with Mike Weller. I had made the initial success for a playwright. The Royal Court capitalised on that work and made it seem as if they had discovered the writer by employing another director for his next play. It is a familiar story.

Before you have to go to your performance, Oscar, tell us about Alfred Fagon's *11 Josephine House* at The Almost Free in 1973 with yourself, Mona Hammond and T-Bone in the cast. This was a full-length play set in Bristol.

JAMES: He said he wrote it in three days. He said: 'Oscar, I wrote this play in three days! Look! Oscar!' He told me how many words it had in it. He counted every single word. He was inspired by being in *Black Pieces* and *As Time Goes By.*

REES: I remember you, T-Bone, saying that both you and Alfred thought if Mustapha can do it, so can we. And it set you writing.

JAMES: *Josephine House* was about West Indians bringing their own culture and community here, into England, into the English culture. Because in the countryside of Jamaica, it is so different to here.

　□ *Alfred came from the heart of Jamaica, Clarendon, where his parents kept a Post Office. I remember how the cast of* Black Pieces *were always sending each other up. But the actor who got most 'fatigue' was Alfred. He was the 'country boy'. The cast used to make fun of his gait as though he was taking large steps through mud! It was all done with great affection.*

How do you keep that going here? There is a unity in that life, whereas the whole English system was tearing them apart. It is about exile. The love and respect that religion imposed on a community in alien circumstances and how it held together. I remember Alfred saying how proud he was of writing it in three days. 'Lawd God, Oscar!' With that I must go and leave the unemployed alone!

FREDERICKS: Oscar was born about three streets away from me in Morvant, Trinidad, the same village! Your grandmother, knew my grandmother. 'Eh, eh, Mrs Eli wha' happenin'?'

KALIPHA: You think dis a play or wat?

JAMES: I'm glad to hear you jammin' all the time. I have work to do. [*Oscar had to go to his performance of* Anthony and Cleopatra].

REES: Gordon and Stefan, you were in Alfred's play *Four Hundred Pounds* and the Brecht play, *Conversations in Exile* in a new version by Howard Brenton. These were two fifty minute plays produced by Foco Novo on tour and at the Royal Court in 1982.

CASE: *Four Hundred Pounds* was about two guys who hanged out together and gambled on pool and then fell out. The £400 symbolised apparently the 400 years that black people were taken across the Middle Passage from Africa to the Caribbean. These two guys loved each other but they fought. They gambled on pool and the black ball became symbolic to my character. He would not pot it because of slavery. By not potting the black ball to win the game, my partner's stake of £400 was lost.

MATURA: You couldn't pot the ball or wat?

Mustapha Matura

CASE: I refused because it was black and the last ball left!

REES: In the Brecht play, you were both refugee scientists from Nazi Germany hiding out in Finland, waiting for news and arguing over the times.

KALIPHA: I was a nuclear physicist.

CASE: I was a socialist engineer.

KALIPHA: It was interesting how you cast the play. Gordon and I were both playing northern European people. We enjoyed the Brecht very much because it was a challenge.

CASE: We had a ball with it. Pun intended! The main thing was we actually played pool during this play. Stefan had never played before. Nothing was set up. We played it as it turned out. So each night, each shot was with different lines. But the other thing was that Foco Novo treated us amazingly well. A car was hired to tour us round the country and we drove it.

REES: It was cheaper than rail tickets. But what most worried me was Stefan's complete lack of sense of geographical direction. I had to pray you would go west for Bristol!

CASE: The relationship in the play, I can say this now, entered into my and Stefan's own relationship. Antagonism but love. It's amazing how Alfred went into the essence of real emotion and feeling.

REES: What was different about these two plays? Had we moved on?

CASE: It was one of the earliest case of open casting. Is that the phrase?

KALIPHA: You must remember I played Galy Gay in Foco Novo's *A Man's a Man* production in 1975 and a Turkish worker in *A Seventh Man* in 1976, with Joan-Ann Maynard also in that cast.

REES: So it was the casting that was the difference?

KALIPHA: You were the only director doing that kind of thing. There may have been other examples but I don't know of them. Now it happens more. For example, I am playing a Spaniard in *Fuente Ovejuna* at the National.

REES: *Independence* by Mustapha Matura, 1979.

FREDERICKS: What I remember from *Independence* was you, Roland, saying: 'Stefan, what are you doing? I can't understand what you are doing!'

CASE: Stefan was saying: 'I'm being independent, man!'

FREDERICKS: It was amazing. It was an important progression in my career. Coming from Trinidad, I was fascinated by the way older actors, such as Stefan, Rudolph Walker and Norman Beaton, could utilise their own accents in English plays and yet keep the essence that made them Trinidadian or Guyanese, etc. Then I heard Stefan was going to be in the play. He was my hero! Stefan was the first Trinidadian I had worked with in England. It was like heaven. It was not like work. And to hear Stefan put the right emphasis on a word, the right Trini 'Eh' or 'Al yer' was pure pleasure.

Independence was about this island which had become independent. The former Governor of the Island and his wife came back to see the sunset a final time, during Independence celebrations. They visited the hotel where they used to take their evening drinks. Now the hotel was rundown. Drakes, Stefan's character, was the ghost of the hotel. He was there to keep the bar going, to make the cocktails, live the part. He was also there so that those English people can never build that place again. My character was there to further himself. Drakes was there as keeper of the past.

MATURA: I came to England in 1962 and did not return to Trinidad until 12 years later, so my first plays were quite happily set in England. And I thought: 'Right, I'm going to be a writer in England.' Then I went back to Trinidad and saw a change in those twelve years. I had left just before Independence. I realised, as it turned out, there were plays to be written about Trinidad. Like *Independence* and *The Coup*.

REES: You were also tackling the colonial past. If you had stayed in England you might not have.

MATURA: I was trying to make sense of our history, And my own personal history. The way to do that was to write plays about it. Trinidad is so interesting with its multi-layered, as opposed to England's stratified, society. Also I found that, in writing plays about England, I seemed to be having to explain my own humanity again and again, saying West Indians are just people. Now I don't mind doing that once but to have to keep writing that sort of play for an English audience who would digest it with no effect at all, was not a progression. There is a strong motivation to write theatre for change. I found my early plays getting like an assembly line. I wanted to resist England too and so writing about Trinidad was another aspect of that.

REES: Norman, in 1987, Foco Novo produced *The Cape Orchard* by Michael Picardie on tour and at the Young Vic.

BEATON: Michael Picardie is a white South African living in Cardiff. He wrote the play in the tradition of *The Cherry Orchard*, hence the title. It was about a white woman, Leonie, who has a fruit farm in the Cape area. She returns from England – where she works as an actress – to bury her son's ashes. The boy has been killed in Namibia, fighting in the South African army whilst doing his National Service. Leonie has an adopted daughter, played by Pauline Black, who is Cape Coloured and she has taken on all the prejudices of a white South African. Into this mileu comes Pieterse, also Cape Coloured, a school teacher, who is very conscious of his heritage, his roots in the Bushmen – he speaks their Khoisan 'Click' language.

REES: Which you so accurately learnt. It was a lot of trouble but it was wonderfully worth it. The sound of it.

BEATON: At the centre of the play was the Black servant, Diane Cupido, played by Claire Benedict, who was very conscious of the struggle going on in South Africa and is herself getting more and more militant. The character I played, Pieterse, was trying to say, look, there is a way forward out of all this violence, away from violent confrontation. And really the play is about that. Unfortunately, what happens is that the holocaust becomes inevitable and we find that Pieterse at the end of the play, now in the future 2005, has also taken up arms.

REES: The Southern part of Africa had become a battlefield. It was a visionary play about a possible future. And it was describing a South Africa in 1987 that political circumstances had barely reached. How did this play strike the audience?

BEATON: People were very struck by the proposition Picardie was putting forward. Everyone is conscious of the potentially explosive situation in South Africa. Here were characters trying to resolve the future conflict by other means than warfare. It was a very rich, literary piece. It transcended not only the English language, but went into the different dialects and languages within the black South African community, including Afrikaans, the language of the Cape Coloureds.

REES: Mustapha, I have directed four plays by yourself and six by Tunde Ikoli. You are, of course, different writers. You come from different generations. You were born in Trinidad. Tunde here in Limehouse. His father was African and mother English. Are there different imperatives for Black writers of different generations and backgrounds? Is this important for an understanding of how Black Theatre has developed?

MATURA: Yes. In as much as it describes and illustrates an aspect of the Black diaspora. Tunde came from a mixed race background and I from a very secure, blissfully happy childhood, and this is where you have to take on board a writer's personal history as well as his cultural history. Tunde's early plays were trying to express and discover his identity, coming from the heritage of growing up in this society. I was a child of Independence in Trinidad. So I was writing two kinds of plays – large political plays and cultural plays. I was not writing just out of personal quest.

FREDERICKS: This brings to light one of the problems when you categorise Black writing and Black Theatre. Tunde is black because his father happens to be Nigerian and because of racism as it is deemed, 1% makes you black. This is not to say Tunde Ikoli is not a Black writer but he is from London, the East End, and writes about those sort of characters. The first play I saw of his was *On the Out* [*produced by Foco Novo in 1978*] at the Bush. I was the same age and social background as the characters. I enjoyed it but did not relate to it. It was as foreign to me as *Look Back in Anger*. Whereas I relate to Mustapha's work. Tunde is black and British and what has happened is that sort of person has started writing now. One wonders why they have not been writing for 200 years because they have been here to do it.

WILSON: Coming from the Caribbean, Mustapha has something to draw from. And not only Trinidad. But the whole of the Caribbean and its colonial past. Tunde has to draw from England where originally there was a small black population. So what he could use as a writer would take time to mature. But now there is growth. Fortunately, part of his parents are Nigerian. So what he does is combine that in his writing. Sometimes it comes out a bit frustrated but he is heading towards combining those elements. Mustapha was the first successful Black writer in England. When people saw *Black Pieces* and *As Time Goes By*, English people were 'seeing' black people for the first time. Now we have to look at which way Black writing is going to turn. The Black writers coming out of England will have to draw increasingly from England. That means understanding more about the society they are living in.

REES: In many of Tunde's plays, which he wrote for Foco Novo, there is an even distribution of black and white, male and female characters. Foco Novo's commissioning process allowed us to look at the kind of characters and thematic development the play might contain. It was a conscious brief to develop a style of play, to respond to large themes with minimal resources, to make a mini-epic form of play.

FREDERICKS: One of the dangers of that is that you think you are doing something new but you are not necessarily putting something new on stage. Alfred had new characters in *11 Josephine House*. Mustapha puts new characters on stage. With this paraphernalia, this integrated casting, you end up with nothing new. Being black is not enough. Being black from the East End and acting, moving, behaving, speaking as from the East End is not theatrically new. One of the reasons Black writers have slowed down is that they are not putting new characters on stage. In Mustapha's *Rum 'n Coca Cola*, you go to the theatre, the lights come up, and you are on the beach in the Caribbean and there is a guy going: 'Rum 'n coca cola!' He speaks. He is new.

WILSON: You must remember you come from that background.

FREDERICKS: But if you don't come from that background, when you see it, it is new and exciting.

WILSON: Black kids born here, who have not been to the Caribbean or anywhere else, are fused up with a kind of English feeling. You cannot actually say that because Mustapha created his characters, there are no other possibilities. You should wait and see how the new Black writers are going to see their country.

FREDERICKS: The first movement ended up with *Welcome Home Jacko* by Mustapha. Then the new writers Caz Phillips, Jaqueline Rudet and Tunde Ikoli started another era. Since that time the energy has slowed down. We are in a lull position.

REES: So you agree something different has happened. Another stage.

FREDERICKS: Yes. Different.

CASE: The approach you have taken, Roland, has certainly moved Black Theatre along. An important part of the definition of Black writing is that it must express black experience. And that can be expressed in many different ways, as Mustapha has said, from all over the black diaspora. Alfred's plays were angry about West Indian life in England. Mustapha's are political and contain a technical virtuosity. But for sheer, raw power Tunde takes it. When you, Roland, started to produce his plays, we had not seen up to that point a lot of black fury and anger on stage. That is the shift – from the West Indies to blacks in England. British blacks do not know the West Indies. That is the important step.

KALIPHA: I would say that the sweetness, Malcolm, you felt in Mustapha's plays, about Trinidad where you were born, is a response to plays about things you know well. You can have Trinidad food, Chinese food, Indian food, but the food you like is from Trinidad.

FREDERICKS: I agree with you. But I still say I look at the British black writers from a distance. The masses of black people who go to theatre and who make our theatre happen, history has not shown that they also have followed.

MATURA: That's a major change. When we started off the composition of the audience was 99% white.

FREDERICKS: And there is danger of reverting back to that. Apart from the plays of Oliver Samuels, the black audience are saying there is nothing we can relate to. They go out to see Oliver Samuels in their droves. That is direct from Jamaica. [*Oliver Samuels: The Caribbean's No. 1 comic actor/writer*].

CASE: Like Boops Theatre.

FREDERICKS: And that is direct from Jamaica!

CASE: Black people go and see Boops but that is like a pair of trousers – it can only last so long. That is the reason Black theatre is not progressing. Every time they think of going to the theatre, Boops and Oliver Samuels is getting the publicity.

   □ Boops *is a Jamaican comedy group which successfully drew large black audiences to their shows at the Hackney Empire.*

MATURA: Gordon, this is a very different kind of theatre you are talking about. The cornier it gets, the less progressive it gets, the more people like it. There is room for other types of theatre.

CASE: How come Foco Novo is no more if there is room for it? Right. That's the point. That's the point!

MATURA: Samuels used their own money. They get no Arts Council grant. They're private enterprise.

CASE: When you say they are doing theatre . . . .

MATURA: Of course, they are doing theatre. They are doing an important part of theatre. Reminding West Indian people of the coarseness, vulgarity of their humour. They say it's alright to laugh at a big bottom woman joke – without any intellectual ideology telling you that is not the right political frame of mind to be in.

CASE: Accepted. But in terms of Black Theatre going forward and to go forward, you have to change, where is that change happening?

MATURA: Both types of theatre have a place. There is the pioneering, breaking new ground theatre like Foco Novo and there is the traditional 'No sex please we're British' type of theatre.

We are subject to the ebb and flow of the culture we live in. [*Interruption from others*] I haven't finished . . . Mr Speaker Sir! We are subject to changes in funding, to the availability of new material, new plays. [*Everyone wants to speak at the same time*] Wait na' man . . . Also what imagination is applied to it. I think a lot of healthy things are happening like Yvonne Brewster doing the classics with black casts. I did an adaptation of Synge's *Playboy* . . . .

CASE: That is superficial. They've been doing that for a long time.

MATURA: It is a factor.

KALIPHA: It is part of the Black Theatre movement.

MATURA: There is a shortage of good new black plays and in order to progress you need new Mustapha Maturas or Mustapharines in the Nineties to write the plays and move the ball along.

REES: There are a number of new Black writers.

CASE: We need an image that is open to new influences. What is thrilling about Boops? We have to move things on.

FREDERICKS: People are doing things. There are new writers.

CASE: Give us an example.

FREDERICKS: The writer at the Court – Winsome Pinnock. She is actually writing from her own point of view, a black woman in England with her own anger and her own judgement of history. She is getting produced. She is also getting 99% white audiences.

MATURA: And Boops gets 99% black audiences.

FREDERICKS: And Tunde is getting 99% white audiences.

REES: I would not think that true of *Scrape Off the Black* at Stratford East and it was certainly not true of the audiences for the plays by Tunde we did in Peckham.

MATURA: The racial composition of an audience is not the way to measure everything.

KALIPHA: If his mother is white and his father black, his plays are for all audiences!

116

BLACK THEATRE 2

BRIAN BOVELL   TUNDE IKOLI   TREVOR LAIRD

Tunde Ikoli has written six plays for Foco Novo: *On the Out* [1978], *Sink or Swim* [1982], *Sleeping Policemen* [1983] with Howard Brenton, *Week In, Week Out* [1985], *The Lower Depths* [1986] and *Banged Up* [1986]. He was a co-winner of the Samuel Beckett award. His film *Smack and Thistle* was shown on Channel 4. He lives in Limehouse. His mother is Cornish and his father Nigerian. He was a member of the Board of Foco Novo for some years. When the Company closed in 1988, as a result of the withdrawal of subsidy by the Arts Council, he was working on a commission from Foco Novo for an African version of *The Tempest*. He is writer in residence at Theatre Royal, Stratford East.

Actors Brian Bovell and Trevor Laird, both in Foco Novo productions of Ikoli plays, *Sink or Swim* and *Banged Up*, also took part. Laird has worked with the Royal Court, the Abbey Theatre, Dublin and the Leeds Playhouse as well as in films *Quadrophenia, The Long Good Friday*. Bovell has worked with the Royal National Theatre, the Royal Court and the Riverside Studios as well as in films *Burning an Illusion, Playing Away*.

IKOLI: I left school at fifteen with no qualifications to my name. In those days, jobs were pretty plentiful. Before I left school, it had already been decided that my future career lay in a factory. I wasn't too disappointed about this. I figured to myself, it would be good to get out on the street and earn money. For two years I was a tailor's cutter in a clothing factory. Walking up and down this factory – it was about thirty yards long – driving myself mad because after three months I hated it, after a year I realised there was nothing new in the job and after the two years come up I was desperate.

Most of my friends had become thieves, drug dealers and those kinds of things. I never had the courage to do anything naughty like that. I thought: 'What am I going to do with my life?' On Saturday afternoons I spent my wages up the West End going to the pictures. I'd go at two in the afternoon and come home at three in the morning. In between I would go to five different picture houses and watch five different films. While I was in these picture houses, I could lose myself. Like I was in the world where the film was, not in the boring world where I was. All the while I have been in the business, that sensation I had when I was fifteen has never been repeated. After seeing *The Godfather,* I think in 1970 or '71, I decided I was going to be an actor. I didn't imagine how difficult that was going to be because I was just a little black East End kid who didn't know anybody or anything, except a youth worker called Dan Jones, who introduced me to someone called Maggie Pinhorn. She managed to turn eight scrappy pages I had written into a script, which got money from the Rowntree Trust to turn into *Tunde's Film* in 1973. I was seventeen.

REES: Then you went to the National Film school.

IKOLI: That's a quantum leap. The British media, as is its wont, loves colourful characters and took me to their hearts. For two weeks, when I was seventeen, I was in The Guardian, every equivalent magazine, and on television programmes, and so I really thought I had cracked it. Hollywood was the next stop! I didn't realise I would soon be yesterday's news. I went from expecting to be a film star to being a nothing!

I got a call from the Royal Court to attend a casting session. As I'd never acted in my life, I thought this was my major breakthrough. So I went along to the Irish club near Sloane Square, and in those days one of the old guard, Oscar Lewenstein, ran the Court. The play, they were casting, was *Play Mas* by Mustapha Matura. I had never read plays, or had what you would call a literate education. I was presented with this script by Patsy Pollock, the casting director, and asked to read. The play was set in Trinidad. I come from an English/Nigerian family and was born in Whitechapel. I don't have a West Indian accent. My version of a Caribbean accent is worse than Jim

Davidson! I was full of hope and confidence and was given this page of script to read. One thing troubled me – I didn't know Mustapha from Adam – was that I thought he couldn't spell. Because a word like 'three' was spelt 't'ree'. Then I read. Within two minutes, Patsy Pollock asked me if I had any other ideas than being an actor? I didn't take this as an insult. I thought she was being kind. I said: 'I want to write and direct plays and films.' So she said: 'Why don't I get you to meet Oscar Lewenstein?' 'Give me his name and address!' We met and in two weeks I was an Assistant Director at the Royal Court on Mustapha's play! And he had written plays for you, Roland, but I didn't know that or know you.

REES: The Royal Court produced in the Fifties and Sixties plays by the Nigerian, Wole Soyinka, the Trinidadian, Errol John, and the Jamaican, Barry Reckord. Barry told me that his play *Skyvers* was produced with an all white cast because the Court told him they could find no black actors. In the late Sixties and early Seventies, I directed plays by Ed Bullins and Mustapha Matura with black casts. A new generation of black actors and playwrights began to see the light of day and they were from the Caribbean. Foco Novo produced your play *On the Out* in 1978. It played at the Bush and on tour. Do Barry's remarks about casting resonate for you?

IKOLI: I really don't believe any of this rubbish about not being able to cast black characters. You make actors. Like with Foco Novo and *On the Out*. When the pleasure of having the token black East Ender running around had worn out and my career was on the downside, I met you. You didn't conduct an interview and ask me if I had studied drama. The play itself and my rawness, freshness was the start-off point. That is the way you find actors.

REES: Why was Ade, your brother, who did not have pretensions to being an actor, cast in the title role of *On the Out?*

IKOLI: For a lot of money that's why! I took ten per cent of his wages! The play is about a guy who comes out of prison. While inside, he decides to go straight. But when he's out, he finds his friends pressing him to go back to crime. Ade was just right for it. It was loosely based on his career. He had been in prison. The director of the Foco Novo production, John Chapman, was keen to use him. I would do that in films now but not in theatre.

REES: In 1978, getting the casting right for *On the Out* was important to you. You were writing plays with characters who came from a different generation and background compared to plays with characters originating in the Caribbean? The casting requirements were very different to those for Mustapha's *Play Mas*, set in Trinidad. You were stating your world.

119

IKOLI: In those days I was into having the actor from the background of my characters and most of my characters were from the East End. I felt at the time that I wanted someone exactly like that. After my experience at the Royal Court, I was not too keen on the older Caribbean actors in Mustapha's play. I thought they had a weird way of acting. Now I feel acting is acting. Acting should carry the play. I was too much in love with the realist concept of acting, thinking that if my character comes from Poplar, so must the actor. Now I don't believe that shit.

That need to copy is like the Peter Hall version of the world. A European version of how verse should be spoken which is presented as the cast-iron way. Drama has many strands but right in the centre is this verse-speaking tradition which apparently only P. Hall understands. In the Seventies at the Royal Court, there was the same perception that some could do one thing and others could not. Though I used to think the perfect actor for a part was the one who came from the correct background, now I know that with work, a good actor will make the performance real for those hours on stage and convince the audience. I now think that all this stuff about multi-racial casting is a waste of time to be really honest.

REES: Next came *Sink or Swim,* the first of a series of plays commissioned about south east London with the intention of playing them in local neighbourhood situations.

IKOLI: I thought you didn't like me after *On the Out* because of my brother. There had been problems with Ade and the play. I thought you was a really strict, hard person.

□ *Ade, who had no expectations of becoming an actor, decided, after the first performance at the Bush, that the play had been done and so why go on for the second performance? We had to hold the show until he could be found and persuaded to perform. Since the tour was to follow, this did not bode well and I had to insist that the director, John Chapman, 'minded' Ade throughout the six week tour.*

You said come and talk to me in Peckham. I'd never been to south London before, even though I live just across the water in Limehouse. I come out of the Queen's Road station and I thought I was in another world. It's flat. No high buildings. Like country. We met at the Bookplace. [*Third world bookshop and neighbourhood meeting place*] Anyway you asked me to write a play about Peckham. It was weird because Peckham was like the East End in the Fifties. It was blocked up with people, just arriving from all over the place – Vietnamese. Turkish, Cypriots, West Indians, West Africans, Irish, Scottish, English. You just had to walk down the street to the bus garage.

Before you cast *Sink or Swim,* there was no script. Although obviously there was a basic idea. First, we chose the characters. We sketched them in. The actors were going to do the research. We had a budget for six actors. We chose three men, three women, three black, three white.

Like *Sleeping Policemen,* [*written with Howard Brenton and also set in Peckham*] it was about dispossession. Rootlessness. We were trying to capture a sub-culture, a separate culture.

REES: That ran parallel to, but found its life outside of Thatcher's mainstream Britain of the early Eighties.

IKOLI: It would be interesting to know where all those six characters in the play have now ended up ten years later. Wouldn't it? There was a Community Worker [*played by Mary Zuckerman*], whose job was to act as a band aid stuck over a big, bloody wound. Trevor's character [*Trevor Laird*] was a young black activist, Brian's [*Brian Bovell*] a youth, keen on football, with Tony [*Tony London*], a Puck-like figure, his white disaffected friend, Tony's Mother [*Pat Leach*] and Janet Key who played a young black girl, forced by her background to be something she did not want to be.

REES: This became an approach we adopted to these south east London plays. It may seem schematic. But in reality it was a response to the diversity of the people in the area, and a desire to create a large canvas on a small budget by employing the six actors, we could afford, to make an epic picture of a local area.

BOVELL: We did two weeks of workshops with improvisations, meeting people, seeing different places in the area, creating the basis for our characters. Then Tunde went away for two weeks and wrote the play. We continued the research into our chosen characters. I spent a lot of time with my 'spar' [*Friend*] in the play, Tony London. We'd go to local community centres where we were going to perform, because part of the play was going to be placed in a community centre. One thing that the play taught me was the existence of the pure characters in that area. So different to mainstream life which can be so characterless. Lots of character, colour and variation.

LAIRD: We went around as a group. The cast, you, Roland, and Tunde. We might have done our own individual work, but we hung together for support, rather than go into an unknown place on our own.

REES: I had set up some meetings in advance, but generally we followed our noses. Going around together allowed us to discuss, on the spot, our reactions to each event and meeting. After all, we had only two weeks, so time was not on our side.

IKOLI: I went to an old People's Pop-in-Parlour. They had places like that in them days. TIN [*Teenage Information Network on the Old Kent Road*]. Roland said: 'Go and see this self-help place on Peckham High street.' [*Then in a derelict state, now refurbished as a black cultural centre called Unity*]. So I go there like a writer researching and knocked on the door. I had on some really stupid, little shoulder bag with my pen and paper, and think this entitles me to go anywhere! This black guy comes out and he's giving me such a look, as if to say: 'Who are you?' I tell yer, I shit myself. 'Oh' I said, 'Sorry. I'm a writer. I've come to see so-and-so.' I was making as if to go but the bloke pulls me in and bolts the door. There is this long, dark tunnel to another door. I'm thinking: 'Oh, my God!' And he says: 'Wait here.' He goes down the tunnel, opens the other door and locks it behind him. Leaving me. I'm thinking: 'They're after my bag. They're going to come down and beat me up! Why did I do this?' The door opens. 'Come through here,' and I walk in with trepidation. I step into another world. Like these houses have been gutted. The place is full of people, sawing and putting this house back together. The guy I met in that place became the basis of your character, Trevor. This self-help guy. The idea was instead of getting white people to do things for you like social services or whatever, you raised money and did them yourself. Managed them yourself. With a workforce of youths.

REES: So he became an important character?

IKOLI: Important for me because of that experience. It made me realise how far I had got away from where I was born. The experience of *Sink or Swim,* became like an event in itself. How we all met up. How we visited different people and places. We had tensions and we paired off. I realise now, but not then, that I was writing about what I had seen you all do in the improvisations, but I was also writing about us, the event. This process with *Sink or Swim* and later *Sleeping Policemen* was instrumental in making me confident about writing.

BOVELL: We played one hall, in Bell's Gardens up in Peckham. Janet Key [*who played the girl who wanted to be a singer*] sang after in the club. That was a good show. A packed house.

LAIRD: We performed in the gymnasium. They went mad. A 99% black audience. A rowdy crowd compared to the theatre, if you judge it like that.

BOVELL: We experience it now. Doing a Black play at the Royal Court for instance. You get the regular *Time Out* reader, you know what I mean, they come from Islington. And it's a quiet night. At the end of the evening they go. Basically I believe their reactions comes off of guilt. The next day if you are doing the play for a black audience, I like to say a colourful richness, the play becomes a different play. It is live. You are getting response and participation. Vocalisation.

LAIRD: That is even more likely to happen if you play a club like we did in Peckham. The audiences were not professional theatre-goers.

BOVELL: Much more refreshing.

REES: Lines and scenes were discussed whilst the next scene was in progress. There was an altercation outside and we had to stop the play for a moment.

IKOLI: All of this comes back to language – how to say verse, the Peter Hall, European, view of theatre. Whatever we thought when we started off, the theatre is a middle class playground and we were half in love with that. When we did *Sink or Swim,* the weirdest experience was actually taking theatre to places where people don't want it! That was the challenge. And that is what I realise now about Shakespeare. His actors had to fight for the crowds. That show began to make me realise what I was in theatre for. To be honest I wanted to go to the Royal Court then. I did not want to play community centres. I thought the rowdy audience response was wrong. I thought it should be like church. You are meant to listen. Later I realised the response was right. It was what I wanted and I got confidence.

REES: The audiences we had in Peckham would normally be watching 'Eastenders'. But in 1982 they got high quality theatre, writing and acting in their neighbourhood. Very immediate.

IKOLI: But we were also guilty of being like the social worker! We went in and did our little bit and then disappeared. Just as you start growing and need to lean on the person who has inspired you, they have gone. I felt that unless we could do a production each year, all we were doing was dropping little pellets. The Arts Council put money into it but, because we couldn't continue, the audience was lost. That's when we realised the kind of resources we would need to continue. It was not a Street Festival thrown together. It was highly skilled people presenting high quality work.

LAIRD: These initiatives of taking theatre to the masses were not carried through, did not encourage that new audience to come to main house theatre.

REES: Interesting that you use the word initiative. The grant from the Arts Council to produce *Sink or Swim* was called a 'Special Initiatives' grant to enable a company to accomplish work, as one Drama Officer put it to me, 'that is different to what you usually do, but not so different as to be unrecognisably your work.' The next year that grant vanished from the Arts Council's books. I had placed great hopes in continuing this strand of the company's work. I spent three months in Peckham, meeting everyone who could help in the setting up of the project, one which was pioneering in every respect. I met members of Southwark's Leisure and Recreational Department, the managers of clubs and organisations which presented us, and, most importantly, local groups and individuals who helped us gather the material for the play. Southwark Council gave us a grant. Not much, but something. The next year, when I returned to do another show that source of subsidy had also vanished!

IKOLI: *Sleeping Policemen,* which we did two years later, was an artistic exercise. In comparison, *Sink or Swim* was a political exercise, because it was the first of its kind. It had a life of its own. You created interest in these places that was next to impossible to follow up.

REES: When I returned to Southwark for subsidy the next year, as far as we were concerned, we were told the cupboard was bare. So whilst our work may have seemed like the community worker in our play, in fact we had made waves that contributed to people believing this could be done. Local grass roots organisations were becoming very active and getting support from Southwark Council to develop their work. You remember Milton Miller with his group, Sojourner Truth, who rehearsed in a school. We did some improvisations with them. Now he is supported by Southwark Council. He has a centre. He was encouraged by our visit. The derelict building you visited with such trepidation on the High Street, by the dint of those people's own endeavour, is now built and called Unity. The great pity is that highly skilled people, presenting high quality work, cannot continue to visit these new, neighbourhood places to enhance the programme they are producing. To further encourage their work.

On a different subject. I was talking to some of the cast of Matura's *The Coup* during their rehearsals. Originally, they had all arrived here in England, from the Caribbean, in the Sixties or early Seventies. Their generation and background provided a different and earlier input into plays and acting compared to yourselves, who were born here. I put it to them that different types of plays now needed to be written in response to a different experience. This was an historical juncture in the development of Black Theatre in this country.

LAIRD: It is a different imperative. Their's is to do plays about the Caribbean, to show where they came from, to show, as an outsider, what it is like to be here. We are from the inside. Our imperative is: 'Why can't we be part of things? We're from here.' Any black actor in a perfect world should be able to represent both imperatives. But that's not always the way things go. At the end of the seventies Black Theatre peaked. Now the development has gone another way. Mustapha uses certain actors to play in his plays – like

Alan Ayckbourn – that can play what he's after. We went into Peckham to create something that had not happened before. So you need a new type of performer that has sympathy with the type of characters we played in Tunde's *Sink or Swim,* that can latch onto their beat.

IKOLI: It's like staking our claim. The old guys, and I don't mean age, had so much shit to put up with. We don't have to carry the weights that bore down on their heads. To me the promise that the Sixties gave, and I was a kid then, was that everything was going to be alright. Teachers, social workers were all talking about inter-racial this and multi-cultural that. So much promise was in the air. Now in the early Nineties I can't see how we thought that.

LAIRD: It didn't materialise.

IKOLI: Races and classes are not intermixed. There's a line in Howard Brenton's *Pravda* about people going into their boxes. That is what is happening now. They've got Vietnamese in that building over there [*We are on an estate off Poplar High Street*] They all stick with each other. If you have two Asian families in a block of flats, they stick together.

REES: When I talked to the actors in Mustapha's *The Coup,* it was put to me that a black play must, if it is to be good, express the black experience, it must distinguish the black experience. There was an inference that black people born in this country were perhaps not in a position to do this.

LAIRD: There is a division. This is it. Their black experience is the experience of the Caribbean or Africa. To us the experience is of black people here. It is also a black experience. But different. Black is just a colour of skin. Their experience coming from the outside, the way they see things, they see they have to impress something on people. The way we see it, we play it – like Tunde writes – we want to show the universe inside rather than conquer the one outside. They're saying: 'Why can't a black person be Prime Minister or do this important job right now?' We're saying this is what we are, what Britain has done to us and this is what's going to happen.

IKOLI: This, the rungs, and this, the ladder.

LAIRD: That's why it needed new and different actors.

IKOLI: They're right about me in one way. I am trying to find out who I am. What is going on in my head? What is going to happen for my children? I don't think that I should sit down and be inspired by something like 'Black experience'. I just write. There's been a Black industry which has not . . .

LAIRD: Helped anything.

IKOLI: If that is what the Black experience is, they're welcome to it.

REES: Mustapha's world as exhibited in his plays, and I take him as the example because he is the flagship for black playwriting, is dominated with and by men. Women are in the kitchen or on the sidelines. White characters, where they appear, in his earlier 'English plays', scarcely go beyond two dimensionality. I don't think this happens in your plays, Tunde. That is a significant step forward.

LAIRD: That is part and parcel of our experience. Those of us born here. That represents the society we live in. The Caribbean is a lovely place. But there is a definite way people are there. And that is reflected in Mustapha's plays.

BOVELL: I dreamed about acting from about five years old. I lived across the road from this cinema and I used to go in there and hassle the projectionist. The man would let me sit up in the box and watch the films. Those films filled my head with a whole heap of visions of this and that. I lived in Tottenham, and I was under the impression through the school system that I had a certain position there, but outside of that I wasn't too strong. I loved the idea of acting, but I never thought I would become an actor. Looking at TV, I was faced with the Black and White Minstrel Show, with Step 'n Fetchit and that whole kind of vibes. It was outside of anything I had experience of in reality. Then one day, I was watching TV and I hear a sound that I know . . . It was Trevor in . . .

LAIRD: My first film, *Playthings*, for the BBC. I was seventeen. Stephen Frears directed it.

BOVELL: Out of the distance came this sound. I know that sound. That voice. That was the first important thing. The second was when I went to see *Welcome Home Jacko* [*a play by Mustapha Matura for the Black Theatre Co-op*]. I wasn't an actor then. Originally, that play was written in Trinidadian, in a swing beat or style. A group of young black London actors took the play and translated the language into black London English.

LAIRD: Rewrote it we did.

BOVELL: Completely translated the play

LAIRD: Matura has never admitted that!

BOVELL: I had been to *Swan Lake*, a couple of operas, a few plays in the West End, which were very stush, which my dad had taken me to, and where you get those glasses for 10p and have a nibble! That's all I was interested in. But when I came to see *Jacko,* it was direct, and I understood the sound and the rhythm of the speech. You remember at Riverside Studios, Tunde, when we first met? I was auditioning for one of your plays and I was thinking: 'He's written this play and I expect things will be the old usual way.' But

From Left to Right. Ella Wilder, Mary Ellen Ray, Carrie Lee-Baker, Trevor Butler and Alfred Fagon in Foco Novo's 1983 production of Howard Brenton's and Tunde Ikoli's *Sleeping Policemen*.

From Left to Right. Rudolph Walker, Colin Tarrant, Maria Charles, Tilly Vosburgh and Robin Summers (foreground) in Foco Novo's 1986 production of Tunde Ikoli's *The Lower Depths*.

they wasn't. I went into the audition and it was easy. You could, with Tunde's characters, be eloquent without having to ape eloquence.

We went to New York and played *Jacko* off-Broadway, 1983, on West 43rd Street. The theatre seated only 150. Black Americans came and they had never seen a play like that. Lee Strasberg students came and couldn't believe it. They had never seen anything like this from England. They expected Noel Coward or the RSC.

That is the essence of the transition. It was plays like Tunde's *Scrape Off the Black* and *Sink or Swim* that enabled me to take the right journey in acting. All of a sudden I felt we had a way.

LAIRD: That's what Foco Novo was about. That's what, Roland, you were doing. Pushing things along in new directions. Now the company is no more. One more opportunity to help new playwrights has disappeared.

REES: Your next play for Foco Novo was *Week In, Week Out*. Again a play commissioned to tour Inner London, this time with a grant from the now defunct GLC. It drew upon your experience of the garment industry.

IKOLI: A leather factory under severe financial pressure in the early Eighties. In my play, the GLC also put up money so the factory could turn itself into a co-operative. But the stresses and strains of working together, as a co-op, became very great. I know the play was going to tour community venues but I have never understood what the word community means. I have never considered myself to be a community writer. I don't believe in making theatre out of the community. *Week In, Week Out* went to places which never normally receive plays. It had a very good cast with Maria Charles and Larrington Walker.

REES: Foco Novo did not think of itself as doing Community Theatre. Indeed we played to all kinds of audiences. Some were absolutely theatre-kosher, such as at the Hampstead Theatre, whilst others had never experienced theatre before, such as the audiences for your plays we are now discussing. This represented our positive policy of seeking new audiences. These performances occurred in venues [*places not built exclusively for theatre use and invariably situated in urban areas*] and this type of theatre was labelled Community Theatre.

In the parlance of subsidy providers, community did not mean an area where there is a homogenous population. Quite the contrary. Community came to mean any place which lay outside the orbit of the community from which theatre drew its audiences. Community meant inner city localities with very little community. And it was to reflect this fact, this sense of cobbled-together modern living, this sub-culture, that I believe Tunde, you, in your plays, and Foco Novo, in its aspirations, seeing it as a major fact of contemporary urban life, wanted to capture a fragment of and put it on stage. Both for audiences in a locality, in our case Peckham, for a real recognition of themselves, and also for theatre audiences to catch a patch of life that normally they pass through in a vehicle or train.

So whilst I understand and share your antipathy towards being, or being called, a community artist, we did, I believe, in these series of plays *Sink or Swim, Week In, Week Out* and *Sleeping Policemen,* create objects that were highly crafted, whose genesis lay in sections of London which had no community whatsoever. Ironically, this was called Community Art!

This leads us to *Sleeping Policemen.* Again a play commissioned about south east London and Peckham in particular. However, this time, two writers were involved – yourself and Howard Brenton. Neither of you had worked with each other before. And the same approach was employed. Certain themes were agreed upon in advance. You were allowed six actors. The economically viable number for such plays in 1986.

LAIRD: It's down to four now. That's inflation for you!

REES: You and Howard agreed you would not double up parts but that you would write six characters for six actors. Again equal numbers of men, women, black and white characters were part of the brief. You each chose three characters. Actors were cast to these character intentions. Then we did a two week workshop. After this, you both went away and wrote your plays separately, absolutely agreeing never to confer. We then met, read out loud the plays to each other and set about amalgamating each play into one play.

IKOLI: The title of the play refers to bumps in the roads to slow down cars. And you, Roland, had been to a public meeting in Peckham about the Council's intentions to put down some sleeping policemen in a particular road.

REES: The meeting became about everything else but bumps in the roads. It was a chance for people who had never before been asked their opinion about anything, suddenly realising their voice. Every complaint about their lives poured out. You both said: 'That's what we'll centre the play on, the meeting.'

IKOLI: People I know, don't get involved in local politics unless bumps in the road or something happens to them. That seemed a good way to draw on all that for the play. We chose the characters – a Labour councillor, a yuppie, a bus driver, an Irishwoman who might have been married to someone in the IRA, the tramp, Bert Bloggs, with two dogs, War and Peace, and a black woman, a single parent.

We both went away and wrote our separate plays in the two weeks between the workshops and rehearsal. Then we met at your house, Roland, and mashed the plays together. With a big pair of your scissors and started cutting! Roland was the arbiter. My characters would have two lines and then Howard's version would take over for two lines. The thing was that people didn't know where a single character would stop saying my lines and where Howard's lines began. Then there would be a switch back. Sometimes the story went in totally opposite directions at the same time. We had two versions of the same thing. You could have a burglary in the first act, written in one way, and then the same burglary happened in the second act in a totally different way. You could have a man running around in a gorilla suit one minute. Then he appears in the middle of a political meeting the next. A woman is looking for her kid one minute, and then is diving under the floorboards where there is a field of mushrooms growing in the damp of her flat, the next. It was like nothing I had done or I think has ever been done before. It was very strange.

REES: A unique occasion for two writers to be brought together in this manner, from such different backgrounds.

IKOLI: I learnt a lot. I have never had a comparable experience. To work equally, with someone of Howard Brenton's calibre, gave me confidence. To know that my individual perception of London in the Eighties was valued. And the work on *Sleeping Policemen* put all kinds of concepts into my head – Cubism, schizoid characters – things I had not thought of theatrically, that touched off my imagination in a way that had not happened before.

REES: Was *Sleeping Policemen* a development on from the previous plays or a new departure?

IKOLI: Basically all my plays have been about London. A strand of London life, not well represented in the media. Writing for Foco Novo changed me a lot. I had been like a reporter. If the riots were going on, someone would ring me up to write something. It was getting easy to slip into that. Especially since I always needed the money. With *Sleeping Policemen,* we did not do the obvious. Nor with *The Lower Depths.*

REES: *The Lower Depths* was a play you had wanted to do for a long time. You admired Gorki and I encouraged you to do your own version of his play. The original is set in turn-of-the-century St Petersburg. I wanted you to make the play about London in the Eighties.

IKOLI: I admired Gorki's *My University.* It inspired me to read much more of him. After doing that and seeing *The Godfather,* I suddenly realised that literature and the arts were not necessarily for the audiences and the class that I always thought they were for, and that maybe I could write about my *own* experiences. I was labelled an urban playwright, and so tackling *The Lower Depths* gave me a chance to develop. At that time, the high standard of productions, which Foco Novo brought to my plays, seeped into my writing. So rather than carrying on with these community plays, Foco Novo allowed me, with *Sleeping Policemen* and *The Lower Depths*, to tackle more artistic goals.

It was in that weird pub in Soho – The French – that you suggested *The Lower Depths*. I thought my real problem as a writer was a lack of mastery of structure. Working with a known text, provided an imposed structure, within which I could create my own characters.

REES: How did you set about the transformation?

IKOLI: The Russian landlord became a Nigerian, married to a much younger West Indian woman. She thought this marriage would make a better life for her. The play was set in the East End, Cable Street down to Aldgate. It was based on my father's early experiences in this country. Quite a few Nigerians owned houses and put up other West Africans, and then later West Indians, when they started coming over, in rooms all over a house. I decided to make one of these houses the location for the play's action, like Gorki's rooming house, and fill it with characters who represented the world I lived in.

So there was a Cornish man [*Tunde's mother is from Cornwall and met his father in London*] with his sick wife who had left home a few months ago to come to London. The only accommodation he could find was a room in Koli's [*Nigerian landlord's*] house. A teacher who had been beaten by the education system in London and had become an alcoholic. He had a room there. An oldish lady once married to a Jamaican guy, the one love of her life who, as a result, has spent the rest of her life as an outcast from the indigenous population and become an honorary member of the black community. She has a room. And Errol, the young black Londoner, who does not see eye to eye with Koli, also does. The important character was Talker, based on a Ghanaian I knew, called Talker. It was an amalgamation of many weird characters who travelled through and across class and race. He had a mysterious history that could have been colonial, could have been criminal. His arrival acts as the catalyst for the play. He exists as most of my characters do, from day to day.

I learnt from Gorki that I must make my characters come to some conclusion with their lives. My characters always used to live *because* they existed. With *The Lower Depths* I learnt I could be in control of them. Once Talker makes everyone attempt to realise their dreams, even though it all goes wrong, they know they still have to live their lives after. But they have changed, even if only imperceptibly. It was all kinds of strands like that which came out and taught me to impose my own world on a play. Like *Smack and Thistle*, [*a film written and directed by Tunde for Working Title and shown on Channel 4, 1991*] it was mine.

From *Sink or Swim* on, you pulled me up on how to write, how to compose a play. You said Tunde: 'There are too many dualogues'. This was because I needed to get information across. You faced me with theatrical questions. How do you get information over without resorting to question and answer? Our workshop processes gave me research time, to digest what we had done, before I had to turn it into a play. That work allowed me to get to grips with character and structure. I could at one time photocopy my plays at the National Theatre. I remember many sessions photocopying rewrites after our discussions.

REES: Was there a Foco Novo way of looking at the presentation of things?

IKOLI: Imperceptible at the time. But now I see the method. On the final play, *Banged Up,* we did it on practically nothing. The design [*by Andrea Montag*] was a real part of the sense of the production. I remember reading *The Elephant Man*, and thinking: 'How are they going to do this without make-up and make sense of the guy's large head? Nobody will believe it.' Me and Lawrentia [*his wife*] was sitting in the front row at Hampstead and David Schofield came on naked and did that transformation [*without the use of make-up*]. Lawrentia wanted to leave after the interval, because she felt sick. She felt he was actually like he was supposed to look. The same thing happened with my productions. They look as they are meant to look. But at the same time they were theatrical.

REES: There was a realism but at the same time there was something heightened.

IKOLI: It was like taking prose and turning it into poetry. In a script I would indicate the need for realism but I came to realise it was not necessary. Now I am writing the way I feel I need to, rather than the way people want me to, which is how I might have gone at one time. You were not afraid to say what would work. You have a very definite vision of what you are doing. But you always took care to explain what you wanted. Your life at the time of working for Foco Novo was as much a part of what the company was, as the play it was producing.

Over the years, the time we was working together, you helped crystalise a view, which contributed even to my film, *Smack and Thistle*. About a cusp of an age we were going through – there were two societies, a mainstream one and a growing sub-culture. It was not like the old class system. People of all classes and backgrounds could exist in either. A different sort of poverty had developed. That idea became like a seedbed for me.

REES: The Board, many of whom were writers and administrators, and had worked with the company in some capacity, constituted a close-knit group.

IKOLI: There was a trust. The way people talked about plays we might do and how they were selected was at first a weird process for me to understand. Nobody had ever asked for my opinion about anything in my life. You had people like Dr. Trevor Griffiths [*The Chair of the Board*], who was a professor, Anne Louise, a theatre administrator, Jon Catty, an accountant, Sheelagh Killeen, a costume designer, playwrights Howard Brenton and Nigel Williams. What was interesting was the perception each person had of the play. Being a board member, made you as a writer more responsible for what you wrote.

REES: Do you remember the discussions about *The Lower Depths* and whether we could produce the play with a cast of ten? [*More than a 100% reduction in cast size from the original*] You, as the writer, had to be involved in the decision, as a member of the board, about whether your own play would be produced.

IKOLI: God, man, yes! In a way we had solved this before. All the previous plays I had written for the company had a maximum of six actors. Audiences, because of the way we approached the writing, thought there were many more characters in the plays. They seemed so full and rich. So I thought we had earned the right to go big. It is like helping a plumber fix the plumbing. All of a sudden, you are faced with the reality of all the boring and mundane things which will enable a production to happen. Will that production get on the stage in the way it needs to? I didn't feel comfortable making those decisions. I don't think writers do.

   □ *After* The Lower Depths, *Foco Novo had to balance their books with a two-hander – the smallest cast play for funding purposes The Arts Council would recognise – Tunde's* Banged Up.

REES: When, in 1988, we were in the process of producing *Consequences,* a play by eight writers, of which you were one, and Foco Novo received a letter from the Arts Council saying no grant would be offered in the following year, the board were faced with an intractable and heart-rending situation.

IKOLI: It was a really depressing time. From the Arts Council point of view, I never knew what their problem was. We were under pressure for two to three years. At first I thought it was the new Thatcherite dogma where you had to prove yourself. We went through all kinds of stages, even before it was the fashion, of discussing and looking for ways to find sponsorship. I remember at Board meetings how this seemed impossible for a touring theatre company in the mid-Eighties presenting new writing of the kind we did.

   We were told all these appraisals were really for our own benefit, and if we did what we were supposed to, we would find ourselves leaner and more efficient in the future. That was the theory.

The Lower Depths really hit off, in a way no other play of mine had. A run at the Tricycle, you would not believe. If we were going forward that was the kind of thing we should have been doing. *The Lower Depths* was the start of something, not an end. I became Writer in Residence with Foco Novo – with financial help from the Arts Council Writing Panel! We had clear plans to incorporate all the work you had achieved, playing theatre to new audiences alongside the more mainstream drama the company produced. I was commissioned to write my version of *The Tempest*. To use the story of that play's shipwreck and make it about a boat, full of slaves, lost on the reefs of the Bahamas after crossing the Middle Passage. All this was going somewhere new. *The Tempest* was causing me problems but I was very excited about it. It was giving me an opportunity to leave the East End behind. Take a leap at wider issues. Then we disappeared overnight.

REES: After sixteen years!

IKOLI: I always had the preconceived belief that I was mortally wounded by not having a university education. The experience of working with Foco Novo, black, white, women, men, old and young gave me an education in itself. A small metaphor for the world you would like to live in. A common purpose the company had.

It was like going to a university nobody else knew about. It was like Gorki's *My Education*. That was my education. I read plays for The Company, I went to plays, I met actors, designers, and I worked with writers I respected and admired.

BLACK THEATRE 3

Photo © John Haynes 1987

CLAIRE BENEDICT

Claire Benedict has worked with touring companies ATC, Cheek By Jowl and Shared Experience, at the Royal Exchange in *Medea*, at the National Theatre in *The White Devil* and for a season with the Royal Shakespeare Company at Stratford. She played Diane Cupido in Foco Novo's co-production with the Theatre Royal, Plymouth of *The Cape Orchard* on tour and at The Young Vic Theatre.

REES: Clearly from the title of Michael Picardie's *The Cape Orchard*, a white South African writer living in Cardiff, his play owes something to Chekov's *The Cherry Orchard*.

BENEDICT: Yes, he did base *The Cape Orchard* loosely on *The Cherry Orchard*. It had that feel, particularly in the Madame de Villiers [*Ranyevskaya*] and Pieterse [*Lopahin*] characters.

REES: The impending threat held over the Farm by the revolutionary ferment, which Picardie painted happening in South Africa, did mirror Chekov's play and Russia of 1904. I think *The Cherry Orchard* was a model for Picardie, which as time and writing proceeded, became less important beside the news from southern Africa.

BENEDICT: The part I played was of Diane Cupido [*Doonyasha*]. She was a coloured woman. [*Cape Coloured*]. Poor as most in South Africa are. Diane worked on the de Villiers farm as a housemaid. She looked after the children, travelling as a close member of the family. They had an adopted daughter Valma [*Varia*] also coloured. So this white, liberal woman, Leonie de Villiers, an actress, adopted a coloured child. At the start of the play, Leonie returns from England where she has been working for some time, to deal with problems looming in the running of the farm.

The workers had become very political. They wanted to turn the farm into a co-operative. Pieterse, local business man and long-time friend of Leonie, in her absence was desperately trying to keep the farm going by obtaining financial backing from the bank to start the Co-op.

REES: The play threw up a lot of ideas about the future of South Africa in an original way. Picardie purposively was suggesting even more widespread, erratic, social unrest in South Africa than there actually was in 1987. The play depicted in the prologue and epilogue, set in the year 2005, that by that time the whole southern continent of Africa would be in a state of conflagration.

BENEDICT: A lot has happened in South Africa by 1991. It has not turned out as Michael Picardie thought. We have a leader in De Klerk who is preparing to meet Black leaders representing the majority. Black Africans do not have the vote there. Obviously that is crucial to fight for. It would be foolish to say positive things are not happening in South Africa.

□ *In retrospect, late 1992, Picardie is daringly and horribly more accurate than we could have imagined.*

REES: With the exception of Leonie de Villiers, all the characters were Cape Coloured. There were no black African characters. What did this choice of Michael's mean for the play?

BENEDICT: Cape Coloureds at one time had the vote, but it was taken away from them. They were a people not liked by the blacks and many whites distrusted them. They were the progeny of white and black, belonging in neither camp. A homeless people. They seemed to have privileges, but in fact did not. My character was militant and so different to coloureds in that respect. She aligned herself with the blacks. Politically, she said I am black. It was the whites who divided and ruled and she knew that was a clever device. A brave women. Her son was also militant – a 'comrade' – and died for his efforts.

REES: Pieterse traces his origins back to the Bush people – the Hottentots – the original inhabitants of southern Africa. In the final scene, year 2005, he returns to his ancestral lands in the Kalahari desert, but is now armed and involved in guerilla struggle.

BENEDICT: Jan Pieterse, played by Norman Beaton, was a very interesting character. Sad. Yearning to recapture all that his ancestors, the Bushmen, meant to his people. He was a learned man. With a weeping going on within him. Yet he had associated with Leonie for a long time, become her good friend, as he was with other white people. He was in a dilemma. He could understand the other side of the story. He loved cricket and Picardie had him read and quote from Heidegger, the German Philosopher. He was in between, aware that Diane had an answer. Her son was one of the young comrades and distancing yourself from the struggle could lead to their answer – a 'necklacing' [When car tyres are attached around a person's neck and set alight].

REES: Were there any things in the play that came unexpectedly to you?

BENEDICT: For me personally the play was a godsend. Because, like other people, I was very ignorant about South Africa. On day one of rehearsal, you showed us a video of South African history from the beginning of the century. It was very explicit. How far back the ANC went. The atrocities committed at different times. It was wonderful background knowledge. I could see where Diane's anger came from. She loved that white farm but she knew it would not help her or her people. She could not let Leonie put her arms around her on her return, as she always used to do. It would make her new political life impossible to pursue.

REES: When the video finished, it was some two hours long, there was a tangible frisson of anger amongst the black cast. I was moved and I felt that it was

137

inappropriate to open my mouth for a moment. But our beloved author was right in there saying: 'See how violence has bread violence!' And: 'There has to be another solution.' That set the cat among the pigeons and a fine argument ensued.

BENEDICT: The audience on tour asked many questions. How does it affect us? How can we change things? What has it got to do with us? So we got mixed responses dependent on how much an audience member knew.

It made me understand that Foco Novo puts on plays which confront issues. Sometimes they are uncomfortable. It was not a South African fist waving play. It tried to present an answer for both blacks and whites. There are terrible atrocities so what is the way forward? It was a complex play.

REES: Most of the plays we see from South Africa are, as you say, of the fist waving variety.

BENEDICT: They have to make plays that way to keep in the forefront of their audience's minds what the struggle is all about. Those plays are a spear they need to have in their hand all the time. Being a black actress, however, I want to be able to play any part if I'm right. Not every white actress gets to play Medea. She may not be physically right to play the part. That should be the same for me. At the end of the day, I do not want to be hired because I'm black, but because of my qualities as an actress. In some shows, I have been involved in, this has happened. It has been a sweet experience, working with a mixed cast. It arms you with a hell of a lot more for today's society, if the play you are doing confronts a range of issues.

REES: Talawa produced an all black *Anthony and Cleopatra*. You were in Webster's *The White Devil* at the National in which one family is cast as black. In both instances, these plays are from the classical repertoire. Do you think it is easier to make this sort of casting with a classical play than it would be with a contemporary play? Does the distancing help?

BENEDICT: With *Anthony and Cleopatra* it works. It is just theatre. It breaks down barriers. It is up to the audience to suspend disbelief, look at what is being offered and not become bogged down with the colour you see on stage. In *The White Devil*, the Corombona family, mother, two sons and a daughter, were all black which also works very well. It makes issues sharper. Not necessarily because of today's society but for the play itself, visually.

You spend three years in Drama School and during my time at LAMDA I played Madame Ranyevskaya in *The Cherry Orchard* and other classical parts. I was made to feel that I *would* be offered classical parts when I left in 1974 and went out into the profession. It came as a nasty shock to realise that nothing of the sort would happen. It is still difficult, but it is beginning to break down.

REES: Did you have heroes/heroines whilst you were at Drama School?

BENEDICT: My heroine at the time was, and still is, Glenda Jackson. She is so strong and powerful. Other people have become important for me like Judi Dench.

REES: Black actors, born in the Caribbean, have a different outlook to black actors born here in the UK?

BENEDICT: I was born in the Caribbean but I came to Britain at the age of five. I have never been back. Younger black actors, born here in this country, have far greater expectations for what they want today in British theatre. They want to be involved in the English classics and in representing society in this country now. A lot do take part in Caribbean plays, but I sense from the actors I know, that it does not make sense to go back into what has been. They cannot relate to it in the same way.

For an actress like Mona Hammond, the island of her birth is within her. She can do all sorts of parts, not dependent on her background, but when she does a West Indian play, the coat fits very well. It's her heritage, her culture. But young black Britons find it much more difficult. They are concerned with what confronts them as someone born here. They want to tell that story themselves.

REES: Young black actors do not want to go backwards. But are new directions happening?

BENEDICT: The classical play and part is an area new to black actors. We want to conquer that. Become part of that. Then you can do other plays, new plays, for the black cause. It's that obstacle we have to overcome, not being allowed to conquer something you are told is out of your reach. I still feel I cannot get to Gertrude and Lady Macbeth. To become part of that, which is also our heritage. Shakespeare's stories are for all peoples. You want as an actor to speak his language.

It is also important to get out of that ghetto situation. It does us no good as black people and black performers. I do want to support black playwrights, the Mustapha Maturas and the Tunde Ikolis of this world. They write very well, but I am about representing *all* people. That is why I am concerned about playing the character and not the colour.

Theatre must be a celebration of rituals over the centuries and not just of a particular culture. If you look at the different rituals around the world, you will find they are ultimately similar.

139

REES: The dilemma I see is this. The newer touring theatre companies and many smaller theatres have made their name recently by producing European classical and modern classical work. Not new plays. Many of the new play producing companies, like Foco Novo, are fast disappearing. Black theatre companies are being threatened. You have made a strong case for the widening of the horizons. But if Black Theatre does not produce new work, encourage the new voices of the black community, something of the continuing essence of black culture goes too. That is the dilemma.

BENEDICT: I take your point. We do need new plays and good ones. Last year I Was in *Death and The King's Horseman* by Wole Soyinka. Written by an African man, it had all the ingredients of a wonderful play. It spoke to all people and dealt with dilemmas confronting black people and white people living in a black society. He wrote the play in the Seventies and people steered clear of it, because they did not know how to stage it. It is a piece of poetry. You need to be brave to tackle it. In the same way that if I pick up *Richard III* or *King Lear*, I won't understand it all at once. But there is something about the writing which informs you.

It is not just the quantity of black writers writing. We need to look at the quality, whatever the origin of the writer. Quality is the supreme goal. Not just issues. I do not want to go the theatre to see a representation of what is going on on the street. I might want to see that but in a different, transmuted way. That's what makes theatre exciting. It cannot just be the photograph. It has to be something else.

BLACK THEATRE 4

Photo © John Haynes 1987

PAULINE BLACK

Pauline Black was the lead singer with the group Selecter for two years, which recently re-formed to tour the States. She was the Presenter for Channel 4's *Black on Black*. At the Tricycle Theatre, Pauline played Billie Holiday in *All or Nothing at All* [1990 OI/Time Out Award] and Masha in Mustapha Matura's *Trinidad Sisters* and at the Hampstead Theatre, Elaine in *Sugar Hill Blues*. Played Valma in Foco Novo's production of Michael Picardie's *The Cape Orchard*.

REES: We are sitting in the Powerhaus, a club in Islington, where you and your band will be playing tonight. You have made as much of a career in music as you have as an actress. Is this combination valuable and important to you?

BLACK: Yes. Some people like to perform. They like the contact with a live audience. It's all in the moment. What I most like about any performance event is that fundamentally you entertain an audience and they go home and hopefully look at things slightly differently, be it through a three and half minute pop song or an hour and half long play. Yes, it is that contact with the live audience I like.

Music came first. I spent two years with my band, Selecter, then I left them in 1981, and I suppose you could say I took an eight year 'sabbatical'. I did a play *Trojans* by Farruk Dhondy at Riverside Studios which was being directed by Trevor Laird. He wanted a singer in the play although I had no acting experience. The whole process seemed so different to what I normally experienced in the music business. The depth of research the actors went into, the time spent together. It just seemed wildly interesting. I thought: 'I really want to do this.' So I just did.

REES: In 1987 you came to work for Foco Novo in *The Cape Orchard* by Michael Picardie, set on a fruit farm in South Africa. Your character, Valma, the adopted daughter of the white owner of the farm, is Cape Coloured. The part has resonance for you, I believe, with your own background?

BLACK: I am of mixed race as Valma was in the play. I was brought up by white parents having been adopted at the age of four weeks. Valma in *The Cape Orchard* struck a lot of things in me. Past experiences that I could draw upon. Valma was going through what I had experienced during my adolescence, maybe up to my early twenties – trying to identify or not identify, as the case may be, with either white society or black society. It was always a question of being in the middle. Almost being ostracised from both. That's a difficult experience for anyone, be they black or white, but it is doubly so when you are not sure which side you belong to. You don't have that parental thing to fall back on anymore. That was the essence of what Valma was going through. Valma did not know what her roots were and nobody was telling her. Basically it ended up in the madness which is exposed at the end of the play.

REES: Picardie saw a South Africa whose future seemed destined for a civil war by the year 2000. It was a play of prophesy.

BLACK: That was *one* way the future could pan out. I don't see South Africa panning out that way at all. I think the projection forward in time to 2005 puzzled people. But the Prologue was enjoyed. The bushman look at life, and the different languages, and contact with nature. Foco Novo was known for doing new plays tackling important issues. Plays about South Africa originating from this country are rare.

REES: Do you find there is a difference in attitude between actors from the Caribbean and black actors born here in the UK?

BLACK: There may be. Because I don't have that tradition of the Caribbean, have not grown up in a West Indian family, when I do a West Indian play I have to approach that play afresh as if I was trying to be a Russian in a Chekov play! But since the Seventies, there is some recognition that there are now good black actors around with a training, who have a different energy. That's all I can define it as. It is a different energy on stage, compared to a lot of white actors I know. Writers and directors exploit that energy by using black actors to 'represent' political themes or social injustice rather than to portray a rounded character.

I would definitely like to see a degree of colour blindness in this country, working to black actors' advantage. Why is there a big hoo-ha about black Cleopatras? If anybody apart from Othello in Shakespeare is going to be black, it is Cleopatra – and why that should generate such a lot of steam and publicity, I find very odd. Yvonne Brewster has got round that very skilfully by saying if you, in the RSC and National won't cast us, then we will do that work ourselves and will cast all the parts with black actors.

I didn't think that a good thing at first, but now I do. I don't see another way of developing black actors to do classical parts, unless we do them in a situation like that. Trevor Nunn is not going to cast us as Cleopatra. But at least that training is achieved in doing our own Shakespeare. That training and experience is lacking and missing in the way we are used in the profession.

There are now more directors around with imagination. It's a time for them to take a chance. Part of the problem comes down to economics. We are now in a situation when we have to get bums on seats. To do that you have to cast 'stars' in leading parts. To actually cast against the grain of what audiences would normally expect to see, such as casting Josette Simon in *After the Fall* is quite brave. But I don't think there is enough bravery going on.

REES: Is Black theatre developing in different ways now? Are there new directions?

BLACK: Yvonne Brewster's work is obviously one. The Tricycle Theatre have a tradition of presenting Black theatre. They did a play by Yemi Ajibade, a Nigerian, about Africans in Soho in the Fifties – something which most people know very little about. The word Black is all encompassing. It is not just the West Indies. There is all of Africa as well. I tend to think those who dwell on the 'Caribbean' experience are a little bit blinkered. But the main thing is to present black people on stage in this country with rounded characters and as human beings. Too many audiences and, come to that, directors, actually consider that black faces on the stage says enough in itself. They don't think there is any need to flesh out a character. I see that a lot. Particularly with a black actor in a small part. The character is there to say something about the play but all that is expected is for them to mirror four hundred years of oppression. That is not acting. That is something else.

REES: There has been an important movement within British theatre to represent women in a more positive light. Do you feel black writers in texts and directors in productions have endeavoured to do the same for black women? Or are the old battles for recognition of blackness still having to be fought?

BLACK: Last year I did *Sugar Hill Blues* by Kevin Hood, at Croydon Warehouse and the Hampstead Theatre, which revolved around four characters, two male and two female. The female characters were truthfully drawn, in terms of the time the play was set, and the range of emotions that could be played. We had a white director for that and the playwright was white. At no point did I ever feel that I could not say what I wanted.

Some black playwrights, I think, don't necessarily write particularly well for black actors anymore than a white playwright writes well for white characters. You have to take it on the merits of the writer.

REES: Are there less parts for black actresses in black plays?

BLACK: The bias there is that most black writers are male writers, talking about black male experience. All black women wait as it were! In the States black women writers particularly novelists, like Alice Walker, have really moved on and out, and talk about the black female experience within that country where it has such a long history. Here it does not have the same kind of history, but it will emerge here in time as more actresses and writers begin to act, write and direct. There are not enough of us at the moment.

There was a tremendous burst of black writing in the Seventies – Farruk Dhondy and Mustapha Matura. Suddenly it was very trendy to go and see black plays. But I think it is symptomatic of this country that the people who went to see those plays then were predominantly white and middle class. The Eighties developed a different kind of audience who wanted to see themselves on stage. So you got different kinds of plays and the black question receded. It has still not been dealt with and I hope new writers will start coming through. Certainly in the music business there is a whole new group of young black people who are saying we can do this ourselves, we are not just going to be a minority, our experience is your experience and you are going to see it. In time the same thing will happen in theatre. But it is much more establishment orientated so it will take longer and also the funding is not there. It will change eventually.

144

STRUTTING YOUR STUFF
Actors talking about their craft

Touring for Foco Novo, an actor was provided a three or four month contract, with the added attraction of a London run at theatres such as the Royal Court, the Tricycle Theatre, the ICA, the Young Vic, Hampstead Theatre or Riverside Studios. This earned national reviews and a resulting high profile.

Equal pay for all the actors and stage management, was company policy, regardless of age or experience, throughout rehearsal and playing, with a *per diem* touring allowance. Each show was a new starting point, but many participants returned, at smaller or greater intervals, to work on further projects with the company.

A number of Foco Novo plays used the past to reflect on the present; David Schofield [John Merrick, the 'Elephant Man' and Quantrill the Raider] and Oliver Ford Davies [Eadweard Muybridge, the early photographer], Fiona Shaw [Mary Shelley]. All the characters played by these three actors are historically based. The fruits of researching the details of their subject's backgrounds, as well as the dangers, are described. But, ultimately all agree that the time comes to let go the research and embrace the character you have created.

In the designers conversation [*See Tearing Down the Curtain*] our attention is drawn to the dangers of using photographic evidence in design. It may impose strict visual representation, without any personal input, while historical reality, as a basis for a play, need not necessarily lead to a documentary. Once historical characters are put in plays, they become fictionalised. For instance, the key to the development of the Elephant Man, John Merrick, is his meeting with Mrs Kendal. In actual fact, this never happened. Through the introduction of this device, Bernard Pomerance could highlight Merrick's vulnerable situation, and make it more real than documented fact.

145

Oliver Ford Davies in Foco Novo's 1981 production of Nigel Gearing's *Snap*.

DAVID SCHOFIELD
OLIVER FORD DAVIES

David Schofield

David Schofield played John Merrick in the original production of Bernard Pomerance's *The Elephant Man* for Foco Novo in 1977. Subsequently this production was remounted in 1980, with some of that original cast, playing for a year on the Lyttelton stage at the National Theatre. Earlier in 1980, he played Quantrill in *Quantrill in Lawrence*, a play of the American Civil War period by the same author, for Foco Novo at the ICA.

Oliver Ford Davies played Eadweard Muybridge, one of the Founders of the Motion Picture, in Nigel Gearing's *Snap* for Foco Novo in 1981, touring and playing the New End Theatre, Hampstead.

David was nominated in the 1980 *Swet* Best Actor Award for his portrayal of John Merrick in *The Elephant Man* and Oliver won the 1990 Olivier Actor of the Year Award for his role in David Hare's *Racing Demon.*

REES: The real reason I was drawn to theatre is that I love telling stories, anecdotes at a pub or a party, hot-trot, meeting people, finding out about other people's lives and sharing their thoughts and ultimately therefore the thoughts of the playwright. I like telling other people's stories to other people.

FORD DAVIES: In the theatre, I discovered I could play aspects of myself I had never previously allowed to emerge in my own life, to release anger which had been stoked down so much in my childhood.

REES: At seventeen, I went along to the Library Theatre in Manchester run by Tony Colegate, now sadly dead. He said: 'Do you want an assessment of your potential?' I said: 'If it's all the same to you, I'd rather have a job!' So I was in theatre, as a student ASM, for two years before I went to LAMDA. It was tremendously helpful to have done that.

FORD DAVIES: In the Fifties, I went to the Old Vic a lot. John Neville and Richard Burton were my idols. But I was inclined towards Michael Redgrave and Ralph Richardson and character acting. I was sixteen in 1956, so I saw the original *Look Back in Anger* and *Waiting for Godot,* and the Berliner Ensemble. I assumed all this explosion of new theatre was what theatre was normally like. Then my heroes became dramatists. Arden, Wesker. At university the big influence on me was a remarkable man and actor, Vladek Sheybal, who left Poland in 1956 at the time of the uprising. He took theatre workshops at Oxford and was a wonderful teacher. An inspiring man. He jumped me into serious theatre.

I was good at passing exams, so I continued on this academic conveyor belt, frightened to step off it. I became a Lecturer in History at Edinburgh University, and continued to do amateur theatre. Then I realised this could be it for the next forty years and it wasn't really what I wanted to do. So at the age of 27 I became an actor. It was my plan to go to LAMDA, but I could not face going back to being a student. So I went straight into theatre without any formal training.

REES: David, in your early career, you worked with Charles Marowitz at the Open Space. Was it the prospect of similar work which drew you to Foco Novo?

SCHOFIELD: I have to say I was looking for a job! The one you offered, seemed exciting. I knew you did new, interesting plays and took them out to where they belonged. Difficult jobs are more interesting than easy ones. Since I have grown up a bit and have 2.5 children, a mortgage and a pension scheme, I find the less interesting jobs sometimes more attractive – they pay a lot better! But I still hunger for adventurous work. A lot of my contemporaries are not interested in putting themselves out on a limb. They want the easy life. I think it turns out to be the more difficult life. Once I read *The Elephant Man* script, there was no doubt in my mind. I would have killed anyone else who was cast as John Merrick.

FORD DAVIES: I knew about *The Elephant Man* but didn't see it. I did go and see *Quantrill in Lawrence* at the ICA [*also a play by Bernard Pomerance with David Schofield*]. So I knew the Company did innovative work, and I also knew that they did not belong to the purely political wing of theatre, that they were more interested in general, social and historical themes. Like David really – and actors always make this joke – it was the job! An actor's career is terribly dictated by that. Those who try to shape their careers – 'This is what I will do now' – have often found it doesn't work out that way.

I went into theatre, curiously enough, exactly the same year as David – 1967 – and there were virtually no alternative touring theatre companies then, so it was not an option to going into Rep. I was there in the last days of the old Reps. Birmingham was a company of eighteen and we did Shakespeare, Ibsen, Shaw. It was a very young company – including Brian Cox, Michael Gambon, Tim Dalton etc – all hired to go and do that work in their early twenties. Timothy Dalton and I made our professional debut on the same night. He was straight from RADA playing a small part in *Richard II*. Now a Timothy Dalton from RADA would be immediately snapped up by TV. A different world.

REES: As you got to know more, did there seem a distinct flavour to the work of the fringe/touring groups compared to mainstream theatre?

SCHOFIELD: As as an actor, you could contribute more to working with Foco Novo or The Open Space than you could in Rep. I did a play in Exeter that was not finished by the start of rehearsal. A couple of us had come in just for the show but the rest of the cast were part of the Rep Company. Many of them were disconcerted and angry that they were being asked to start rehearsal on an incomplete script. Yes, it was hairy but it was exciting. I could not believe there were actors going around at lunchtimes, saying: 'I've had enough of this. Unless we get a complete script for that scene tomorrow, I'm going.' I said: 'Use your imagination. Contribute something yourself.' So that was the difference.

FORD DAVIES: There *was* a difference. Alternative theatre in the Seventies was quite definitely wanting to challenge the status quo. It actually wanted change. This came out in the work. It might be asking you to look afresh at the American Civil War or an historical person, or it might be presenting an overtly contemporary, political play. But there was definitely a feeling that there was a status quo to be challenged. That was not what was happening in Rep. There was a divorce between the work I was doing and the beliefs I held. In the Seventies most of my political beliefs got channelled into Equity where we were struggling for a branch and delegate structure, whereas my work was mainstream and classical.

REES: David, you were saying that working with the Open Space or Foco Novo allowed an actor to be more involved in the work process. Because the organisation was smaller, it provided the actor a greater sense of responsibility.

SCHOFIELD: Both the systems have pluses and minuses. I think the Rep system can teach you amazing things about discipline, reliability – Page One, Rule One in the theatre. I did find that a lot of companies, who counted themselves as fringe/experimental, practised what we called scratch-your-arse acting. As long as you scratched your arse a bit and tried to look like Marlon Brando or James Dean, and went against the normal conventions of theatre, that was exciting. It wasn't of course. You needed to bring the two things together. The freedom of expression that experimenting in theatre can give you and the discipline of Rep where you have got to take care of business. I never knock the Rep system.

FORD DAVIES: I would add a corollary to that, as a result of doing a new play, *Racing Demon*, by David Hare, who came out of that whole Seventies political tradition. He has honed his style to a point where he writes in terse, spare sentences. And doing this play with actors like Michael Bryant, Richard Pasco, Barbara Leigh Hunt, one found that people, who had got this enormous wealth of classical training, understood instinctively how to get absolutely behind the line and centred on it, and then hit it right down the middle. Because the line does not work unless you are centred on it. Their training allows them to keep a speech running at a considerable pace yet they could still observe the full stops.

The whole tradition of TV acting is that you take no notice of the full stops. On the whole you run over the full stops as much as you can and take your breaths during the next sentence. The whole effort is to naturalise it.

Working with David Edgar and David Hare, I have noticed how much they relish finding classically trained actors handling their language, punctuation and full stops, exactly as they have written it. I agree with David. I don't want to deny the Rep system at all.

REES: Which in the form you knew it, is now being dismantled. Ironically, it is the Fringe which might be said to have taken over the role of being a training ground.

Much of Foco Novo's work has been about historically-based people and events. Does this present a particular edge to the business of creating a part? David what drew you to Merrick?

SCHOFIELD: I was drawn to the play for the reasons Oliver has been talking about. Some writers write so concisely that there is no point in paraphrasing the dialogue, no point in doing anything except getting behind what the writer has put down on paper. And my first impression of *The Elephant Man* was: 'What a fantastic script. What a wonderful telling of a story!' I liked the humour Bernard had put into the script. I have personally yet to meet a disabled person who is not funny, who is not self-humorous. It is us able-bodied who find disablement uncomfortable, until you get to know the person.

REES: In *The Elephant Man* there are two characters called 'Pinheads'. In order to understand how to play these parts we set about finding out why somebody was called a Pinhead. First, we saw a film about a circus by Tom Brown called *Freaks*. In this Circus, there were performers who were called Pinheads. They had conical shaped heads, were very gregarious yet naive and child-like in their demeanour. But we needed to understand their condition more intimately.

I contacted Dr Martin Bax [*Editor of Ambit*] who effected us an introduction to Friern Barnet Hospital and arranged for the two actresses playing the Pinheads – Jenny Stoller, playing Mrs Kendal, was doubling as one and Judy Bridgeland, the other – to meet patients who were regarded as Pinheads.

☐ *Foco Novo had a cast of seven for all of the many parts, whereas when the production was remounted at the National there was a cast of twenty plus – a lesson in the use of subsidy!*

They took us into a Nissen hut, standing in the middle of the spacious grounds of the hospital. After seeing the film, I had to say: 'I am sorry but I don't think that there are Pinheads here.' We were taken to another hut. Still I had the same reaction. The doctor escorting us said: 'We will take you to a further hut but we need to know that you are prepared for it!' Immediately we thought we are being taken to where the so-called maddest of the mad were kept. And indeed, the smell on entering that hut was more pungent than any we had previously experienced.

But there were some Pinheads! They were drugged up to the eyeballs and so unable to communicate much. However, everyone else here was very friendly and curious, plucking at our clothes and repeatedly saying: 'How are you? How are you? What's your name?' After we had been there some time, talking to the Pinheads, although their responses were anything but child-like and gregarious as we had seen in the film, I felt an overwhelming desire to start laughing. No sooner had I started than each person there copied me and soon the whole hut was awash with laughter. This made me, Jenny and Judy giggle and laugh even more. And again we were copied. Everyone was rolling around on the floor. And I thought this is it, I have caused a riot! Afterwards, the doctor told me that this was probably one of the best afternoons they had spent for a long time.

SCHOFIELD: I didn't go on that trip because Merrick's disability was not one of the mind. Unless I was to meet people with neuro-fibromatosis or Von Reklinghausen's disease, I didn't want to meet anybody whose mental capabilities were impaired.

REES: Did there seem huge problems to solve in the representation of Merrick?

SCHOFIELD: When we first met during casting, you said you had no idea how this is going to be done. But the theatrical devices we evolved were absolutely stunning, and so simple.

REES: In the text, Bernard indicated that Merrick should be played probably without make-up. We decided to take that route. But what that meant was up to us.

SCHOFIELD: I remember spending a week in the rehearsal room above the Eton pub on Adelaide Road, near Swiss Cottage, with empty ice cube boxes in my mouth trying to speak!

REES: Merrick had a cleft palate amongst many of his infirmaties.

SCHOFIELD: He had a cleft palate, severely deformed mouth and jaw. His speech was unintelligable to most people.

REES: Many of his bones and limbs were abnormally heavy.

SCHOFIELD: He had difficulty walking, sitting down, doing anything. We tied weights to my legs to get a sense of a much heavier leg.

REES: The key to the physical portrayal of Merrick became the scene of Treves' lecture to students and doctors at the London Hospital, exhibiting Merrick and enumerating his bodily deformities. [*Treves was the surgeon who took pity on Merrick and got him admitted to the Hospital*]. You were naked, David, arms outstretched and in perfect health. However as the lecture proceeded, illustrated with the original slides of Merrick taken in the 1880's at the Hospital, you transformed yourself from this vision to the deformed physical specimen of Merrick, so imperceptibly over a space of four or five minutes that an audience would scarce have perceived movement. The vision at the end was how you would portray Merrick's physical presence for the rest of the play. No use of make-up.

SCHOFIELD: It was a case of studying the photos and taking up physical postures. I could not have a huge flipper-like right arm or a distorted hip or a partly dislocated jaw. By God, I have to say that by the end of the run, my shoulder was partly dislocated. So was my jaw and back.

Photo © John Haynes 1980

Roland Rees, Peter McEnery and David Schofield rehearsing Bernard Pomerance's *The Elephant Man* at The Royal National Theatre.

REES: At Hampstead when the run was extended, your back needed urgent attention. Bernard has added to the text that no actor with back difficulties should perform Merrick.

SCHOFIELD: I actually got one of Merrick's problems from doing the play, Scoliosis – curvature of the spine. And it wasn't until a few years ago that it was straightened out for me. To this day, if my back gets in the wrong position, I can be bending over a basin, cleaning my teeth, and experience the full effects of whiplash!

REES: I remember being in rehearsal, still flummoxed as to how we would present Merrick. Then one Sunday at a friend's house, whose father had been Keeper of Prints at the British Museum, flicking through a book of Leonardo prints, I came across that image of the naked Vitruvian man, arms outstretched and of excellent physique and knew at once that that was the answer – from beauty to the beast!

SCHOFIELD: Yes, yes. That's right! How things should be. The accepted norm. As Treves on one side of the stage described Merrick's physical condition, the audience watched the actor on the other imperceptibly change his posture, and then they looked at another slide on the screen in the centre of the stage, and when they returned their gaze to the actor something else small had altered. The whole staging was marvellous.

On tour between scenes, we had a blackout which hid me as I changed position. When we got to Hampstead, a scene change light was introduced. I got very thrown by that.

REES: You didn't have your protective blanket of darkness. You reverted to you, David Schofield, between the scenes.

SCHOFIELD: I stopped the tech and said: 'I cannot take this anymore. I'm expending all this energy and emotion to create this illusion and it is being destroyed at the end of every scene.' And I remember getting the only note I ever got from Michael Rudman [*then Artistic Director, Hampstead Theatre*] who shouted from the back of the auditorium: 'David, its okay!'

FORD DAVIES: And a very good note too!

SCHOFIELD: That is a nice thing about how a show can grow. I had to be convinced and take it on board. Once the penny dropped, it became one of the high points. Between the scenes the audience were constantly reminded that here's a normal guy.

REES: Merrick lived in the latter part of last century, Muybridge at the beginning of this century. Does the historical basis make a difference to the creation of a character?

REES: I do have certain spiritual thoughts. I do believe we've all been here before, that we'll be here again. So I felt a greater responsibility to the role knowing this young man had lived and experienced a lot, grateful that I was·only portraying and not experiencing them. I found it celebratory to tell Merrick's story. So it did make a difference.

FORD DAVIES: I'm interested in this question as an historian. I enjoy going out and doing a lot of research. It stops me having to rehearse. I relish all that. You often dig up details about a person that sets off an enormous train of thought. When you discover that the young Humphrey Bogart kept his upper lip stiff, a trademark of his acting, so as not to show his bad teeth, such details can reveal a lot about a person.

But there are two big warnings I give myself. One is, you must not play what is not in the text. There is no point in playing the fact that you have found out that the character was actually recovering from a terrible operation at this point in his life, if it is not mentioned in the text. You are simply muddling the audience. Second, you don't get any marks for getting all your research right. You can say you crammed all the 160 salient features of Napoleon into one performance, but what use is that if people get no feeling of Napoleon from your character?

At some point you have to loose yourself from the historical and recreate the *spirit* of the person. So if this character was a perfect bastard, but enormously charming, you cannot say I will recreate Napoleon's charm. You have to find that charm from within yourself. A member of an audience should be able to say: 'I understood the spirit of Napoleon from your portrayal and why people followed him for so long.' But it is a delicate moment when you decide to give up the research and start going for the spirit of a character, which only you as an actor can create.

When I was preparing the part of Muybridge in *Snap*, [*The serial photographer who made his name in California by proving a millionaire's bet that a galloping horse has all four of its hooves off the ground at one time*] I asked myself where his first name Eadweard comes from? Is he Dutch? Then one of the first things you discover, is that his name is actually Edward Muggeridge and during his life, he set about slowly altering his name. That kind of detail immediately sets you off on a character.

Muybridge was born in Kingston-upon-Thames. I visited his house and library. I long to see the plaque go up 'The Father of the Motion Picture'. The house is now a shop that sells bridal gowns.

Muybridge had such an extraordinary life. He had this strangely blinkered vision – immense concentration on certain things going on in his life, entirely blind to others. The obvious example being that his wife had a child by a lover whom he had employed as a model in his studio. On realising this, he travelled 200 miles to Napa County, Northern California, and shot the man dead and claimed: 'I'm innocent. It was a crime passionel!' Apparently he was the last man in California, if not America, to be acquitted on such a basis. After his case, they changed the law. These kind of details are very interesting, and the photos of California in the 1850's showing how primitive it was, and how a photographer would have flourished there.

REES: Nigel had written a play of cinematic images in which Muybridge was also called upon to play cowboys and indians and other stock characters from motion pictures. The play was set inside the black box of a camera obscura. The use of stroboscopic lighting effects illustrated the method Muybridge adopted when he photographed a single subject with a series of still images, turning these 'stills', through the use of his zoopraxiscope, into 'motion'. It was highly theatrical.

FORD DAVIES: *Snap* was immensely ingenious and owed a lot to Nigel having worked for a time in Paris. I thought in many ways the English audience was unprepared for this box of tricks. Parisians would have taken it in their stride. It was a bit too clever for the English. A terrible indictment of how isolated we were.

REES: Turning back to *The Elephant Man*, David, the play, when we first did it at Hampstead, was received with considerable favour. Quite remarkable things were said about it and your performance. A year later it was put on in New York, first off-Broadway and then on Broadway, becoming the longest running straight play Broadway has known. It was this Broadway run which

155

gave the play its notoriety. David Bowie played Merrick for a while, although in a loincloth. When I saw the show in New York, I could not but notice how many aspects of our original production had travelled across the Atlantic. I saw Philip Anglim playing Merrick. He had seen the production at Hampstead and persuaded Richmond Crinkly, the producer, to put it on in New York.

Not the least of which were the individual elements of your portrayal of Merrick. How did this strike you at the time?

SCHOFIELD: At the time, I didn't know anything about it. I had moved onto other things. But I knew the play was going to be done in America and that there was, for various reasons, no possibility of anybody from the London Foco Novo production being allowed to go over and do it. So I put it completely out of my mind. Then some months later, a girlfriend of mine, Stephanie Fayerman, came back from New York having seen the production with Philip Anglim. She had gone to see him after the show. And my name came up in the conversation whereupon he looked startled and said to Steph: 'You know him? Well, that's wonderful, because I owe him everything!' I just wished that, rather than his good wishes, he had sent a cheque!

I think it was Olivier who said that all actors are thieves. If something's good, you take it. But I think there might be a difference between taking the spirit of what somebody is doing because they have hit on some kind of truth and just copying what another person has done.

REES: When I saw the New York production, I could not help noticing that many of David's individual and idiosyncratic mannerisms cropped up in Anglim's performance. Little physical gestures, dexterous vocal sounds he had created. Now this cannot be achieved, I would have thought, as the result of one seeing of the play. Anglim would have had to have seen our production a number of times, to achieve the verisimultude he did.

FORD DAVIES: The original production of *Equus*, for example, had a set that fitted the play so well, that if you were doing the play again, you would have a difficult decision. You would have to say, do I copy that – and so acknowledge it as the only solution – or do I do something different just for the sake of being different? If somebody decided to do *Snap* again, would you want them to throw away that whole idea of the set, the camera obscura?

REES: If there are tricks to be solved and you solve them, those solutions become part of the play. I think David was making the point that aesthetic satisfaction in our wayward profession is not enough when so little and then so much money, can be made out of the same product.

The remount of *The Elephant Man* at the National was very successful – it ran for a year – but somehow it did not seem to receive the extraordinary critical attention we got the first time round. Perhaps because of its immense success on Broadway, it was now tainted for London critics. It was no longer a discovery.

SCHOFIELD: Perhaps many of them were surprised the first time to see a play about someone with such terrible disabilities, that was full of so much humanity. The second time around, the critics went a bit more for the jugular of what Bernard was saying politically with the play. I have to say I am not a political animal. Like Sam Goldwyn, I let that message be taken care of by Western Union.

FORD DAVIES: Critics get caught up in the business of fashion, in the business of the moment. A play rapidly becomes last year's play. Old hat. It is pernicious, the way we write off quite recent plays.

REES: In the plays you did with Foco Novo, both of you had to appear naked on stage. Did this bother you?

FORD DAVIES: I have never been asked to do this before and probably will never be again! The first time I actually took my clothes off in *Snap* was in a late run through at the Roehampton College where we were rehearsing. It was daytime. There were no theatre lights and, standing in the wings, it was very cold. I came to that moment, when you actually remove your knickers and hand them to a female ASM, and step on the stage naked for the first time. There were only six or seven people in the auditorium, but a hush fell upon the proceedings. You could hear a pin drop. But after that initial time, it didn't bother me ever again. The first time is the worst.

I felt that the other three actors had been partly chosen for their very beautiful bodies and in the play they actually appeared naked first. I was playing a much older man, so when I appeared, I got a definite feeling, particularly during matinees on tour, that old ladies were saying: 'Ooh! They've even made that poor old man take his clothes off!' There was a great wave of sympathy! We had one good moment at Plymouth, where the Arts Centre had double booked, and they placed us at the Quaker Centre. We thought the Quakers would object to the nudity, but they either stayed away or took to it like a duck to water. That's what Quakers approve of – letting it all hang out!

REES: You felt it was an essential part of the production.

FORD DAVIES: It was integral to the play. Muybridge took over ten thousand pictures of naked men and women, including himself. And you explained what was involved in full at our very first meeting. So I was left in no doubts about what I was taking on!

SCHOFIELD: It didn't worry me unduly. I know actors are always told that this nude scene is really important to the role. Most of the time it isn't. It's just gratuitous flashing of bum and tit. Very often, on screen, you see women naked but men sleeping in their underwear. There was no question of whether the actor playing Merrick should appear naked at the beginning of the play. It was making a very particular statement about a normal body, without blemish, becoming, in front of the audience this man with terrible deformities. It constantly reminded them that a normal able-bodied person was trapped inside a very uncomfortable body.

There was only one occasion it bothered me. On a Foco Novo tour, the audience can be within literally inches of you, so you're there warts and all. Now in a regular theatre, you will have a proscenium arch, an orchestra pit or something between you and them. At one particular tour venue, Alsager College, the front row was eighteen inches away and unfortunately sitting there was a gentleman of a certain persuasion, who spent quite a lot of time staring. This did not make me feel uncomfortable but it did make me angry. If he wanted to see a naked guy, he should have gone to a gay strip club. He was sexually harassing me in my place of work!

REES: Oliver, your first contact with Foco Novo was seeing the production of *Quantrill in Lawrence* at the ICA. David, you were in it, playing *Quantrill*, the lead part. This play had a cast of thirteen and, by our standards, this was a large show. We were only able to produce it as a result of the small but very welcome percentage Bernard insisted the producers provide us from the Broadway production of *The Elephant Man*. It was a play I had always wanted to do. And we chose to perform it at one single venue because its size made it inappropriate to tour.

FORD DAVIES: It was a very arresting and original play and you did it in a very striking manner. I was annoyed I had missed the *The Elephant Man*. I knew the names Foco Novo and Pomerance. That combination made me go to see it. One of the aspects of group work is that audiences went to see that group and that writer. I don't think they were so bothered as to who was in it. That was a very healthy development of the Fringe.

REES: The play took place during the American Civil War in Lawrence, Kansas and its environs [*where William Burroughs now lives*] and centred on a gang, led by Quantrill – Quantrill's Raiders – that included Jesse James and his brother. For the wrongs he felt done to him, Quantrill abducted the daughters of the Mayor and major citizens of the town and held them to ransom.

SCHOFIELD: It was an extraordinary play. It was not unlike a less unpleasant version of the Manson family. This man seemed to have power over people. He liked women and introduced people to drugs. I once asked Bernard what the message of the play was and he thought for a moment, as he did, and then said very quietly: 'Never trust a guy with a private education!'

REES: Muybridge, Merrick, Quantrill – do these kind of parts often turn up?

SCHOFIELD: I didn't have parts as challenging, interesting or as exciting as Merrick and Quantrill for ten years after that. Recently at the Manchester Royal Exchange, I did a new American play, *Winding the Ball*, by a young Texan writer, Alex Finlayson. That was an extraordinary play and took me right back to the time I spent with the Open Space and Foco Novo, the two most exciting and challenging times in the 23 years of my career to date. They were new plays, about historical people. I have played parts that are considered the great classical roles in the theatre, but they were not for me as challenging or exciting. Although extremely demanding on many levels.

FORD DAVIES: Muybridge was interesting and challenging too. I often joke with my agent and say that I play good friends and mad scientists. I used to keep being offered Horatio – five times so far – that's my good friend part and I really longed to play a mad scientist and Muybridge fell into that category. I really want to play the mad scientist in *Back To the Future 7!* That is living proof you can play a big performance on the screen [*Christopher Lloyd*] and get away with it! It's extraordinary to talk in terms of types. But one does find oneself type cast a lot and I now find my type-casting has extended to human failures. I'm playing a lot of failures lately – top Civil servants disintegrating under the weight of secret vices!

REES: The relation of actors to directors. Are there do's and don'ts, you would advise directors upon?

SCHOFIELD: One of the nicest things I ever heard a director say, was on the first day of rehearsal for *Anthony and Cleopatra* at the National with Anthony Hopkins, Judi Dench and Michael Bryant. On that first morning, after saying, 'welcome,' the first words of Peter Hall were: 'I hope you will all be glad to hear, I don't have a concept!' That was good news to me because, when I was working with another large organisation, the concept was everything. The whole production was twisted to accommodate the director's and designer's concept. For one play I was costumed from head to toe in black and instructed to wear very pale make-up and eye shadow to deepen my eyes. The whole costume was topped with a black, widows-peaked wig. Then I was told *not* to play a villain!

FORD DAVIES: I'm a believer in the fact that a director is the best audience you will ever have. You should be able to trust the taste of your director. That is vital. I also think a director should create a climate in the rehearsal room in which everyone can work creatively. A director should open up choices. Actors usually see two or maybe three ways of doing something, but a director can do a great service by opening up a fourth and fifth choice. With young actors, a director should be very encouraging. Actors blossom under encouragement and they also blossom by being told that's fine but you can do it even better. I think actors with love and encouragement can be pushed out of their shells, out of the safe things they do, into being bolder and freer.

SCHOFIELD: The director, Peter Wood, after I had done something which was more than acceptable in rehearsal said: 'Yes. And? We know you can do that. We've seen you do that. That's easy. What else can you do with that section?' Of course, then I had to think again, past the acceptable, interesting choice to the second and third choices and suddenly I was saying to myself: 'I didn't know I was going to do that.'

REES: Thelma Holt told me how keen Robert Strua and Ninagawa are to work with English actors. She said they liked the open market and the fact that English actors had minds of their own. And for the way they put in hours of work after rehearsal and came back the next day with a different offering. The implication is that they considered their own company actors were puppets, vessels waiting to be filled. Here, we have two directors showering admiration on English actors whilst, we, English actors and directors, have been enthralled by the work these directors have achieved with their own companies, the very actors they now desire to escape from! I am fascinated by this cross-over.

FORD DAVIES: What Thelma is saying is the old Tyrone Guthrie expression – 'Astonish me in the morning.' If you come up with an idea, go away and work on it. Don't do what you did yesterday!

SCHOFIELD: The difference between watching Japanese actors working under Ninagawa's direction and English actors is striking. The Japanese actors, regardless of whether they had done their homework, were absolutely one thousand and one percent, every single one of them, in that play. The same collective intention. They invested the production with an enormous passion, all too often lacking in English productions. The enormous power of the play, and what the play had to say, came right out. I have to say watching English actors in a Ninagawa production it was peopled with actors giving their own isolated performances. I lost the play as a result.

REES: So much for the open market.

FORD DAVIES: An essential part of a director's job is to hold a balance on what an actor is doing. Actors with minds of their own, will end up doing their own thing, if that balance is not held. There is a story how Brecht suddenly stopped rehearsals one day and said: 'An actor has to serve the intention of his character but he has to serve the common cause of the play.' Which I think we would all agree, is fairly good Stanislavski. But he then went on to say: 'All creativity in acting lies in the contradiction of these two things and the dynamic relationship between these two things.' I think what a director should do is to spot where an actor is either spending too much time serving the common cause of the play, and too little time putting forward the intention of his own character, or vice versa. These two things are hard to hold in balance.

So often actors are accused of being selfish, that their ego shows too much. In theatre as great a danger is too much selflessness. Whereby everybody is filling in, doing their part, and making the scene work instead of contributing to a creative conflict.

SCHOFIELD: Peter Wood said to a great actor, Michael Bryant: 'Can I just ask you something, Michael? You know, you have two performances. Number two, where you give everything to the other actors and then you have your number one, where you look after yourself. And I think we need your number one in this scene.' Peter Wood was pointing out that balance, that exact balance you were talking about, was tipping the wrong way. It was because of an actor's selflessness and generosity.

FORD DAVIES: In a drama, one is usually dealing with the most critical three days in a group of people's lives. The stakes are high. Some characters do react by internalising and taking a step back from the crisis. But every actor must be aware, however their character deals with the situation, that the stakes are high. Very often you go to see an English production of Ibsen and you don't seem to be made sufficiently aware of how high the stakes are.

REES: Young writers can have one show on at the Bush and are straight away writing a series for TV. There seems very little intermediate ground. Is this happening to young actors? Do they look at the industry in a different way to when you started your careers? You described your early days in the Rep system. Do they bypass that now?

FORD DAVIES: Young actors say there is an enormous pressure on them during their first two or three years. They may be offered five or six really good parts on TV during that time. They are being constantly judged that if they do not make a significant mark with these parts, they will be dumped. That pressure is far greater than when I started in Birmingham Rep in 1967. It was a period when we were still learning. Agents and producers did not come down to see what we were doing. Those days are gone and I think that is serious.

English actors are looking much more towards America than we used to 20/25 years ago. More and more actors spend half the year in LA sniffing around. They are after status and money rather than learning their craft.

REES: The disparity between what you can earn in theatre and what you could earn in a few days TV work, has made a total difference to the practice of theatre.

FORD DAVIES: I don't think actors think about the West End at all. There are not many plays on in the West End and below the leading parts the money is really not very good. Not good enough to counter balance having to sign on for nine months or whatever. The theatres in London which pay well are the National and RSC.

REES: Those two institutions solely and alone?

FORD DAVIES: That's right. You can live on what they pay. But that is an unhealthy situation. Whenever a Company starts to do exciting work like the Almeida, it immediately runs into financial problems.

REES: Many companies like Foco Novo had a principle of paying the same to everyone. It was practical too. Otherwise my administrator would have ended up on the phone for days of conversations arguing with agents over £3.75. I think the knowledge that everyone is paid the same, creates a good climate. Very different to the experience where actors are going around trying to find out what everyone else is getting.

FORD DAVIES: My early experience of Rep is that a situation, in which people discover that they are on different money, can become very divisive. You suddenly discover an actor, straight out of Drama School, is on higher pay than yourself. I am a passionate believer in companies of actors being paid the same. I joined the Cambridge Theatre Company in 1973/74 and we were all paid the same through a season of nine plays and we all genuinely played little parts and big parts. That was great.

REES: What lies in the future for theatre?

FORD DAVIES: There will have to come a point when money from TV and Film gets ploughed into theatre. The high standards on TV are due to the high standards of training people get in the theatre. TV acting will become safer and safer and more boring, as actors cease to work and experiment in theatre.

For years we quoted Germany as the example for the support of the Arts. But look also at France, Sweden, Italy, Holland and Canada. All spend a higher percentage of their gross national product on the Arts. [*Sweden spends £33 per member of the population on the Arts, France £23 and the UK £13*].

So quite apart from government subsidy, I think money will have to come back from TV into theatre.

REES: Each company bidding for a particular TV Franchise has to put down a stake, which goes to the Exchequer. A percentage of this conglomerate stake money, should be earmarked for the performing arts. After all, these companies benefit from the work experience of playwrights, actors and directors trained in the subsidised theatre.

SCHOFIELD: I agree. TV companies, who have got their license to print money for another ten years, should put some of that into their research arm – theatre.

FIONA SHAW

Fiona Shaw has played many leading parts including Hedda in
Hedda Gabler, Abbey Theatre, Dublin and The Playhouse, London,
Julia in *The Rivals* at the Royal National Theatre, Kate in *The Taming of
The Shrew* at the RSC, Stratford. For her portrayal of Electra in *Electra*
at the RSC, Barbican, Shen Te/Shen Ta in *The Good Person of Sechuan*
at the Royal National, Rosalind in *As You Like It* at the Old Vic, she
won the 1990 Olivier Award for Best Actress. Fiona played Mary
Shelley in Roland Rees' original Foco Novo production of Howard
Brenton's *Bloody Poetry* on tour and at the Hampstead Theatre
in 1984.

SHAW: The desire to perform is the desire to make sense of the world through performing in it. The question arises, are actors made or born? I believe they are born and that many more are born than become actors. I enjoy the element of changing reality. Like a lot of children, I think the imagination is a great place to retreat to, from a world often out of one's control or, in my case, from a world which was big and domineering and full of rules. Performing means you can have the world on your own terms

Acting is still anti-bourgeois in its lifestyle, although I know many actors are very bourgeois. I love living my life outside the regular rhythm of nine to five. Having said that, theatre has very strong in-built disciplines. Rehearsal at 10.00am – at least it's not 8.00am! And, of course, you are learning lines and working on the play way after you finish rehearsal. So I let acting discipline me. The great thing about that is you turn up to rehearse, have a cup of tea, the director gets you started and then you enter this imaginative world and you are there until it is time to go home. Your day is decided by these events. You worry or argue about pieces of text but mentally you are worrying about versions of reality.

REES: You did Philosophy at Cork University?

SHAW: If I ruled the world, I would make everyone take a philosophy degree. It helps you to look at a piece of text and know what to do with it. It allows you to think differently for each writer, to be able to take their approach. That's a good basis for acting.

REES: When you were at RADA in the early Eighties, did you think their particular training prepared you for the profession any differently to other Drama Schools?

SHAW: Unlike Drama Centre, RADA did not try to rely on any one method of training. It was not against 'The Method' but it did not put people through it. Drama Centre was about deconstructing yourself before you were ready to perform. Quite a lot of them fell by the wayside, whereas at RADA, you could behave as badly as you liked because whatever your route to being an actor was, you were supported.

REES: One of your first jobs after leaving RADA was playing Mary Shelley in my production of Howard Brenton's *Bloody Poetry* for Foco Novo.

SHAW: Rumour was rife about the companies actors wanted to work for. Foco Novo was one of the vibrant companies who toured. So an actor would feel they were really doing their job because more people would see you in more places that way.

REES: The play is about the meeting at Lake Geneva between Byron and Shelley with Mary Shelley, whom you played, and her half-sister, Claire Clairmont and that quartet's subsequent exile in Italy at the beginning of the 19th century.

SHAW: New writing was always terrifying to me. The most fantastic thing about *Bloody Poetry* was that it was a new play but it was also set in a classic time. In retrospect, what I learnt from the Foco Novo job was the way the emotional present is what you are always playing out, even if the piece is set in the past. That was what was marvellous about that play and that production. It did not require a particular skill to deal with the past. You really had to be *there* for what was being said about the present.

REES: Does it make a great difference playing someone who 'historically lived' in comparison to playing an 'historic character' who is an invention of the playwright?

SHAW: It does. Brenton was trying accurately to capture a spirit of the time. He was also exploring his own life and world. I remember reading that big biography on Shelley [*The Pursuit by* Richard Holmes] and, of course, we read Shelley's own prose and poetry. So I was keen to be true to what I learnt. The whole thing was so educative. You get very excited if you are learning about something from scratch.

When I met you about the play, I was filming and thought the film process, which involved hanging about a lot, a bore. The job was so defined. It did not seem at all what I had been trained for. At our meeting, your enthusiasm for the play and the fact it was unfinished – there was a script but it would be altered – all this seemed terribly exciting. It was a play about people and about people hitting up against their lives in a very grand manner. I was a late starter in life. I did not really have my undergraduate days until I went to RADA. *Bloody Poetry* happened soon after and I did not fully understand the size and bravery of those people's lives.

REES: You mean Shelley's relations with Mary and her half-sister, Claire, and Claire's simultaneous relationship with Byron?

SHAW: Yes. All that losing of your virginity on a grave – things seemed slightly unreal. (*Mary and Byshhe first made love on a grave*). I loved playing it but it took time to sink in that it was that real. I had not lived enough. I saw the play again at the Royal Court and by that time, I knew more.

REES: Shelley was in pursuit of his life come what may, including exile in Italy, and babies who died as a result of this pursuit. Hence the word '*Bloody*' in the title of the play.

SHAW: A play like *Bloody Poetry* is so important because more and more America is setting us a terrifying example where freedom becomes consonant with homogeneity. And the most astonishing thing about that period and that play is that it reminds one that people have always behaved

Photo © John Haynes 1984

From Left to Right. Valentine Pelka and Fiona Shaw in Foco Novo's 1984 production of Howard Brenton's *Bloody Poetry*.

extraordinarily and it is important that they do. The breaking of social barriers is what cleans and refreshes society. People in America think they are free and they all drink coca cola and wear sweat shirts. That is freedom, to be exactly like your neighbour. Imagination is a word almost outmoded now. It is not considered to be what people function from. It is, but they don't know that. The term is thought of as romantic but it isn't. It is fundamental for opposing depression.

I remember that rehearsal process more vividly than many others. We rehearsed in Leicester (*Co-Producer Haymarket Theatre*) and we became this little family. We were taken out of our contexts like the Shelleys because we relied on ourselves and each other. (*Shelley called his attempts at creating communes with Mary, Claire and others, 'His family'*). It resonated. We were all strangers. You were directing actors you did not know. We were always waiting for you and Howard to tell us what you wanted from us and, in that way, it was your baby. I would be more useful to you now because I would know what to come into the rehearsal room with.

We were nearly all, new young actors finding our way. (*Valentine Pelka, Jane Gurnett, William Gaminara, Sue Burton with James Aubrey, who played Byron*). We were 'inspired' by these characters in *Bloody Poetry*, also finding their way, who, in their turn, were representatives of the originals who committed massive acts of self-destruction.

166

I remember the absolute joy of Howard Brenton coming in one morning with a new speech because he felt he knew the rhythms of my voice. I was enchanted. To find I was speaking the lines of the character but with the in-built inflexions of my own voice, seemed to me the point where art happens – the fusion of performer, director and writer in one moment. I have never had that experience again. To become the muse of a character. Nothing short of thrilling. And to hear another actor do that speech, as I did at the Royal Court, meant you are able to watch it become something else again.

Touring meant you got very different audiences. Reps do potboilers and occasionally something experimental. We were the latter. We did not have full houses in Leicester but we did at Theatr Clwyd, Mold and at the Hampstead Theatre. The play got massive publicity and caused quite a stir.

I felt privileged to be in at the end of that spate when playwrights wrote something because they wanted to. I fear the two National Companies could become colonial – sole purchasers and doers of new plays. When the reasons for their existence are to represent Shakespeare and World drama.

REES: Is there a different approach to work between a building-based company and a touring company? For instance, everyone in the *Bloody Poetry* company were paid the same wages?

SHAW: You see I did not realise that then. Shortly after Foco Novo, I went to the RSC and that was another chapter altogether. It was like going to Versailles or going up to Oxford. Joining the RSC, you join an institution which appears to know what it is doing. People are pensioned there. The date the company moves to Stratford is like the glorious twelfth. You almost learn the rules of hunting. You get a cottage in walking distance of this astonishing ship, this jam factory of a theatre. Whereas small, new play producing companies are important because they happen in the moment. Their demise is occurring for reasons outside of their responsibility.

Recently in Dublin, I realised the city is hot for new plays. Everyone talks about them – the bus driver, the taxi driver. Whether it was a good play, a hopeless play, doesn't matter. The important thing is that a relationship is seen between the play being produced and the public at large. Then it becomes not an academic but a cultural exercise. When I toured with the RSC, *The Merchant of Venice* and *Much Ado*, one, if not both plays, were on that year's school curriculum. So we found that the audiences were full of teenagers. Their presence was built into the production. A new play cannot have an in-built audience but a healthy relationship to new writing could. It is a great loss that people do not think going to see a new play is as important as staying in to watch *Coronation Street*.

REES: Stephen Rea says touring is the cutting edge of theatre. Could you be attracted to touring Ireland?

SHAW: He may be right about the cutting edge. But for me now, there are difficulties involved in touring. I am not so keen about lumps of the play being left out when you reach the next venue because the set does not fit. If one is trying to keep the production at the same boiling point it had, at that last run through in the hall, then by comparison touring is a state of emergency. However if a play is under-rehearsed or not ready, then touring is fantastic, because it needs that added energy in performance. With a new play and a writer working on it, touring can be most beneficial. Then it is the cutting edge of theatre.

I am keen that the audience gets the best possible experience. For that reason, I would not tour *Hedda Gabler* because it would crash into itself all the time. That cast shared the same imaginative basis for the play in Dublin. When we came to London, we were presented with a different shape in our minds. We had to re-remind ourselves of the universe we were inhabiting. In Dublin, we were familiar with the red-bricked building across the road from the theatre. You can take it with you but in the end the place you perform a play has an effect on both you and the play.

REES: I went to a weekend seminar conducted by a former Hollywood film director, Paul Grey. More than once, he said that stage actors are entirely different beasts to film actors. I put it to him that this may be true of the States because film is the dominant form, but that in the UK and in all other theatre and film producing countries, there is a constant to-ing and fro-ing. But he remained adamant.

SHAW: I don't think film and theatre actors are different beasts. Theatre acting, at its best, is more advanced and, at its worst, less advanced than acting in films. It is the circumstances where theatre takes place that can be at odds with the actor. I did a film last year, *Three Men and a Little Lady,* in which I had to play an obscenely cliche-ridden text. If I had not had the theatre experience I had, I don't think I would have been able to do it. I developed this character from mining the few words she was given. Most of the text in a film is the debris of what people say and not the actuality. I find it terrifying in film that there is so much cheating. The emotional state is not experienced, it is provided by the editor. For which reason, actors make the cross-over but not always easily.

Undoubtedly, film has suffered from theatre performances, but I think, on the other hand, film has not suffered enough from theatre performances. I think film suffers from filmic performances.

REES: American actors measure everything by the number and status of their appearances in movies and English actors who go out there are drawn into the same game.

SHAW: America has lost its theatre because it is so overshadowed by the film world – success and wealth being the motivation. Their theatre has not advanced like it has here. They don't have a language with which to rehearse theatre. I have learnt so much from people who know what the language of theatre is.

REES: Shakespeare's language provided the visualisation, the setting, through the mouth and performance of the actor. In contemporary plays the actor uses language through which character and plot are conveyed. In film, where the language is, as you say, the debris, the camera has wrested the job of delivering language from the actor. So the actor has a different job to do. An actor's physical presence on film becomes part of the decor of the camera. I believe it is this that Paul Grey was referring to in his seminar. But this does not mean actors cannot cope with both media.

SHAW: America is suffering from an acceleration of diminished language, losing words by the minute. Film is no longer about expression but non-expression. The content of films is about people who cannot express themselves – the 'Road Movie' is about people disenfranchised from expression – and the form of film follows this. On top of this, the editor makes another decision about reality. What is unprecedented in our experience, is that across many thousands of miles of the American continent, people are using the same shared nuances – a catchphrase – so that their experience of life becomes about these catchphrases.

When the actor playing Richard III comes on stage, his personality goes into the part even though the character is historical. The more idiosyncratic the actor, the more this influences the interpretation of a Richard III. The problem with American texts is that when you read them, you know exactly how to say the lines – 'Hi, how are you?' and 'Fabulous' – there are only so many ways you can say these catchphrases. There is a rhythm in them that is already given. There is a musical notation at play with such phrases which you could work out on a computer.

REES: Thelma Holt, who is producing you in the title role of *Electra*, is an impresario who has brought many foreign companies to London. She is now bringing directors – Ninagawa from Japan, Strua from Georgia – to direct English actors in English plays. She told me that both these directors loved English actors because they said they have minds of their own and always come in with something new the next day. The implication being that actors in their own companies, whose work we have so admired, are puppets in comparison. I was fascinated by this. They wished to give up what we regard as a great strength – strong company acting – in order to embrace our market economy of casting actors. To me, this is a great irony.

169

SHAW: Thelma wants to plug into a reality beyond nationality, which is difficult to define. I think the clash between a Japanese director and an idiosyncratic company of English actors would provide a synthesis which neither party expected. That's the idea.

But you're right. What is wrong in England is that we have no theory of acting and directing, so, dangerously, we end up with people doing their bit. There is no school for directors here. They seem to be accidents of nature. You meet a director and you wonder how they became one. They say I did this and that and then: 'I became a director'. You would not say: 'I became a brain surgeon.' The language of directors is not defined here. Whereas the foreign directors you mention, know what they want to do, maybe to a fault, because they have been proceeding like this for twenty years.

REES: They have not had to operate within a market economy which promotes film and television at the expense of theatre. In the UK, you earn less in theatre. So here actors commute between the media. They cannot afford to remain working in theatre for a lifetime. Whereas Georgian actors clearly could in the Rustaveli Theatre company, as indeed actors do in German Municipal theatres because they are paid much better there for theatre work.

SHAW: I would be happy enough to spend my whole life in the theatre but as you said, sadly, here we do not have the economic stability to do this. I am about to play *Electra* at the Riverside which will be popular and sell out, but for which I will be paid the Equity minimum wage. I am 33. It is quite late in the day to be on Equity minimum. I need to be able to buy the groceries. If you think you are doing important work, you need to have some economic recognition. The French have a truly intellectual tradition. The Government and Arts bodies spot people they want to fund. In England, we fund institutions.

REES: You have criticised the lack of a philosophy of acting and of directing. This means English actors above all are empirical. What is your approach?

SHAW: Deborah Warner applies this fantastically non-interventionist approach, which is not a conscious choice but more the result of her Quaker background. It involves sitting and waiting to see what moves the spirit. One's relationship to truth and reality becomes sharper with experience and so whatever method works, use it. I have many different approaches to preparing a part, but finally it is about knowing it is right. That's enough. And being absolutely honest when it is not.

You notice when actors come on stage if they have just eaten biscuits and had a cup of tea. Too much of that is tolerated in this country by other actors and the audience. And these are the things which get applause. The theatres are emptying because the performing is bad and it is bad because there is not a rigorous enough watchdog on acting. Actors think the audience don't notice. The whole thing should be cleaned up.

We also do not have any properly developed theory of criticism in this country. The arbitrariness of critics is terrifying. There are good critics but in the end it comes down to taste – finally *only* down to personal taste.

REES: Preparing a part for a film, there is neither the time or money to sit and wait for the spirit to be moved. Do you adopt a different approach?

SHAW: For over six or seven years, I didn't go near a camera. I always feel there is an 'L' plate on my back when I do. I marvel at people like De Niro and Meryl Streep who seem to know exactly how to get the time to do their homework. For most of us, you do not smell the film until you're doing it. It is emergency time.

REES: Are there parts that you have mentally earmarked which you want to do?

SHAW: Yes. My great sadness is, that despite being so privileged to have played a whole spectrum of parts other actresses of my age have not had a chance to do, we don't live in a milieu where writers are inspired to write for performers, plays and parts of great size. I hope this is not the result of my personality, I don't think it is. I do get the odd letter from a writer, having seen something I've done, saying they are inspired to write something bigger. But the world seems to have retreated into its drawing room, although, having said this, the drawing room of *Hedda*, in which I am acting at the moment, allows a massive drama to unfold. I wish things were being written with a greater size of aspiration. I'd love to play Cleopatra!

What cannot be overstated enough, and I am sad to say this, is that I see my colleagues and contemporaries and those older than me, waiting so long for a part, that the desire to be an actor is destroying their lives. And they go on waiting. It is detrimental to their development. They would be much better to explore the world by another path. But then it seems too late. An actor not acting can become a non-being. I know a famous actor in America to whom this happened. It gets to rot your stomach. You become less equipped. Theatre is an emotionally dangerous world.

REES: Is theatre going to survive as we know it?

SHAW: If actors work largely in Film and TV and not in theatre, then theatre will diminish its own possibilities. People get tired and do something else. Let's hope theatre is not losing good people. Those who had massive energy. With Foco Novo, you spawned people who went elsewhere. But Foco Novo had to commit kamikaze to achieve that. It is very sad.

Skill gets lost. The Fringe can only benefit younger actors and writers if the experienced directors remain. The big flagships will shoot themselves in the feet if they cannot draw sustenance from a healthy root. If the old Fringe companies are going to have to go because their associations are historical and not of our moment, then something else must grow up.

Stephen Boxer as D.H. Lawrence in Foco Novo's 1985 production of *The Ass*.

THE ASS

A Music Theatre show based on D.H. Lawrence's poem

The interview with Mike and Kate Westbrook, composer and singer, and the actor, Stephen Boxer, is about *The Ass* and the notion of 'Music Theatre'. It is a genre where people desire to synthesise different performance elements on a shared and equal basis. When Stravinsky composed *The Soldier's Tale* and William Walton, *Facade,* they did not leap to quantify what they were doing. It was music. To the credit of the Westbrooks, they are sceptical of naming genres but, at the same time, they feel the need to distinguish what they are doing, particularly when there is, presently available, such a variety, cross-over and fusion of music. Essentially, Music Theatre requires the music to be on equal terms with the narrative text, and for the dancers, musicians, and actors to recognise that they are sharing their skills, not contributing separate roles.

Mike Westbrook's background is Jazz, music with a structure which at the same time encourages improvisation. Joshua Sobol, describing the formal characteristics of polyphonic dramaturgy, uses Jazz as an analogy. 'Jazz is very democratic. Every voice takes the place it deserves, according to its inspiration at a certain moment. Jazz is like an open platform on which each voice can speak out what it has to say, fully, without restraint. When you come to a Jazz performance, you do not know what will happen.' This describes why Jazz admirably suits the needs of Music Theatre and is itself polyphonic.

Of the 38 productions Foco Novo presented, thirteen used live, specially composed music. The Jazz percussionist, Nigel Morris, provided a touch of 'film noir' and the voice of 'nemesis' in the first show, *Foco Novo*. In Brecht's *Edward II*, the percussion of Eddie Sayer was both the voice of battle, and the eerie sounds of Edward's inner life. Dave Brown played and composed the music for Adrian Mitchell's *A Seventh Man*, evoking the travel of 'guest workers' from Turkey, by means of shawms and pipes, to Frankfurt, Germany where their reactions were captured with electronic sounds. In *Needles of Light*, Cengiz Saner used his Turkish musical tradition to great effect, in creating Basque music, in a play about the Spanish Civil War.

MIKE & KATE WESTBROOK

STEPHEN BOXER

Mike Westbrook   Kate Westbrook   Stephen Boxer

Mike and Kate Westbrook, have been working as composer and singer respectively for many years, touring the UK and Europe. Whilst their creative origins lie in Jazz, they have explored many facets of music with their bands, Solid Gold Cadillac, The Brass Band, and with their trio, performing Jazz Cabaret. They were the composers of *The Ass*, a show they adapted from D. H. Lawrence's poem of that name, and produced by Foco Novo on tour and at the Riverside Theatre in 1985. *The Ass* premiered in Nottingham as part of the D. H. Lawrence Centenary Festival.

The actor, Stephen Boxer, has appeared in plays at the National Theatre, the RSC, and many Reps, as well as with numerous Fringe and touring companies. Stephen played D. H. Lawrence in *The Ass*.

REES: Mike and Kate, you have increasingly combined music and theatrical devices in your performances. Was *The Ass* a 'Music Theatre' production? What does the phrase mean?

M. WESTBROOK: Musical events, which are not known categories like opera and musical comedy. A further category is needed, for some reason, to describe other approaches to music which people are making.

K. WESTBROOK: We always have great difficulty in describing what it is we do. The term we came up with in the Seventies was 'Jazz Cabaret'. That was a bit unsatisfactory and so is Music Theatre. They are not very specific. The sooner we talk about *The Ass* we will know what Music Theatre is, since the show was a supreme example.

BOXER: The show defined Music Theatre.

REES: What are its origins? Was Stravinsky's *The Soldier's Tale* or Brecht's early experiments with Weill, Eisler and Hindemith, at the Baden Baden Modern Music Festivals in the late twenties, Music Theatre? Has Stravinsky or Brecht influenced you?

M. WESTBROOK: I think Brecht probably has. When we started doing the Brecht songs, we thought of their lyrics as being something very different compared to the lyrics of our normal repertoire of Jazz standards.

□ *American popular songs of the Thirties and Forties used as vehicles for improvisation.*

We did the Brecht songs with 'The Brass Band' and this was a new departure. Something else became involved and it has to be called 'theatre'. But there is still a narrow dividing line.

K. WESTBROOK: Having played a repertoire with The Brass Band, a real mish-mash of songs, pieces from all different sources, we decided to do a show with one central theme which we called *Mama Chicago*, performed in 1978 at the Open Space Theatre on Tottenham Court Road. To sell the show, we needed to describe it and we called it a 'Jazz Cabaret'. As far I know, it was a not a term which had been used. It was new at the time. It was the nearest we could get to describing what we did. We didn't know the term Music Theatre. The important thing for us was to devote a *whole* performance to one theme. To present a completely composed piece with lyrics, music and a certain amount of visual imagery. With that show we crossed over into something else. And we have stayed with it.

M. WESTBROOK: I don't know what Stravinsky called *The Soldier's Tale*, but it was certainly a model for us. And that came out of wartime conditions, shortage of musicians, the difficulty of touring.

BOXER: *Facade* by Edith Sitwell with music by William Walton was genuine Music Theatre.

K. WESTBROOK: I don't think that the Brecht/Weill partnership produced Music Theatre. I would have said it was 'Theatre with music'. Music Theatre implies interdependence. You could do Brecht without music.

M. WESTBROOK: But what is the difference between a Brecht/Weill and, say, a Cole Porter musical? There is dialogue and there are songs. In this respect, is *The Threepenny Opera* different to *Porgy and Bess?*

REES: Brecht would have said so. Large parts of his theory of theatre were based on this difference. He looked at the form of the musical as a 'culinary' experience, making the material palatable for the public by using music to underscore the achievements of the text. He emphasised the need for the autonomous but complementary contribution of music to a show.

K. WESTBROOK: However, *Seven Deadly Sins* is a piece of Music Theatre. The singers have to be trained yet it is different to opera.

M. WESTBROOK: Do you remember Jack Gelber's *The Connection?*

REES: That was a play about jazz musicians, some of whom were waiting for a 'fix', hence the title, in which Jazz was played but was not compositionally central to the play. Text and characters were what the play was about.

M. WESTBROOK: Yes, that is it. The difference lies between music being incidental and music being central in a show. We saw a show about Jelly Roll Morton [*American composer, band leader and pianist*] talking about his life. Every so often the band played one of his numbers. The music was not integrated within the show. It was a documentary.

REES: After *The Ass* we wanted to make a Jazz Opera.

M. WESTBROOK: We did one in Quichotte, France, but that was really a straight opera even though the promoters wanted to call it 'Opera Jazz'.

BOXER: In opera, the medium is very much song backed up by the instruments, but somehow there is more of a trade off between the word and the music in Music Theatre. The spoken word is probably used as much in opera but for Music Theatre properly to realise itself, it needs to have a show underscored with music throughout, as happened with *The Ass*.

REES: Let's turn to *The Ass*. Which came first, music or text?

M. WESTBROOK: The text. Kevin West of the D.H. Lawrence Centenary Festival approached us in 1984 to contribute some work to the Festival. He had seen things like *Mama Chicago* and the Jazz Cabaret and I think he imagined that we would come up with something like that. His brief was for us to produce something based on D.H. Lawrence's animal poetry. Apart from that, he gave us carte blanche.

K. WESTBROOK: I have always thought *The Snake* is one of the great English poems but too complete in itself to use as a basis. So we started reading the animal poems and came across *The Ass*. It offered itself up, visually, verbally and, by what it suggested, musically. Not the greatest poem ever, but a starting point for something strong.

M. WESTBROOK: At one stage we were looking at three poems – *The Bald Eagle, The Humming-Bird* and *The Ass*. We thought we might combine the three animals into one story. Finally we decided to concentrate on *The Ass*. So we started with the text of this poem. This included the parts where the ass is called upon to bray – a crucial step towards the 'sound' of the piece. It became a long process. We visited Sicily – Taormina – where the poem was set and where Lawrence lived for a time.

REES: Before you went to Taormina, you came to me with a text which included the poem, with certain sections transposed and sometimes repeated, and fragments from Lawrence's letters of that period.

K. WESTBROOK: We wanted to go beyond the cabaret style designed for one-nighters. We wanted to make a Music Theatre piece which we had never done or had the resources to do. Mike had written music for Adrian Mitchell's *Tyger* for the National but this was the first time we were going into a theatre production of our own. So we came to Foco Novo.

REES: Prior to *Tyger*, you had worked with the Welfare State. They are a theatre producing company but not of a conventional kind and not in theatres. Their work was about the integration of different forms and must have influenced your interest in theatre?

M. WESTBROOK: I first met John Fox, the Artistic Director of the Welfare State, at the end of the Sixties and started to get drawn into the kind of events which in those days were called 'happenings'. There would be an originating idea – some kind of a vague ceremony in a public park – and people would just turn up with instruments which we would co-ordinate. Out of these events, crystalised The Cosmic Circus, which was a multi-media group combining a real melange of semi-improvised theatre and classic circus acts – fire eaters, conjurors, trick cyclists – with music and visual effects, slides and film. My band Solid Gold Cadillac accompanied the shows .

In 1973, this development culminated in a show at the Tower of London called *The Apocalyptic High Dive Into a Pit of Molten Fire*. If you pass the Tower now you cannot imagine having done such a thing. It involved people diving from the battlements into a foaming cauldron. It was the time of the Roundhouse shows, like The Grand Magic Circus, Red Bhudda, all going on. A very successful period.

The impetus for this kind of work had come from the Art Schools. Roland Miller and The People Show, John Bull's Puncture Repair Kit. Forms of event and practice were introduced which people had not seen before.

K. WESTBROOK: 1973 was the tail end of that whole movement. I was teaching painting at the Leeds College of Art which was then a very lively place, although little painting was going on. John Fox, Jeff Nuttall and other performers made a creative ferment there, producing events. Jeff Nuttall's influence was seminal. He wrote *Bomb Culture*.

And the unsatisfactory thing, I remember from that time at Leeds, was the way these 'spectacles' were so much grander in intention than the event. This was partly due to underfunding but primarily it was the weight placed on the grand gesture with no attention to the text or to detail.

What I loved about *The Ass* was the craftsmanship and attention to detail, how it all came together. The Solid Gold Cadillac band and the Welfare State ought to have been absolutely stunning. Intellectually it was, but, so often, one was unmoved. It was big gestures but no craft.

M. WESTBROOK: I had the opposite experience when I did *Tyger*. The Kenneth Tynan era at the National commissioned Adrian Mitchell and I to do a show about Blake. The production process for *Tyger*, compared to our work with the Cosmic Circus, was entirely different. With the Circus, much was heralded and promised but usually fell far short of the intention. We never had enough rehearsal.

With the National, we had a long rehearsal period with two directors, John Dexter and Michael Blakemore. Everyone, I remember, was extremely nervous as to whether they would attain the high standards required. We had chorus masters, ballet masters, an enormous amount of money spent on sets and costumes, to the extent that when the time came, the sets would not fit into the Lyric Theatre in the West End. They had spent thousands on scenery which could not be used. It was so wasteful.

An extraordinary contrast between people, with brilliant ideas working on a shoestring, who could not realise what they want and people with enormous resources, achieving what? There was such a potential there, that needed the resources the National and the Royal Opera House had, to use in a way that they, the flagships, never would have done.

REES: Jazz is a strong and abiding part of your music. Is it the primary impulse and tradition within which you work?

M. WESTBROOK: It's where I started and where I came from. It was in the late Forties, whilst I was at school, that I became interested in music. Jazz was popular and so it made a big impression on me. I worked my way through the history of Jazz until I stood on my own. I was not classically trained. I am self-taught. To feel part of the Jazz tradition is for me important. Even though things we have been involved in lately are not classifiable as Jazz. Nevertheless, the origin and philosophy behind Jazz is there.

I was just old enough in the early Fifties to have been around when Trad Jazz and Modern Jazz, the committed, experimental side, were both popular. Bands toured the country and had an audience. Whereas Trad Jazz expressed a nostalgia for a bohemian past and an ethnic music thing, there was also a progressive attitude, a new notion of society, and with it the welfare state, which required a new kind of 'modern' music. When I first came to London there were clubs all over the place, playing Modern Jazz. It was the hip thing.

Then this music with a thumping beat, nice lyrics, lots of fun came along and audiences left Modern Jazz for Rock. Maybe Modern Jazz was experimenting too much, getting too elitist and so was losing their audience. Then Jazz went underground. I think Jazz has remained underground ever since. There are some big Jazz names like the late Miles Davis, who was a star in any firmament. And Jazz has acquired a commercial edge in the last few years, throwing up musicians like Courtney Pine who get big audiences here in the UK. But the vast majority of the Jazz community do not benefit from this. Jazz is potent but in mass cultural terms it is not.

REES: There have been theatre shows about Billie Holiday, Fats Waller etc – figures of Jazz history – which relied upon the music of their period, but very few shows, if any, which have used original Jazz, composed and improvised, as the mainstay music of a show, as we did in *The Ass*. Nearly all of the show, 95%, had a musical base. With opera this is usual, but not in theatre. Words usually have a separate space and dominate.

BOXER: I'd certainly never done anything like it before and I think that's why I did it. If you work in the theatre, you are like a junkie for the new, you need a fix every six months. That was what was so lovely about the show. It required from me a very different discipline and combined people with very varied talents, which we ultimately all shared. It was unique. I have never done anything like it again.

K. WESTBROOK: I cannot think of a situation where the visual, the musical and the choreographic held an equal status. We started rehearsal with a warm-up, both for the voice and body. I thought if synthesia is a goal for us all, then *The Ass* was, as near as dammit, *it*!

REES: Indeed the composer, Mike, acted in it, danced, played percussion and commanded the band from the concert piano.

M. WESTBROOK: The People Show integrate production elements. But the integration in *The Ass* was absolutely fundamental.

BOXER: It was finely honed, without loose ends. It was a whole with a beginning, middle and end and was not a series of ideas and sketches like The People Show. Everything in the show found its source in the poem.

REES: The show was set in Taormina's town square, in Sicily. A huge donkey dominated the proceedings. Its tail could be pulled, causing its head to move, and under and between its body and legs lay the main gateway from the square into the town – the Porta Cappucini. Lawrence sat alone writing at a cafe table. Gradually, he became embroiled with the townspeople, in this instance, a local Sicilian band composed of a pianist, accordion player, singer, violinist, and a saxophone and clarinet player. The music reflected Jazz and was improvised but at the same time, there was a Sicilian atmosphere visually created by the designer, Ariane Gastambide, and by the choreography of Pat Garrett and aurally through the music.

K. WESTBROOK: The poem is about Lawrence fantasising about being a donkey, and the history of the donkey, which includes taking Christ into Jerusalem. It makes Lawrence take off in many directions with the donkey as the central image. The music was not a slavish attempt to reproduce Sicilian folk music. It was improvised Jazz and Sicilian folk music, mixed with other strands of European music including the Stravinsky stable. The characters were also like that, each taking off from the basic character into other areas.

REES: What this form allows is, as you say, the freedom for characters to 'take off' at will, whilst still remaining constrained within the musical structure. It is that structure which coheres rather than a narrative structure.

M. WESTBROOK: We had an overture during which a succession of slides of Kate's donkey paintings were projected.

K. WESTBROOK: The lighting by Dick Moffatt was extraordinary.

REES: Particularly during the overture, which was not presented as seven musicians sitting down and playing music. It was a continual and sinuously moving event, as the band grouped and regrouped for different combinations of instruments. And the donkey was a bunch of lighting tricks.

BOXER: It had all the ambition of the Welfare State with the discipline of the Royal Opera House.

M. WESTBROOK: We had been involved in so many of these sorts of things, tried to make them succeed but always with great difficulty. It was marvellous that you and Foco Novo made it into a complete production, that we were able at last to move beyond the situation of a Jazz band doing a gig. I don't think there is anything we have enjoyed so much. Okay, it was small scale, designed to tour into small venues. But when it reached Riverside Studios, it filled the space and looked as if it was designed for that theatre.

Unlike most Music Theatre I have seen, usually the Jazz element – the improvised part – is kept under wraps because it is deemed not interesting to watch a musician improvising. Pete Whyman on saxes had long solos, at one point playing with the ass's head on, the instrument poked through its mouth. A most remarkable image, a donkey playing a saxophone!

BOXER: From my point of view, it flowed into the acting sequences. That bit, where Pete sexually assaulted me from behind with the bell of the sax every night, was never the same twice!

M. WESTBROOK: The point, where Stephen as Lawrence was becoming the ass and began to bray, stays with me. It was so powerful and moving. It was harnessing the power of Jazz and making it work for theatre.

K. WESTBROOK: Because you know and love Jazz, Roland, you were able to accept three members into the company, the musicians, who had no experience of a six weeks tour, presenting the same show each night. I am used to one-off concerts, working like hell on my own until I have learnt the material, and then performing it. Mike and Pete Whyman are used to the same thing. The other three Stephen, Lesia Melnyk and Trevor Allan were used to theatre practice. It was a brave thing to take on such a mixture.

REES: Stephen, *The Ass* was not like a conventional play where you have a text which provides you with indications of character. You had to provide a lot of Lawrence from your own research and resources.

BOXER: I had a notebook which I used during the fifteen minute overture. I was looking back at the notes I made, the other day. It was all pseudo-Lawrentian. I wrote down, at each performance, what I had done that day and tried to do it as DHL. Some notes are tedious and pretentious, others are amusing. The show gave you that energy. Whilst you did your research and reading, the show itself provided you with a great imaginative platform. It's not the sort of thing I could do in another play.

M. WESTBROOK: Looking back, we all feel this was a very special show. But I never felt the response equalled our own excitement.

BOXER: Like a lot of little gems, every so often you meet someone who says that was simply original and marvellous.

REES: There were theatre-goers who had trouble with a lack of obvious narrative line, there were jazzers who had trouble with words. Music and theatre has different audiences and the audience who will embrace both, perhaps are yet in the minority.

M. WESTBROOK: It matters so much in London how you describe a show. We could have called *The Ass* an opera. Thereby attracted that audience. Then people might have looked at it differently.

K. WESTBROOK: We also came across a very strong prejudice against D.H. Lawrence. His enemies are outspoken. I can understand that he was a very irritating figure in the English literary canon. Until you read him, then he illuminates. If people were unmoved, they have too much head and too little heart. The show was funny, sad and angry.

BOXER: We were aware of the two audiences. It was greater or lesser depending where we were in the country. There were places where the Westbrook's had a following and others where Foco Novo did. Sometimes they synthesised. There are honourable failures. On its own terms, this show worked brilliantly and there were enough people out there, who appreciated it, to justify doing it. You knew you were working with something extraordinary. People out there shared that.

M. WESTBROOK: Maybe I am wrong to expect more. I thought it terribly important for the show to be recognised not only because of the piece itself, but also because of the manner in which so many elements were successfully integrated. I never felt that was fully appreciated.

REES: Theatre is the whore of the performing arts. An opera, a musical, a ballet are defined genres with particular disciplines. Theatre permits the possibility, if people are creative, to congeal different disciplines under one roof. Theatre likes to be stretched, likes the unusual and seemingly contradictory. Consequently audiences, who are used to responding to defined and cut-glass genres, are with Music Theatre in the position of the horse which shies at an unfamiliar fence.

BOXER: The Jazz audiences were more open minded than theatre audiences.

M. WESTBROOK: Because, for Jazz audiences, there is still the tradition, which I mentioned, of welcoming new ideas and experiment.

K. WESTBROOK: If we feel we did not reach the amount of people the show deserved, we must remember the appalling record in this country. We have witnessed the cutting of funds to Foco Novo, one of the few radical and innovatory touring theatre companies. So many pleaded on Foco Novo's behalf to no avail. The climate has changed so much during this decade that it is hard to remember what things were like. Subsidy used to go to work which had a philosophy behind it and which was not the creation of market forces. So I feel we have worked in very honourable company. It is a crime and a tragedy that the climate has changed so much.

FOUR PLAYWRIGHTS TAKE UP ARMS

HOWARD BRENTON
PAM GEMS
JOSHUA SOBOL
NIGEL WILLIAMS

New plays and their production were central to the genesis and survival of the new theatre. Two Arts Council schemes were fundamental to this development. Contract Writers Awards enabled companies to commission playwrights, and the Royalty Supplement Guarantee Scheme guaranteed a minimum royalty level against the customary $7^1/2$ per cent of the low box office expectations of small auditoriums and their subsidised ticket prices.

First and foremost, Foco Novo was a new play producing company. But the commissioning process provided a further advantage. The company could originate its own idea for a play and then approach a playwright with a brief. By this means, new writers were brought out of isolation and a relationship created with them. Those writers knew their plays would, in all probability, be performed, and they would receive the benefit of the guiding experience of the company, versed in the production of new plays. Foco Novo was a seedbed for this process.

The majority of its productions toured the Arts Council-supported small scale circuit. Additionally, the company developed a series of plays for special, neighbourhood situations. In the Seventies these toured the coalfields and in the Eighties, plays for and about Peckham, London, were produced. A third strand of Foco Novo's work comprised adaptations and our new versions of modern classics by Brecht, Buchner, Genet and Duras, playwrights who held a prime significance for the contemporary writers the company produced.

Foco Novo had on its Board the writers, Bernard Pomerance, Jon Chadwick, John Hoyland, Mustapha Matura, Howard Brenton, Tunde Ikoli and Nigel Williams at different and over-lapping times.

In 1988, at the time of the withdrawal of subsidy by the Arts Council, the company was preparing a production, contributed to by eight writers – Trevor Griffiths, Howard Brenton, Nigel Williams, Nell Dunn, Tunde Ikoli, Olwen Wymark, Joshua Sobol and Snoo Wilson – based on and named after the game of *Consequences*. The production had to be abandoned. Its theme was the Thatcherite inheritance.

From Left to Right. Vincenzo Ricotta and Sean Bean in Foco Novo's 1985 production of Nigel Williams' translation of Jean Genet's *Deathwatch*.

NIGEL WILLIAMS

Novelist, playwright, television and film writer and BBC producer for
Arena and *Bookmark*. Stage plays include *Class Enemy*, *Sugar and Spice*
[Royal Court], *Line 'Em* [National], *Country Dancing* [RSC] and *Nativity*
[Tricycle]. Williams made a new translation of Genet's *Deathwatch* for
Foco Novo. He was a board member of the Company and
contributor to Foco Novo's *Consequences*.

REES: New writing was a primary aim for many companies in the Seventies?

WILLIAMS: I think the new writing movement is now completely finished. What it did in the Seventies was to give access to an enormous body of material because it did things very cheaply. It did a lot of rubbish, but it also did a lot of good stuff. It did at least keep it coming. I guess it is coming in different areas now.

There have been a few writers who have been allowed through. But various others have no outlet. For example, Ted Whitehead is a very fine theatre writer – one of the finest plays of the Seventies was *The Foursome* – a writer who has not forsaken theatre, but the theatre has forsaken him. He is still writing very good work.

REES: You also give the impression that your theatre writing is behind you, despite the fact that your plays have been produced at the National, Royal Court, RSC, Greenwich, The Tricycle?

WILLIAMS: I now make my living out of writing TV scripts and novels. Novels are my passion. I feel completely excluded from the process of theatre, so I have more or less given up writing stage plays. I don't feel a kinship with any stage in the country, apart from the National. I do think Richard Eyre has done a good job. I enjoy watching many things there although inevitably they are very traditional.

The focus for new writing or rather 'old' new writing has become: 'Are you going to write a play which will be successful on Shaftsbury Avenue?' And a bit of you finds it very difficult to do that.

REES: Were there distinguishing features to the writing and work of that period?

WILLIAMS: The distinction between say the Royal Court and Foco Novo in the early Eighties – I joined the Board of Foco Novo late – was that my sense of the Court was that it was fantastically difficult to get your play on with all those pressures of fashion. Coming to a touring company like Foco Novo felt just like the very first company that ever gave me a job – Avon Touring – which was run by Howard Davies and Bill Alexander. In 1977, Howard directed my first play, a socialist pantomime. That company was absolutely about a bunch of people in a garage, fantastically democratic in mood and feeling and that comes from touring. You pile into the van and go to the venue. There is no institutionalism. That was not true of the Royal Court or the RSC. They are very hierarchical institutions.

Foco Novo was you and your enthusiasm. You were encouraging in a non-specific way. Whereas those big institutions had their idea and something they had to do. The touring gave it an incredible freedom which I don't think the building-based institutions had. That's classically true of theatre.

REES: So the distinguishing features are the encouragement for new writing and a more democratic approach and access to the work.

WILLIAMS: When I say democratic, it is in much the same way I run *Bookmark* at the BBC. You knew what you wanted to do and knew who you wanted to work with and within those limits you were nice and equal-minded with people.

REES: Did touring bring distinctive features to the work?

WILLIAMS: You could not say touring meant something radically different to mainstream theatre. But I did get the feeling that the relationship with the audience was much closer.

When I did the translation of Genet's *Deathwatch* for Foco Novo, I remember a discussion we had after the show at the Birmingham Studio Theatre, the sort of occasion you would never have had in London. Ordinary punters from the city of Birmingham came and saw the play and stayed behind to express their views on it. A sort of teach-in. I thought that was terrific. There is not nearly enough of this in London, where theatre has inevitably to be smart and on the cuff. That slight touch of missionary activity I liked.

I think the touring companies were very much about encouraging new writing in the area between the commercial theatre and the mainstream. The Genet was a case in point. Nobody put Genet on and certainly not that play.

REES: There were a few writers who particularly influenced those starting their writing careers in the Sixties. Genet was one of them.

WILLIAMS: I translated *Deathwatch* from the original. The Frechtman translation is good in many ways but it wasn't very theatrical and intense verbal theatrical language is what I have always liked in the theatre and, what I feel is completely lacking from our theatre now. Foco Novo had a poetic interest in drama. I do not mean poetic drama, but drama in which the play itself is a lyrical expression, which is what drew you to Genet and to getting Michael Abbensetts to do a version of Lorca's *Blood Wedding*.

REES: What did you want to achieve that was different to Frechtman?

WILLIAMS: One of the hostile reviews of the translation said Nigel Williams always uses three words where one would do. On reflection, I found this a compliment. One of the things about French is that it has a much more limited vocabulary, so a single word has to be used again and again to describe a particular emotional feeling. 'La gloire' always means something! The word Genet uses a lot is 'rayonner' which means to be radiant, to radiate. He doesn't just use it to mean radiant, radiant, radiant. It carries other meanings, whereas English, with its larger vocabulary, is a much more elusive language. So I saw it as my task to try and render the Genet prose. It is of a high classical order because the major influence on his reading was the result of the fact that French prison libraries were incredibly well stocked. If you go into Fresnes Prison where Genet was banged up – I filmed there whilst making the Arena programme on Genet – you can see the library where he started to write *Notre Dame des Fleurs*. You will not find Freddie Forsyth on the shelves or for that matter Jeanette Winterson. You will find Racine and the classics of French Literature and little else.

If you are there for twenty years, reading those books is bound to influence your style. What I tried to do in the translation was echo his feeling for language. The fact that so-called lower class, common people can speak poetically in the theatre has always been most important to me. So I really enjoyed doing the job for that reason.

REES: *Deathwatch* is a play set in prison in a murderer's cell with two other prisoners occupying it. A triangle. It is one of the least produced yet most powerful of his small cast plays.

WILLIAMS: None of them are done much. It was written in 1949 and put on one side. Then Roger Blin did it with *The Maids* in Paris, I think. Your theatre was very like that – two people and a dog. That was what was good about Foco Novo was the two men and a dog aspect. I never saw the dog.

REES: When you did the interview with Genet for Arena, it had to be conducted for various reasons in considerable secrecy? Did he make conditions for the interview?

WILLIAMS: He was paid ten thousand pounds up front. He had only given two interviews before.

REES: Ever?

WILLIAMS: Ever. He gave one interview with a chap called Hubert Fichter for Playboy. It's all rubbish that he never wanted to be interviewed. It was partly because nobody was interested.

REES: What persuaded him to be interviewed by you? The ten thousand pounds?

WILLIAMS: The fact that I'd translated his play was a factor. His agent in London, Rosica Colin, knew I genuinely liked his work. That's always important to a writer. He just felt like doing it at the time. And he was, as you say, well paid for doing it.

In the interview, I asked him: 'Why don't you write plays any more?' He said: 'Well, some people liked them and then it turned out they didn't, so fuck 'em.' So I thought well, that's fair enough.

REES: He would not meet any of the cast or see the show. He was very secretive.

WILLIAMS: Genet just turned up at my front door in Putney for the interview.

In Paris, I met the director who did *Les Paravants* [*The Screens*] in that theatre outside Paris. He was quite well-known. I cannot remember his name, Jean Paul something. Exactly the same sort of bloke you get in the mainstream subsidised theatre in this country, well-heeled, charming and fluent and somehow fantastically phoney. We had a very nice chat and he told *me* what a genius Genet was, and I told *him* what a genius Genet was, and he told me Genet turned up to rehearsal once and then walked away and that was it. Just one day.

I don't think Genet was quite like that. That disinterested. Like older gay men, he had a number of lovers and existed on the edges of a large family and in hotels wherever he was. His address on his passport was his publisher, Gallimard.

REES: A lot of your generation wrote plays with public themes which took place in public places. Even if they were about a small group of people, the play would attempt wider social implications than those individuals. My sense is that nowadays new plays by younger writers are always small cast, four actors for economic reasons, and remain centred on personal passions without tackling the kind of themes and issues that attracted writers in the Seventies and Eighties.

WILLIAMS: I think that is true. I cannot think of a new play by a young writer that breasted the swell of the usual stuff that goes on, that for me stood up and you thought: 'Jesus that's amazing'. This may be my ignorance. Or maybe this afternoon I cannot think of the play. I did see a play by Winsome Pinnock at the Court which was great. Very strong narrative skills, beautifully touching. I really liked that play. From an identifiable tradition of Caribbean story telling. Now, she is writing for a mainstream TV Series. Nick Ward, good writer. But really he is doing Channel 4. Take Lucy Gannon, a very good writer. She goes on to write *Casualty* for TV. It happens incredibly quickly. But where are the writers who are channeling all their energies into the theatre?

REES: Theatre had a definite tradition in the Seventies. There was a marked difference between writing for theatre and writing for TV and Film. This meant there were writers who specialised in each media. Now cross-over is the tradition.

WILLIAMS: Theatre used to be much more self-funding. There was money. Look at the fact that Foco Novo got its grant withdrawn. The government under Thatcher did some things right and some wrong. One of the wrong things was to withdraw subsidy from enterprising artistic activities and to

189

try to cut off the legs of the BBC and the National Health Service. Those will be seen as complete fuck-ups. It certainly did that to theatre. No question.

It is no longer possible to make a living in theatre in the way it was in the Seventies and early Eighties. Howard Brenton is a successful writer, still earning his living as a playwright. But what about the writer who would be like Brenton now, aged twenty-five to thirty? How do they get by? They end up writing for TV. I was different. I had a day job, always did. I started writing plays very late thirty-one/thirty-two.

REES: You were a member of the Board of Foco Novo from the early Eighties. I shall never forget the astonishment which crossed your face when you met a Drama Officer from the Arts Council for the first time at a Board meeting.

WILLIAMS: It was extraordinary. I do remember never having been so angry. It reminded me of being at school. The questions were all like: 'How many marks out of ten are we going to give this?' It was a nightmare. I remember him sitting there saying: 'Well, it's not good enough. The norms are not sufficiently met.' It was like Stalinism! And yet he never showed any inclination that he had responded to the play. [*Howard Brenton's* Bloody Poetry].

REES: Informally, he had told me, that of the subsidised productions he had seen that year, *Bloody Poetry* was the best. Then he came to the meeting and berated us about touring dates.

WILLIAMS: He came along in a sports jacket and tie and behaving like a little Hitler. Like the worst sort of VAT man. He had come along to a meeting to read the riot act to this group which was not doing right by its norms. In no way, did he see his job to motivate or enthuse those who were working hard for the greater good of the Arts, and in no way showed generosity towards the people sitting around the table. He seemed a dull little man. I was appalled that this person should be in a highly paid job. Certainly paid more than you. I remember having a very strong urge to hit him.

It is a stale cliché for those working in the theatre that others, such as journalists like Michael Coveney, earn more than most of the people whom they review in plays. I think that is shocking. But I do think that people in the business of handing out money to artists and writers should look at their responsibilities. Their responsibility to their client is a serious one. At the meeting at which I was present, the mood was of sullen bureaucratic arrogance. Like: 'It says here on this bit of paper that you have to do 32 productions with 'P' in the title in a seaside town during the summer. You haven't done it!' At the BBC, it's the same. As long as you get the programmes out, it doesn't matter what the people watch.

190

I would not have met Howard Brenton if it had not been for the Board meetings. Mustapha would come along and be very humorous. I have always enjoyed his plays and company. There was a good mood. Writers are very good at not wasting time. They would come and say what's the point of doing this? Okay if you think it's good, lets do it and get it on. Thelma Holt was there. I thought it was a fantastically interesting gathering. It was not so much the serious stuff but the asides. 'Oh Christ, we're not going to do that!' The gossip. 'What's the show like?' All that. It was obvious you were running the show, doing what you wanted to do and employing people who believed in what you were doing, so it was a good atmosphere.

But you were fantastically aware that the economy of this operation was dependent completely on the word of one bureaucrat. That is why I used the word Stalinism. One person could say I'll have you, but not you, so that little man had the power to hire and fire. When our grant was cut in half we should have gone commercial there and then. The ethics of the market place have proved to be bloody right, for example, in Eastern Europe. To get funding for theatre, maybe we did wrong to trust the government. Maybe Sainsburys would have been better. It couldn't have been worse!

REES: I wonder whether you are going to be proved right about Eastern Europe! And going commercial as you said would probably have meant touring plays you would not have wanted Foco Novo to do. A radical version of *Arsenic and Old Lace?*

What of the future of theatre in the times of international exchange? Can we cross the language barrier? Or does the way forward lie with the visual spectacle, as seems increasingly to be the case?

WILLIAMS: Like *Cats?* I think that what you said about English theatre in the Seventies and Eighties was true. It drew the eyes of the world upon it because it discussed openly and strongly wide issues. The difficulty in narrative theatre is to combine that with a lively sense of story telling as Shakespeare does. That depends on the power of the English language to summon up an entire world on stage. The mixture of visual and linguistic elements are always part of theatre but I think theatre is primarily a linguistic and not a visual medium.

Most writers I know have given up on the fact that the day for writers earning their living in theatre will return. There are a few but even for them, you feel its a much more temporary field. Most writers I know lurch from job to job in a chaotic way and that is to do with the fact that companies like Foco Novo have ceased to exist. My last play was done at the Tricycle and Nick Kent said that his staple diet was Black or Irish plays. Extraordinary.

REES: He's serving a catchment area.

WILLIAMS: Exactly. Its like those marketing things in Threshers. They have two kinds of off-licence – The Wine Rack or the Drinks Store. The working class have the Drinks Store in their neighbourhood.

REES: It's the same with the Peckham Sainsburys. We have the D version not the A. There are certain things you cannot buy there.

WILLIAMS: No wonder Howard Davies complains about not being able to get aubergines in Peckham/Camberwell, wherever he lives.

REES: We have talked about the fact that dramatists were prolific in the Seventies and Eighties. Even if they were being critical about their own backyard, the important issues seemed centred there. The big events over the last few years are occurring elsewhere in Central and Eastern Europe. How will English writers respond?

WILLIAMS: I have just written a series for Channel 4 called *Tales for a Circus* about the recruitment of circus performers in Eastern Europe, buying talent cheap. It is a Central European movie. We are getting closer to working with people in Central and Eastern Europe. I think it is terrific about all that stuff going on there. Nobody wants any ideological crap any more. After all, the whole system and the pretentious rubbish written about it, and I wrote plenty, has disappeared. I think that's good. But it makes writing harder. There is no crutch to fall back on. I think it means there may in the future be a way through to writing more social plays again. England will be as well placed to write them from as anywhere else. The world is smaller so they will apply all over. But that is always true of literature. Evelyn Waugh writes about England but it could be somewhere else. Ultimately I am an optimist.

PAM GEMS

One of Britain's leading playwrights, her plays include *Piaf*, produced in the West End and on Broadway, *Dusa, Fish, Stas & Vi, Camille, Blue Angel* produced in the West End, and *Queen Christina*. Five of her plays have been produced by the RSC and many abroad. Roland Rees directed the first play of Pam Gems, *Betty's Wonderful Christmas*, in 1971 at the Cockpit Theatre.

REES: Are you a writer for the theatre first and foremost?

GEMS: There's nothing like live theatre. It's where the real action is. I was stage struck from childhood, having a good Junior and Grammar School, where we did a lot of live theatre. As a writer, I was a late starter, always intimidated by the world of television and movies. Having learnt the craft of playwrighting, the notion of taking on screen-writing was too much. Anyway it was not what I wanted to do.

I did not have to make my own living. I was married with another source of income, our studio factory making display figures and wax models. I was not a single parent who had to write an episode of *Crown Court* to survive. So I had no excuse not to do the hardest thing – write a stage play.

REES: Did having another career before you came to playwrighting, help or hinder?

GEMS: I was 45 when I came back to live in London. Now that the children were at school, I could visit lunchtime theatre which was springing up all over the place in the late Sixties. It was before OPEC and the oil crisis. There was money about. An open society with promise of change. Being a middle-aged woman with no connections in the theatre – wrong age, class, size, wrong everything – I was lucky that it was a time when it was possible to start working in theatre, to get together with groups of women and do things for ourselves with no money. Without those Fringe theatres, I would have had no chance.

REES: Looking for a space to start a theatre in Notting Hill, I got you and Keith Gems along to look at one. We tested the neighbours' attitude to having a place of public entertainment on their doorstep by letting a rock band rehearse there one evening, followed up with a local poll.

GEMS: Sir Malby Crofton, head of the Chelsea and Kensington Council, was adamantly against any theatres in W2. He said this was a domestic area. Go to the West End if you want to see theatre. But there were good potential spaces for theatre here and a good catchment area for Fringe. There was the Mercury Theatre, the Coronet, now a cinema, and a theatre in Westbourne Grove used as a furniture store. Now we have The Gate.

REES: I directed *Betty's Wonderful Christmas*, your first stage play, in 1971 at the Cockpit. You called it a Christmas Tale. It threatened to tear apart the conventions of what a Christmas show might be.

GEMS: It was my very first stage play. In my ignorance, I thought: 'I don't know how to write a stage play. So if I write a children's play, I'll be able to just tell a story. It will be an easy structure, that way I'll learn.' I had four children. Children have always been my deviation, I have a weakness for them. I showed the play to Clive Goodwin after Tony Garnett introduced us. Garnett liked a couple of television plays I wrote which were never done, being too radical for the time.

REES: Clive Goodwin was my agent. He gave me the play. I liked it and took it to David Aukin.

GEMS: I've never known that! I was always too timid to ask. I was terrified of you, I might say. I didn't know my role as a writer, what a writer in rehearsal does. It seemed magical working with professionals, making it happen. Everyone got on with it. There was none of this film-style, fur-collared overcoat bitchiness and drama, I had imagined it was like.

The story was partly autobiographical. A family in the early Twenties, my own period, with a depressed widowed mother, of which there were many after the First World War, living in great poverty with three children. Betty is asked to a Christmas party, has nothing to wear so goes in a paper dress. At the party, it is accidently ripped off. Betty rushes out of the house and into the storm. There is an implication that she is attacked by a man called Alf Silver. Then the story goes into fantasy. Betty is trying to reach the palace to meet the prince. When she reaches it, he is no great shakes. The Goths arrive on a motorbike, in the form of that American actor you had worked with, Richard Pendrey. There is a dragon, who was played by the Jamaican actor Charlie Hyatt, with a tail that was stamped on. At one matinee, his own children rushed on stage and stopped the play, saying to the characters: 'Don't do that to my Daddy.' There is a revolution, they all lose their crowns and it ends with Betty back in the forest, found by the villagers. She is offered a place by the Lady of the Manor but prefers to live with her mother.

It was a brutal tale and in directing it, you did not avoid that. People were startled by it. I've sat through many children's plays with my own children and slept. A good fairy story should appeal to everyone. That was what I was trying to do with *Betty*. There was a sub-text for those who wanted to pick up on it and there was a strong story. People still speak to me about it.

REES: It exploded open the possibilities of what could be achieved with a known formula.

GEMS: A lot of writers write down to children. I hate that, as I hate the mod-cute approach: 'Let's not do Hans Anderson, let's do one about a supermarket.' That is just as bad.

REES: As a result of this, what direction did you go in next?

195

GEMS: Visiting The Almost Free Theatre in Rupert Street, I met Ed Berman. He said he had this Fun Art Bus: 'Would I write two "sexy" pieces for his programme?' It was the heroic days of neo-Feminism, so I was insulted. I thought: 'No, I'm not going to give you tit and bum!' Just to annoy him, I wrote two strong monologues. One had a girl sitting in a prison hospital waiting room. We gather she has murdered her child, stuffed it down the lavatory. The other is about a woman, a suppressed middle-aged spinster, who does all the work at the office, is paid less than anyone, and is sneered at. As a horrible joke, someone posts her a vibrator. She wants to take it back to the shop but eventually decides to use it. A bit difficult on stage, but with decorousness you can get the effect without being prurient. The point of the piece is, if nobody else will love you, then love yourself.

Pedr James, the director, and I took the play to Jan Henfrey playing at the Savoy Theatre. She said: 'I'd love to do it but I cannot do the last bit! We'll have to cut that.' Green as anything, overwhelmed at being in a West End dressing room, I said, 'sorry about that,' and got up to leave. I knew there was no play without the end. If you cannot be radical on the Fringe, with no money to make, where *can* you be? I reached the door and Jan said: 'Hang on a minute.' She did it and amazingly Ed said he'd do the play.

REES: Ed took on a lot of plays that others would not touch at that time.

GEMS: He started a lot of things. The first piece was difficult. On Friday before we opened, Pedr called me into rehearsal and said: 'You cannot do this on stage. You are going too far!' Sheila Kelley, a good actress, was playing this very rough girl. I said: 'She's got to come out with all this stuff.' With both pieces, I was not trying to be deliberately offensive but pushing the boundaries of what could be said about women in public, by women to other women. You could not use the word 'period' then.

Pedr said: 'I'm sorry but I am not going to do this.' I turned to Sheila; 'Are you on?' She looked at me carefully. 'Right, turn to page one.' We went right through the play. She knew exactly what it was about. In performance, she was ferocious, frightening. There is a Greek book about a midwife, who goes around villages murdering babies because, eventually they will die in the winter or of starvation. In this way, she will save money for the family. It is an ironic, horrifying book. That is what I was trying to touch.

We filled the Almost Free. It was a double bill, lasting an hour. Ed got very excited. There was clearly a hunger for this sort of play. Ed said he would do a series of plays by women for his autumn season. So the phone was hot. We formed a group which met in a room in my house in Kensington. We read all the plays, choosing the season very democratically.

REES: Which writers were in the group?

GEMS: Jennifer Phillips had a play in the season, directed by Liane Aukin, so did Jane Wibberley, her play was all in long-hand, and Midge McKenzie directed two short pieces.

One of the other plays we chose was *Swallows* by Michelene Wandor. There was a big row over this. Ed said: 'I am the Artistic Director and the decision about the choice of the season finally rests with me.' He didn't like *Swallows*. He said it had no structure and didn't make sense to him. To the group, it was the play which we all responded to most. We said to Ed: 'We want to direct, design and light the plays.' He said: 'Okay. You can do the plays you want, but you have to paint out the theatre!' He was testing us, trying to put us off, saying all the old things about women not being able to carry the lights and do the electrics! So we did it. And the basement, turning it into a creche. It was a very successful season. Women were hungry for plays about women. They could not believe it. Women were the protagonists.

In a business with eighty per cent unemployed, the position is tough anyway. The guys will not move aside. Where would they go? So it made us take our destiny into our own hands. Out of that season was formed the Women's Theatre Group. Our policy was: 'Come one, come all.' That resulted in a split between the libertarians, who said any woman should be allowed to join, and the professionals who said: 'Hang on a minute. I am an Equity actress, out of work for eight months. This lady is a well-paid secretary who has just said she cannot rehearse tonight, because she is going out with her boyfriend. There is a discrepancy here.' So we split.

The Women's Theatre Group stayed with the libertarians and The Women's Company went with the professionals. With great reluctance, I sided with the professionals for old-fashioned union values, protecting a living, and because the libertarians were implying there are no skills in theatre, anyone can do it. It has taken me twenty years to learn how to write a play! Both groups applied for an Arts Council grant and The Women's Theatre Group got it!

The Women's Company included Annie Mitchell, Marji Campi, Yvonne Edgell, Sue Todd, myself and Shirlie Stone. Shirlie worked as the publicist at the Roundhouse and asked Thelma Holt, the Director, whether we could use a 'dark' week to put on a show. I was just off for a cheap, winter, holiday via the French Railways in Menton. They asked me to write *Go West Young Woman* on that week's holiday! It's always been 'Go west, young man' but the men having got there, needed clerks, teachers and a softening influence. The history of the heroic days of capitalism are in women's diaries. I had enough material for ten plays. I knocked out the play and came to rehearsal to discover why the week was dark. The Roundhouse was being renovated. They were throwing baulks of timber from the roof, so it was a tough rehearsal period. On opening night there were two interruptions from two separate militant feminist groups, objecting to the fact that we had men on stage. Feelings ran high in 1974. The show died on its feet with these rows going on. They were coming down the aisles trying to get on the stage. Finally the Front of House called in the police. We, The Women's Company did not like that. It made us look the baddies!

Sue Todd directed the play. Annie Mitchell and actors, who had been in Drama School with her, were in the cast. Later that connection with The Women's Company got me into trouble. I was tied down with a handicapped child. But in 1976 Lalla went to school, so I was free for the first time in eleven years. That's when I wrote *Dusa, Fish*. I had a six piece band living underneath me with an excellent girl singer. So I wrote this play with gaps for songs to carry the emotion whilst the dialogue, in comparison, would be quite dry. That's when I had the problem. I realised I could not offer it to The Women's Company. They were young matrons, I needed 28 year olds. It hit me because they were out of work. So I put the play in the drawer for a year.

REES: You needed to distance yourself from a group of people, with whom you had closely worked, so you could eventually cast from the whole market place. You would be the playwright, not a company member.

GEMS: It never works cognitively like that. Ann Jellicoe came to review the play at the Roundhouse and gave us a glowing notice. She was Literary Manager at the Court and opened the doors to writers. You had a pass and could observe rehearsals with the consent of the director. Writers always feel tangential and indeed have to be. They bring the news 'from the Rialto'. Ann asked if I would like a commission. It is the only one I have taken or been offered. I said: 'Do you mean for upstairs or downstairs?' She said: 'It depends on the play.' I thought: 'The chances of getting it on are slim, so if it fails, it will fail for downstairs!' I wrote *Queen Christina*, which is very dear to my heart, and is the best thing I have written. By the time I finished it, Ann and Oscar Lewenstein had left the Court. Nick Wright and Bob Kidd ran it. I still have their rejection letter: 'It is a bit sprawling. It would appeal more to women than men.' Can you imagine saying a play would appeal to *men* more than women. It made the mind boggle, particularly since more women go to theatre than men.

I had always wanted to go to the Edinburgh Festival with a play. So I showed *Dusa, Fish* to Nancy Meckler, who I had met through you. She said: 'I cannot do the Festival because I have these small children.' I don't know why I wanted to do the Festival. Nowadays I would avoid it like the plague! So I gave the play to a director, who was part of the company, Caroline Eves.

Ann Jellicoe gave a party at the Court for writers. She introduced me to Lindsay Anderson, for whom I had great respect. He said something about women writers and Ann said: 'Now Lindsay, we want more women writers and directors working here.' 'As long as its not Pam Brighton or Jane Howell,' said Lindsay. Well there were only one or two others! And the year before, 1975, Buzz Goodbody died. Buzz was our ikon. She had been to stay with me at our house on the Isle of Wight. She had this bright, definite manner. There was no indication of what she was obviously going through. It was fatigue. Your mind starts to give you false signals. She was a great loss. The fall-out was not good.

So in 1976, we took *Dusa, Fish* to Edinburgh. We had Lindsay Ingram, Leslie Joseph, Sally Watts and Jenny Stoller in the cast. Paul Sand wrote the lyrics and music, Barbara Jung was the singer. Two Japanese guys, a furniture designer and a sculptor, did the set.

REES: Where did you perform the play?

GEMS: Maggie Jordan, the actress, and I co-produced a whole programme, from noon till two in the morning, which we presented above the Wax Museum, happily next door to the Fringe Club. *Dusa, Fish* was part of the programme. Victoria Wood and Quentin Crisp came and did shows for nothing. People crowded in from the Fringe Club, which closed at midnight, to listen to our band which played until two. At The Almost Free I had made food every day. It was too much to do there, so we got a local women's group to do it. I became knackered by this early morning to late night schedule. After the Festival, to thank Quentin Crisp, I invited him to tea and cakes, which I heard he liked. I was sitting there with the others from the band and suddenly felt a terrible pain. I thought: 'Fuck, I'm having a heart attack!' It was pleurisy.

During the Festival, David Aukin, Manager of Hampstead Theatre, came to see the production. He said: 'I will do it at Hampstead if you agree to a new cast and a new director.' Leslie Joseph said you cannot just drop us. It was very difficult for me. My second dilemma with the casting of the play. I thought: 'Should I turn the offer down?' In the end, I accepted and said to the cast: 'If I were your age I would stick out for the principle, but I am twenty years older. I cannot turn down Hampstead. I need it as a learning process.' We did it at Hampstead with Nancy Meckler directing.

When rehearsal started I was full of anti-biotics. Going to lunch with Nancy at Hampstead, with David and Michael Rudman, the Artistic Director, I was feeling very unwell. Rudman greeted me with: 'I suppose we can call you and Pam Brighton the earth mothers of the theatre!' I said:

199

'Because we are obese?' I made an enemy for life. It was the anti-biotics talking.

I don't know why it was a success. It was Christmas, raining all the time. Everyone I knew had a kid who was ill or had a lover who had just left them. We all had something wrong with us. I just don't know why it worked.

REES: You touched a moment – four women – on their own.

GEMS: Yes, it was that moment when people, women, responded. It was an important time for women in theatre. Actresses who had been trained to wait by the phone began to realise they had to motor their own career: 'I can do a one-woman show, I can practice my craft.' Five years out of drama school, the boy is twice as experienced as the girl because he has been offered twice the number of parts. Then they say the girls cannot cut it. Look at the lists in the Radio Times, there is still twice the work for boys.

REES: That period, late Sixties to mid-Seventies, produced work which made an impact on the the mainstream of theatre and the business in general.

GEMS: It has changed things. When I think of what went before. And I am an old and passionate enough theatregoer to know. I hitch-hiked up to London during the war to go to theatres. It was a period when you needed colour and light-heartedness. Then we had the so-called 'Angry Young Men' – Wesker, Arden, a great playwright. But apart from Ann Jellicoe, Shelagh Delaney, where were the girls? As for the bourgeois theatre, there was Lillian Hellman in the States. Those years, we have been talking about, were a window. People could do their own thing for a bit. Until OPEC and the oil crisis, then the money went away.

In our village, Bembridge, on the Isle of Wight, red-neck territory, the wife of the local newsagent got onto the local council. Before that it was all Lieutenant-Colonels. There was real change in the air. Then it stopped. Once the money runs out, nothing becomes possible. An awful dilemma. Then the whole emphasis is placed on getting money, having money, taking money away from someone else. But that time from Jim Haynes on, that lovely time when youth was celebrated with all its dangers and silliness, but with all the good things, was precious. People talk of The French Revolution as if it was only about blood running in the streets. But it changed the world. The beginning of modernism and the end of nepotism. These brief periods make such an impact.

HOWARD BRENTON

Howard Brenton is one of the most provocative and renowned playwrights writing in the English language. His plays include *Magnificence*, *Brassneck*, the first collaboration with David Hare, *Weapons of Happiness*, for which he won the 1976 Evening Standard's Best Play Award, *Sore Throats*, *The Romans in Britain*, *Pravda*, again with David Hare, at the Royal National Theatre, *Moscow Gold* at the RSC, and most recently *Berlin Bertie*, at the Royal Court. Foco Novo commissioned from him *Conversations in Exile*, an adaptation of Brecht, *Sleeping Policemen* with Trude Ikoli and *Bloody Poetry*. Brenton was a member of the Board of Foco Novo and was one of the eight contributors to *Consequences*.

REES: In a preface to a volume of your plays, you said that one of your impulses to write for the theatre was archaeology?

BRENTON: Layers on layers. The feeling that this is a society which has been stamped over a lot. Literally. A heel has been on every bit of ground. And also that our institutions, our way of life and our class structure are sort of battered.

I can't understand why I write. What the impulse is. It's very difficult to know. I don't know whether in a way, you're sick in the head. Maybe it's show off. Writers are very close to actors in that writing a script is something of a performance and when it's done, it's often hard to rewrite because during that time you were doing this play, if it is botched, I am afraid it's botched.

REES: Nigel Gearing, the playwright, likes the fact that, temperamentally, you need to be able to work on your own and know that your best means of expression comes from this, and that also, as a writer, working in the theatre, you will go from this enormous privacy to equal gregariousness in the rehearsal process.

BRENTON: As a young writer hanging around the Royal Court, very shy and embarrassed, and being straight in a somewhat queer world, shall we say, one day I was burbling to Bill Gaskill about wanting to learn all about the stage and the lights, the profession, so I could really write for it properly. He said: 'Don't bother, writers belong outside the theatre. We, the directors, know how the stage and the lights work. We are the ones who don't know what's going on outside and so writers should bring their scripts in.' I remember feeling mortified at the time, but it was terrific advice really, for playwrights to not be in the theatre all the time.

REES: Did you work in theatre at Cambridge?

BRENTON: Yes. Towards the end of my time at university I wrote a long, unworkable play which was put on to universal derision. I remember Germaine Greer printed a bad review of it in *Varsity*, where she actually said: 'I am doing the British theatre a service by stopping this man now.'

So I rewrote that play and we did it for a week in the summer at the Oxford Playhouse – the dead part of the year when that theatre took in anything. The cutting made it that shade better. It was always a humourless Genetesque piece – rotting meat, butterflies, butterflies and rotting meat!

Then some friends of mine got together and somehow we toured Ireland. In those times, things were so cheap. There were some drop-outs from Central School and some university actors. I wrote a short play on a double

202

bill with John Grillo. I acted in his play and he in mine. Because I had been so frightened by the first play going down, the second play really worked. It was very funny, and so I got going. I had the romantic idea I should learn about the theatre by doing physical work in it. I became a stage manager at weekly Reps. I was the last man out of the bankrupt Worthing Connaught. After that I bummed around London and the Court did a one-act play on a Sunday night. Then I went down to Brighton to join the Combination.

☐ *A small performing space run by Jenny Harris. Later Harris and the Combination opened the Albany Empire which ran successfully for many years in Deptford and now sadly like the Half Moon, north of the river, lies dark.*

By now I was beginning to write all the time, all short plays. Chris Parr, who had directed my play in Ireland, went to work with students at Bradford University. He was hired by the Student Union Entertainments Committee. He commissioned his mates to write plays which were performed in the intervals of Rock concerts. So again this was the fear of God early on.

REES: At the Ambiance Lunchtime theatre, then situated in Norman Beaton's Green Banana in Soho, I did some short plays of yours, *Gum and Goo* and *Skinney Spew*, with Michael Feast and Frances Tomelty in 1969.

BRENTON: Two of those were originally done for Bradford and the other one for a Teacher's Conference at the Combination in Brighton. The Brighton Combination was a whole landscape of the mind. This was 1967 and all the contradictions were there, which are still with us in our lives in the theatre. Some people saw it as a political crusade, some as an artistic enterprise and others as sociological – cheap dinners for people who didn't have a roof for the night. The Combination was art, plus rock music, plus political agitation. There was always a tension you felt in yourself. I wanted to make my scripts very beautiful, others wanted real right on stuff.

REES: In the late Sixties there was a big mix of forms and styles and then in the Seventies people pursued more specific paths. There was what we have come to call 'Performance' theatre – Welfare State, John Bull Puncture Repair Kit, The People Show. And there were those who pursued what was then termed 'Political' theatre. And as you say these divergent impulses are still with us.

BRENTON: It still gives you bad nights. Sometimes you still wonder whether you have taken the right course.

REES: What led you to the Portable Theatre? Were you involved in its formation with David Hare?

BRENTON: I was never a director. They were doing Kafka and odd bits and pieces. They asked me to write a play on the history of evil which I thought was a pretty awful idea. My wife and I had a flat in Notting Hill and to our alarm we discovered it was around the corner from the pub where Christie used to drink. So I thought instead of the history of evil, I'll do *Christie in Love*. It is a play which has prospered. It still gets a lot of performances. Yet it is a play without any meaning. It illustrates the difficulty with the Brighton Combination in that it end-stops any sociological explanation of why Christie was a murderer of women. Because, you know, there are *other* people from Yorkshire living in London who were abused in their childhood, and who also find it difficult to relate to nurses they want to pick up, but they don't kill them. I wanted to capture that inexplicable madness. It was a very anarchic piece. Like a lot of the stuff around then.

REES: Portable Theatre was about new plays and touring.

BRENTON: Yes. But it was intended to be a theatre of high excellence, almost through anti-excellence. They turned down the first offer of an Arts Council grant. It was almost literally possible then to swing it, to survive by losing a bit of personal money, fifty or a hundred quid. Sets were simple to make. The pig pen in *Christie* for example. Awful to act with but it only cost £20. That was the Portable philosophy.

REES: Did you have particular heroes at this time?

BRENTON: Jean Genet. He was like a hero I had lost contact with because his plays are great unworkable pieces. They are like political poems, impossibilist theatre. I like that. I've always wished that Marlowe had lived and been our great playwright. They call him an over-reacher and he was. Genet was an over-reacher and so was Oscar Wilde. I always liked Oscar Wilde, partly because I was Jack in *The Importance* in a school play! And that struck me as a play that could never be explained, yet was clearly full of meaning. That puzzled me as a young, hot-headed man. It seemed to be against the political grain. So Genet and Wilde attracted me first, rather than Brecht, who I began to understand later.

REES: Do you think the new theatre you are talking about had different ideals to mainstream theatre?

BRENTON: At the time, yes. When I first came to London in '66 there was one Fringe theatre, where I had a play *A Sky-Blue Life* put on. It was the Little Theatre, off St Martins Lane, run by a strange and rather dear lady. The only other place was the Royal Court Theatre which was occupied by a very confident, second wave generation. David Storey, their writer par excellence, and Lindsay Anderson then at the peak of his career, clearly hated our stuff. A hatred we returned. There was a generational and professional dust up between us and them, with them saying you are not going to get your hands on our theatre.

David Hare founded Portable Theatre in 1967 because of that. There was a touring circuit just beginning. Two years later there was an entire circuit. Places began to mushroom like The Green Banana, where you did my plays. I am suggesting that the only new play producing theatre was the Royal Court and that theatre was not amicable to our work so we had to make our own arrangements.

REES: Touring was crucial to the development of this new theatre. We wanted to find a new audience, one that was of our generation and one that was not attracted solely by mainstream theatre but who we believed would come to our theatre.

BRENTON: That's true. The People Show, Pip Simmonds – anti-theatre outfits, performance art, music and dance-based people, wild performers, magnificent stuff – Ken Campbell Road Show which used pub jokes. But all of this was not script-based. Portable Theatre joined in this melée but we did not improvise our plays. There was a group called Freehold which Nancy Meckler ran. The idea was eight to ten excellent actors just exhausting themselves with improvisation to produce incredibly well-honed, very physical shows. *Antigone* was the apogee. But very anti-script.

So Portable Theatre and its writers, Snoo Wilson, David and I, we were plugged into the new circuit, but we were not liked. There was antagonism. There were other writers who are sadly not around now – David Mowat was excellent.

REES: Foco Novo did Mowat's *The Guise* on tour and upstairs at the Court and earlier I had done two short pieces of his at The Green Banana – *The Normal Woman* with Doreen Mantle and one partly written in Inuit, the language of Eskimos, with Tony Rohr and Hilary Westlake.

BRENTON: So there was a group who were looked on with great suspicion by the Sixties lot. Ideologically we were similar but it was quite clear that the *writers* carried the banner into the difficult Seventies and Eighties. With the exception of The People Show that original performance vein of work has not survived.

REES: The Welfare State?

☐ *The Welfare State were one of the earliest of the Sixties experimental theatre groups, centred on a community in Cumbria. Like The People Show, they have survived into the Nineties.*

BRENTON: The Welfare State were always into something different. There were two huge Festivals at Bradford University, major events, and they were filled with all the young Fringe people. I wrote *Scott of The Antarctic* for the

Mecca Ice Rink for actors, lots of local dancers, and the local skating class who were the fairies of the South Pole – a marvellous chaotic undertaking. That kind of event was terribly easy then. At the next festival, I wrote a show about John Wesley to be performed in a local church. These were two highly scripted shows, an ice panto and a masque play. Straight writing. At the same time I think Welfare State was born at these festivals with the idea of the public display. I remember wandering around the seedy area of Bradford one night, looking for a curry with Jeff Nuttall, a corpse over his shoulder, an immaculate dead body made by one of his students at the Art College!

REES: There was also a strong and distinct sense of being with a group. Instead of hiring actors, many companies based their work on the composition of the group members. People stayed together, to work together.

BRENTON: A lot of our actors were renegades. Some have become very successful. Stephen Rea is one of the great actors of our generation. He was in Freehold. He did not want to do the RSC stuff. A lot of our actors were out of Drama School and feeling: 'I don't want to do the David Storey trip at the Court or go to the RSC.' The arrogance of the Sixties was born out of a time of full employment. You almost had to be deliberately smelly under the armpits in order not to get employed. I was trying to explain this to my kids the other day. There was a strong bohemian, Baudelairian spirit which came with the various substances we consumed. And talking of substances, another important input at the time, was the Mickery Theatre in Loenersloot, outside Amsterdam, a former farmhouse owned by Ritsaert ten Cate

Portable was able to run because of the Mickery. Portable's final show – *England's Ireland* – which closed them with a debt of £900, had a cast of eleven actors and was about Northern Ireland. Only four theatres would touch it in the UK, but Ritsaert toured it in Holland and so the guilders made it possible. I first met Ken Campbell at the Mickery. First Saw The People Show and La Mama there rather than London. Went to workshops with them. It was a terrific liberation.

I was always a straight playwright, who in spirit, loved the Fringe, the alternative society, but, in practice, hated its lack of discipline and its self-destruction. The way it was institutionalised as well. The circuit quickly became 'The Circuit' and then they were onto Arts Council this, that and the other. People started talking about the acting not being as good on this tour as the last. Instead of about the morality of Christie, the murderer, or Snoo Wilson's extraordinary vision, they were talking about a play being sort of like 'alternative' Congreve. So you thought: 'Fuck this!' In fact, the circuit was quite small, usually university based, a few labour gigs, a few genuine above-pub venues and Arts Centres. But in reality, it was tiny. Everyone began to know everyone else and that was not good. Theatre needs strangers.

REES: There was that circuit. But some groups wanted to reach another audience all together, within the Labour Movement. To play their shows in the places of entertainment connected with local communities and places of work. Foco Novo toured shows through the auspices of the NUM [*National Union of Mineworkers*] in Wales, Yorkshire and Scotland.

BRENTON: Now it is very easy to dismiss the idea of the alternative society. But in 1968 you did not know what was going to happen. You didn't know what 1970 was going to be like, let alone 1980. You thought by 1980, we may all be dead. The Cold War was still being fought. A revolution broke out in France and even in 1970 the business in France was still there. It seemed there was a revolutionary movement in progress and you wanted to belong to it. But it was not easy to belong. None of us had money. We scraped together these plays which were inflammatory and a lot of them got bad reviews. Yet it seemed it was going to flourish. Then the hard dawn of failure. It became clear there was only one society. In other words, that politics are horribly straight and that a country, especially this one, is very homogeneous. If the left is not in power, if the angels aren't governing, then nothing can be done in an alternative way. There is nothing to be done down in the cracks except to stay in the cracks.

In the 1970's, during the tyranny in Bulgaria, I went to a cabaret in Sofia. They slagged off, by name, the President, his wife and the Secret Service; this was during the Brehznev era. Licensed blowing off for privileged people. That was what the alternative society was in danger of becoming. And it duly collapsed. In other words it did not take over.

And then we became more serious about our politics. In fact, we discovered politics. There was a crisis for many around 1972/73. This may seem awful to many people but there became the question whether to become an urban terrorist. This is what this era of love had by 1972/3 become – The Angry Brigade or Baader-Meinhof – in support of the dream of a free way of life which was increasingly impossible to articulate. Mind sets twisted out of shape, and for some it seemed that the only way to defend that way of life, of which you could not speak, was to take up the gun. Amid the tower blocks, there moved the armed spacemen: the situationist image.

I thought that was wrong. Twenty years later it seems rather a wise choice. But then, it was agonising. All that stuff at the Brighton Combination about the assault on society, burrowing underneath, finding new forms of ways of life and speaking, new sex, new politics, new religion, new atheism. This was not to be found in the Labour Party, certainly not in the Communist Party. The great libertarian ideas ended up, degraded in the politics of the Baader-Meinhof gang. They inherited the ideas, filtered through years of drugs, decay and above all the collapse in France.

I wrote a play called *Magnificence*. Like you do with plays, you don't know what you think when you begin it. I imagined someone I could admire who was an urban bomber and I thought, at the end of this play, I will know whether I am for 'or agin' him. I tried to dramatise the play through his world and ended up thinking this was a tragic waste. I called it a *Tragedy of Waste*. So from 1973, I was more mainstream. I was a left Labourite.

A lot of us went through that. John McGrath [*7:84 Company*] was not a left Labourite, he was sort of a Trot who has, as far as I know, never joined any party ten years later. Because of Michael Foot, that magnificent lost cause, the prospective Prime Minister who wrote books, I couldn't help joining the Labour Party. We remember all that with great affection. It was defeated, but we were not.

REES: During the Eighties, you wrote three plays for Foco Novo. What attracted you to the company?

BRENTON: At first, I was a bit frightened of it. I thought it was a hard company. John Berger wrote for it. I thought: 'My god, this is steel-teethed theatre.' It looked a formidable outfit. Then I met you and saw the humanistic heart. I saw your production of Brecht's *Puntila* in a matinee at the Ashcroft, Croydon, and I remember the physical sensation of it – a very bright, hard-edged set, uncompromising Brechtian light, gleaming out into this Saturday matinee, a third full, not bad for Brecht in Croydon – with our very young first son, Sam. He has never forgotten it. Sam can still tell you the story of *Puntila*.

Before I wrote my first play for you, I remember coming to a run through of a production. I cannot quite recall what it was, but I do recall the set of sliding screens at the back, and that you got very agitated and were picking flecks of dust I could not see off the stage. You were really in a runt-arsed mood and I remember you coming to me and saying: 'That's not going to be like that!' So my image of Foco Novo was of a hard outfit. And I think that the three shows we did together had that hard-edge to them. Rough theatre but oddly, emphatically stated which I think my work rather likes.

REES: The first one was a commission to make an adaptation of Brecht's play *Conversations in Exile*. The original was a long, discursive but provoking piece about a German physicist and an engineer, whiling their time away in a Finnish railway station, hoping to catch fresh news about their homeland from another new arrival, fleeing the Reich. Much as Brecht, himself, must have done on his nomadic travels after he too left Germany, travelling by way of Denmark to Finland, through the Soviet Union and finally ending up in Hollywood where he stayed until the war ended. You managed to dissolve the three and a half hour original into a fifty minute play and we wanted this to complement, in tandem, with the same actors, a two hander *Four Hundred Pounds* by the Jamaican writer, Alfred Fagon.

BRENTON: Brecht was extraordinary at this point in his life. Eternally travelling, writing compulsively. *Conversations* is a wonderful piece.

REES: Brecht was important both as a dramatist and theatrical experimenter. Foco Novo purposefully pursued a new writing policy but we recognised the seminal influence three writers, Buchner, Genet and Brecht had upon the contemporary writers we wished to produce. So we wanted to produce their plays to discover the roots from which our work came and the new directions in which we might travel. What is your attitude to Brecht now?

BRENTON: It interesting that his plays still fill the theatres. *The Resistible Rise of Arturo UI* was playing at the National. I did a version of *Galileo* in 1980, directed by John Dexter with Michael Gambon as Galileo, which packed the Olivier theatre. There is a secret in the theatre that says Chekov empties the theatre but Brecht fills it. How the English theatre establishment wished it was the other way round! But it's not. The reason, and it is very odd, is that behind Brecht there are some old fashioned influences.

One is Max Reinhardt – the spectacular show with the big main part at the centre which Brecht always delivered. *Mother Courage, Galileo, Puntila.* There is also this fabulous debate about lighting in his theatre which also stems from Max Reinhardt. Brecht's obsession with clarity comes from a view of lighting. It was Brecht arguing in his mind with Reinhardt. When he was in rehearsal and was annoyed, Brecht would say: 'Max would never do that!' Left-wing actors would say: 'He's talking about Max Reinhardt, that dreadful old camp has-been. He's throwing Max Reinhardt at us!'

The other interesting thing about Brecht was that he called for a kind of acting with the 'A' effect. This was an ironic, laid-back approach with an actor always on their dignity – 'I am an actor doing a job so don't give me a hard time,' and, 'I give you this story about this woman, this man.' That sense of irony is naturally English. That, I believe, is why he did versions of *Coriolanus, Measure for Measure* and Marlowe's *Edward II*, and why he liked Charles Laughton, that great camp actor. Brecht was fascinated with the sense of dignity which a great camp actor will always have. They will always be on the back foot, in cricket terms, and will be oddly exploitative at great emotional moments. You think as a member of the audience: 'I must not weep or the actor will laugh at me.' Brecht liked this because he was after a story telling form of theatre.

REES: When Brecht was young and was working with German actors at the end of the First War, the tradition was one of operatic and expressionist gesture. Reacting to such a climate, he would, if he he'd been able to have contact, have responded to English actors. As a result, we would never have had all those manuals. He was, and still remains, an abiding theatrical influence, and in some cases an influence on the very avant-garde who would say he means nothing at all to them.

BRENTON: For actors there are two poles – Stanislavski and Brecht. English actors are naturally Brechtian. A boulevard actor like Nigel Hawthorne is born to perform in Brecht. Given a good version, he would be magnificent. He would be a great Azdac. John Dexter, who has so sadly died, and a man I wished I had worked with more – I only got to know him in his last years – said the point about Gambon is that you cast a light actor as Galileo because a light actor will understand it – Gambon was known, as an exclusively Ayckbourn actor. People then said, after seeing the show: 'My god, what a heavy-weight actor!' But not at all, the part of Galileo is very waspish.

You and Foco Novo were a godsend to me. I had had a hell of a time with *The Romans in Britain*. I was 37/38 and really on a roll as a writer. I thought that *Romans* was a wonderful play, my best play yet, but not only did I have bad reviews – except for a good one from Bernard Levin, an ambiguous compliment, although I was very grateful to him – we also had to suffer all the nonsense of the court case.

☐ *Mary Whitehouse, self-styled public watchdog, brought a private prosecution under the Sexual Offences Act, as a result of a particular scene in* Romans, *against the Director of the play, Michael Bogdanov.*

It was the sort of mess that could sink a writer. You might never write another word. Particularly since you believed in it so much. Then you came to me and for the next three years, 1982-85, we put three scripts on very quickly, each a very, very different task. It kept me enormously busy as the fall out from *Romans* went on.

REES: Stefan Kalipha and Gordon Case played Fagon's two Jamaican pool hustlers in *Four Hundred Pounds* and then the two German characters in Brecht's *Conversations*. Whilst you were not directly working with Alfred, it was a close collaboration. I remember the enjoyable poetry reading you both gave in the Theatre Upstairs. Alfred played a part in the next play, *Sleeping Policemen*, you wrote for Foco Novo. Had you worked with black actors and writers before?

BRENTON: I hadn't. Alfred was a really interesting man. He was a self-taught scholar, a street scholar, how the British working class used to be. Alfred's knowledge of Milton was fantastic. He could quote reams of it. I gave him a copy of *Paradise Lost* in the original spelling. I loved talking to him about Milton. He was a boxer, been in jail for a while, and an excellent actor.

I was trying to bring something elusive out with the Brecht. Alfred kept things spinning in his play. You thought you were listening to something as remorseless as a Bach sonata in *Four Hundred Pounds*, a clavichord piece, but actually it had no internal logic and I was very interested in matching that. I chopped up the Brecht violently to stop the obvious dramatic development. There is a revelation at the end of *Conversations* as there is in *Four Hundred Pounds* A sudden turn around. But Alfred's writing had that wonderful quality of floating. You thought you were listening to something formal but you weren't.

REES: I wanted to connect the plays through the game of pool. So the brief I gave you both was for the two pool hustlers from Alfred's play, whom we never saw playing pool, to play a game in Brecht's play, whilst these characters talked about the state of the world and Germany in particular. The actors had to learn the game which, in Stefan Kalipha's case, meant starting from scratch!

BRENTON: It was a nightmare. I cannot remember if we wanted a moral point to be made by who won the game or not, the bourgeois or the worker!

REES: The games were never the same. There was a different winner each night!

BRENTON: New writing has got a bad name in the late Eighties. There is an idea that it is a supine activity, whereas Foco Novo at that time was a premier new writing theatre company, demanding plays about specific topics, and going out to find the writers to do them. The three things I did for Foco Novo were as a result of you approaching me as a producer. You were operating as a goading producer. If I had not delivered, you would have gone to someone else. That was how you operated.

REES: In a small company, the artistic director is dramaturg, producer and director. One of our most fruitful activities was our method of commissioning. Wanting plays about particular themes and finding the writer who shared our mutual enthusiasms.

BRENTON: I think that is where the Royal Court has made a mistake. That method you are describing is how you should run a new writing policy. For example, I think Max Stafford-Clark probably wanted to do a play about the City so he got *Serious Money*. I don't know if he wanted to do a play about the art world or whether that was Timberlake Wertenbaker's idea. But an artistic director saying we must summon into the world a play about 'X' – and therefore who is going to write it, who design it, who play in it? – is a good way to run a new writing policy.

REES: *Sleeping Policemen*, your next project for Foco Novo, represented another strand of the company's policy. We wanted to present modernist, classical writers, such as the Brecht you adapted. Another strand was the presentation of shows about a community or neighbourhood – examples being the shows which the NUM sponsored and promoted around the coalfields in the Seventies, and the inner city shows we made in the early and mid-Eighties. We wanted to capture local politics in action and their attempts to deal with the reality of Thatcher's inner city life in boroughs like Southwark, where a sub-culture had developed by the early Eighties, running parallel with and separate to mainstream life. In Peckham, where I live, with its multi-variety of population and its dimension of basic human problems – therefore the receptacle of every new-fangled government scheme going, ironically much as Peckham had been in the early part of the century – this sub-culture had become the 'mainstream' way of life. So here lay a rich earth from which to draw sustenance for such plays. Not as data for research, but as the fertile example of human endeavour.

Tunde had already written a play about Peckham, *Sink or Swim*. He and I were fascinated by the population composition with people from all over the world and still, just, including some few who were born in the area. It is not a ghetto for any one community.

BRENTON: There was a population survey done about Peckham. Only ten percent of those living here were born here. For some it's a haven, for others it's a dumping ground – problem families and some of the worst housing is shovelled this way.

REES: I wanted to bring yourself and Tunde together to write a play about the area because I wanted two different visions in the same household.

BRENTON: We spent a year on and off meeting, deciding what it should be about, who the characters should be. You gave us a brief of three white and three black characters, three men, three women. This was a kind of trade off between a working class black writer and a middle class white writer. We were two disparate writers, nervous about whether we would get on. Tunde is twelve years younger than me. He is a black guy from the East End and I am a white writer who had a premier English education, brilliant Grammar boy and Cambridge. We could have got up each other's noses. We might have come to blows. I know you purposely put us together, but it took a year on and off getting on course.

REES: The show was going to be workshopped for two weeks. You were then going your separate ways to write your play after which we would collect again to amalgamate the two plays into one.

BRENTON: After a year of excellent food and meetings in this room, lengthy phone calls and swearing love, we finally arrived at the workshop with six characters and six actors to represent them. Collaborations are difficult enough between writers because each has their own way of firing. It is tricky to make that happen simultaneously. Tunde and I had to keep a united front in the face of some very intelligent and aggressive actors. We loved the workshop, because it meant we could go away afterwards and say that we are not letting these people tell us what to write. It bonded the writers in a curiously successful way. And because the relationship between Tunde and I was becoming a precious thing, we began to need the workshop process less and less.

REES: There were actors in the workshop who had experienced this process before, and from that experience felt they were contributing to the writing of the play, and so deserved a portion of the royalties gained from its authorship. They asked for this after only a few days. Neither Tunde or you were having any of this. Foco Novo in this situation was caught between writers and actors. The actors wanted the writers to alter their contract, a contract that was with the company and not them .

BRENTON: They did indeed. We had done the work and were convinced we could write it. We thought that there were these terrible, awful, appalling people trying to wreck our work, and ask for some of our money, so let's ring our union. We rang the Writers Union and the actors called Equity in and it got mad!

I remember the day all this blew up, there had been a thunder storm and it struck and split the fig tree in your garden. We thought: 'What a premonition!' I remember saying: 'Everything's fine, we can write the play anyway.' We should have closed the workshop there and then, after three or four days, but you said: 'I've got the funding and we have to spend it!'

REES: I did a workshop recently with a young writer, Sebastian Baczkiewicz, at Goldsmiths College, University of London, and some professional actors. Sebastian and I came in to take the workshop on a theme of our own devising. We made a short, very interesting play about Central Europe and after, on hearing that he might develop it into a full length play, the actors wanted to know the same thing – would they become part of the royalty earning? They felt they had contributed to the writing in the improvisations.

BRENTON: There is a misunderstanding about workshops. In the workshop plays in the Seventies when Joint Stock, under Bill Gaskill and Max Stafford-Clark, honed the process into a wonderful way of working, there was never any split between actors and writers. Actors acted and writers wrote. I did one with Joint Stock called *Epsom Downs*. I had announced it would be about racing. The actors would visit a bookmaker and say: 'Howard, the bookmaker said this,' and I would write it down and they would throw the lines about and would show you things. Technically the actor had been a researcher, but whether that material was included in the play or not, or in what way, was utterly up to me. All we were trying to do was enhance both writing and performance, increase the definition. As time went on this process decayed. *Sleeping Policemen* was a late, decadent, workshop-movement workshop! The point about a workshop on a new play is it only works if the writers are in control of the text and the actors of the performance.

So the workshop was terrifically successful because it bonded the writers at the expense of the actors peace of mind. But then this was an experimental piece of theatre.

REES: After the workshops, you were going to retreat and write each your own plays, separately. You were not to converse in any way.

BRENTON: Both our texts were substantial. When we came to meet and read the plays there were 150 pages here on this table at which we are now sitting. We cut it in a day. It worked like a dream.

REES: With a large pair of tailor's scissors, we intercut sometimes a line, sometimes a speech, sometimes a scene. It became a mosaic of both writer's work and was, as you used to say, a cubist cut-up job. I remember we took ourselves off to the Cubist exhibition at the Hayward.

BRENTON: This was experimental writing for the theatre. Now experimental work is never acknowledged in the arts because it becomes, like everything else, an evening out, whether it is experimental or not. But this was really experimental work and has informed a lot of stuff I have done since.

REES: Michael Billington called it an urban *Under Milk Wood*.

BRENTON: It's much more than that. Our play was warm but not sentimental. I was talking to David Hare about this weird thing of getting old, and are our plays going to be done after we slip over the sides of our yachts in the South Atlantic? David said it's pure chance whether some great director revives *Plenty* or *Sleeping Policemen* forty years from now. If Tunde's and my work gets dug out of obscurity and receives a smashing production, it becomes well known. I have great faith in the play, more than many I have written, some of which I am sure are destined for the dustbin.

REES: The play worked very well everywhere on tour except for the Royal Court Upstairs audience. We played the Albany Deptford straight after the Court and it was a different play.

BRENTON: Out on the road, I thought we had a major sensation on our hands. It was taken as bad news at the Upstairs. It was incredibly glum. None of the many jokes worked. People were very frightened of it. They thought some terrible obscenity was going to take place. This educated, theatrical, audience eager for sensation were disappointed. The chattering classes thought: 'Oh, look how they are suffering out in the working class suburbs.' At the Albany the audience fell about. It was taken as a comic piece about life on the street, as a joke about people at the end of their tether in south London, which is how we wrote it.

When I was a stage manager, those many years ago, I was making tea during a performance in the green room and I had a rather dicky, odd ASM on the book and this noise came over on the tannoy. I rushed onto the stage to find this poor guy was in tears. For some reason he had brought the curtain down three pages too early before the murderer is revealed in the last line. The audience applauded and left the theatre perfectly happy. The question was what were they watching? The play was a 'Who Dunnit', yet they did not care who did it. They were reading the play in a different way. I suspect as a weekly Rep, they were watching their boys and girls being clever and lovely. They did not care who had murdered whom. There was a terrible enquiry and my ASM was fired.

How do audiences read plays? *Sleeping Policemen* should be a totally incoherent disaster but nobody ever asked: 'What's going on?' There are two different accounts of six stories: twelve stories going on simultaneously on stage. It should not work. It is the great problem Edward Bond has had. His plays are very simple and clear, very humanistic and should be very friendly. People think they are difficult, obscure, dark. It is a very interesting question – what does the audience see?

REES: The third commission was *Bloody Poetry*, 1984. I had read Richard Holmes' book *The Pursuit*, a biography of Shelley, in the very early Eighties. It influenced me enormously, returning me to re-read his poetry and introducing me to his prose. The story of Shelley's life was so exciting and resonant that I became immersed in it and I immediately wanted a play written about it. I approached you and at that point you felt you couldn't or wouldn't write a play about Shelley and then you rang me some time later and said, 'you're on,' and that you would do it.

My original interest had been in the variety of Shelley's interests – his political beliefs, his experiments with electricity and hot air balloons, his dissemination of pamphlets, his commune in Wales, the pot-shot taken at him, his support of the Irish, the fact that the Home Secretary kept a watchful agent following his every move, his vegetarianism and, not least, his relationship with his wife Mary Shelley and her half-sister, Claire Clairmont, in the same household. He seemed such a modern person.

Michael Coveney reviewing the play commented that in an age of small casts, your solution was a model of how to make a play both personal and political, epic, with a cast of six.

BRENTON: Isn't it amazing how you forget the good reviews?

REES: This was the only time I commissioned a playwright who used less actors than the brief offered!

BRENTON: How many did you offer?

REES: Nine.

BRENTON: And I used six and two were peripheral. It's odd how much that play helped me. The play I have just written for the Court – *Berlin Bertie* – has only five. It became wonderful that form, a cast of six with four leads.

REES: Did you know that I had gone to see Richard Holmes to talk about Shelley? It turned out that he was terribly keen to write the play. I said: 'Can you provide an outline for us to make a decision.' We then received half a Shelley play. I was in an awkward dilemma. After all, he was a very fine writer and knew more about the subject than anyone else, and yet I did not see a play sufficiently there. He had a striking visual conception, but I was not sure that the characters would live.

BRENTON: Did he see *Bloody Poetry?*

REES: I don't know, but I don't think so.

BRENTON: So many people think they can write plays! Plays are strange things. They are minimal with only a few words on a page, 85 to 90 pages long. They have a powerful undertow, which people who are not playwrights are not aware of. It's an odd business. Excellent novelists cannot deliver plays – they think it is easy because they are so short. Plays are full of ghostly sub-lines, tides going the other way. Line by line.

I read Holmes's book which I loved but my initial reaction was that I don't like the idea of writing about writers. As a playwright, although I may do it by accident, I don't like deliberately writing about myself, or having an alter ego in a play. When you write about a writer you hugely admire, nay worship, such as Shelley, there is a danger that you could self-aggrandise. There is also the *Amadeus* trap in biographical plays, where you propagandise a life to support a view of the theatre or the world. Mozart was a hugely successful musician who spent and drank too much, and unfortunately caught Asian flu. *Amadeus* is a totally false picture. There can be a terrible trap with writing biographies.

I only twigged how to do the play when I thought of the quartet – the two men and two women – Byron, Shelley, Mary and Claire Clairmont. I was thinking of the feeling that was coming over us in the early Eighties – of the whole political project that started with freaked-out anarchists of the Sixties, who begun to think politically in the Seventies, joined the Labour Party, had Harold Wilson back, tried to keep the faith, went east to see what it was like there, all this, and then suddenly the country goes into this reactionary mode. We had a strong sense of internal exile in the Eighties. Lots of writers picked up on it. I think Martin Amis wrote one of the definitive Eighties texts – *Money* – round about the time *Bloody Poetry* went on – a satire of internal exile. Our play was one of being exiled from England. So that's why I thought let's do their last years in Italy with this endless optimism – Gramsci's great saying: 'Optimism of the will, pessimism of the intellect.' Let's try and dramatise the last year of that and do it honestly. Mention the dead babies and the fuck-ups and the terrible behaviour. Do you remember at Leicester when we had the debate with Paul Foot [*whose great hero is Shelley*] and he said why bring up the dead babies?

REES: I was amazed at his attitude.

BRENTON: The search for a revolutionary hero was very intense then. It was a terrible time – the early Eighties – and we were keeping the faith going.

REES: The original commission was to write a play on Shelley. But Byron became very important to your story?

BRENTON: I thought I could write the play when I saw the split between the two. This is a classic writer's dilemma, if you are going to write about writing. You have got the brilliant vision-led writing of Shelley, not messy and Dionysian, but vision-led. Then you have got the political, rational writing of the Apollo-like Byron: 'I'm of this world, my clubfoot is in the shit and from that I draw strength.' If Byron was broke he would have changed his name and done, in our time, twenty Eastenders under a pseudonym. He wouldn't have cared. Shelley would, in our time, not even have had an agent to suggest such a thing!

REES: Byron was independently wealthy and published, Shelley eked out his dwindling inheritance and remained unpublished.

BRENTON: Shelley had no concept of writing for money. Byron would do a deal with the publisher before he committed a word to paper.

REES: One of the abiding things I remember about Shelley was that much of his prose work and many of his poems were distributed through the Labour Movement, particularly by the Chartists, while he was in exile a thousand miles away in Italy. He died in ignorance of the knowledge of how he had moved and influenced people.

BRENTON: I wanted *Bloody Poetry* to be an adventurous play; to do some high, hysterical writing. The characters live on a plane of high, sexual tension and intellectual play. Their bodies and minds are at their most extreme.

REES: Is *Bloody Poetry* performed more than others of your plays?

BRENTON: It is done quite widely. It goes on and on. *Bloody Poetry* is of a peculiar genre. It is a 'good men fail' play. They have a potency. The greatest of them is *Death of a Salesman*. A minor genre. Look, I knocked it off for you in five weeks.

REES: I was waiting for the second act whilst casting the play!

BRENTON: I thought, 'Oh God, this is so hard to write, I'm going to take the typewriter downstairs and write it in the living room,' because it was so late. I owed it to you. There have been three versions of it in my attempt to solve some of the problems I didn't solve for your production.

In all I did three experimental pieces of theatre for you. We knocked them off within three years. You were doing other things as well and so was I – a play at the Court, the RSC, a TV play and *Pravda* with David Hare. A lot of energy came out of Foco Novo for me as a writer. And that was after a personal disaster – *The Romans* – which according to all the laws of theatre life should have sunk my career. Terrific body of work those three plays.

REES: You wrote an article about touring with Foco Novo whilst we were rehearsing *Bloody Poetry* in Leicester. Touring is important to you?

BRENTON: Actors and writers both love and fear trying to convince strangers. Strut your stuff before strangers. That's what touring is about. What's hard, is you don't know whether the work is deteriorating or getting better, moving from one place to another. But meeting strangers is one of the main impulses.

REES: You were on the Board of Foco Novo. What do you remember about that? The relations with the Arts Council?

BRENTON: I was hopeless as a member of the Board. I always assumed I had been put on as a 'yes man'. And was indeed quite happy with that. I found that whole business with the Arts Council very distressing. At Board meetings I always wanted to go on the attack and say perhaps the rude, juvenile thing. My instinct was always to make trouble. The Company got a reputation for being difficult, which we should not have done because we were doing gorgeous work.

When I was first aware of the Arts Council at the Brighton Combination, I remember Dennis Andrews [*Then Deputy Director Drama. ACGB*] coming to Brighton and giving us several hundred pounds in cash, hand to hand, to keep the Combination going. They had no structure then of how to distribute money to a new, small company. By the end of the Eighties when Foco Novo folded, there were endless structures. I never understood why you should employ someone for £15 grand a year to turn up late to Board meetings and be called a drama officer.

REES: Nigel Williams said that those who administer the structures of funding bodies for the arts make more money than those whom they are officiating the structure for, those who create the work and provide them with a job.

BRENTON: Indeed. Foco Novo's debt when it folded was, what, £55 grand? How many drama officers salaries would go into that – four or five?

But that was not how Thatcher's world worked. It was odd that individualism was not encouraged in the Eighties, when, theoretically, it was called the age of the entrepreneur. Who knows perhaps Foco Novo lost its subsidy because we were pinko entrepreneurs, doing our job too well, bashing our work around the country!

But I fear that we may have got institutionalised, because we got so worried about the position of the company. Our fears were not about our audiences or the work or what we wanted to produce but always first to do with the grant. This worry took over all the theatres – the RSC, and the National and the Royal Court. You end up worrying more about the grant than you do about addressing the audience. Money was coming from bums on seats and still we worried. I feel it was awful, the end of the Eighties – the way this institutionalisation went on, at a time when buccaneers were meant to prosper. We were certainly buccaneers.

For Foco Novo to prosper at the end of the Seventies/early Eighties, it needed to expand, to become a major touring company. I remember when I first joined the Board you were agitating for that. You toured *Edward II* and *Puntila* on the middle scale. You played the Roundhouse. We needed to be recognized as a middle scale touring company and the Arts Council would not fund the company to do this. They wanted to keep us down in the small scale circuit. They were living off a version of alternative theatre that we knew was long dead. The artists had abandoned that concept ten years before. But the Arts Council were still thinking along the lines of these wonderful, vibrant, grubby shows visiting student and Arts Centery places, whilst we were saying: 'Look, we have shows like *Bloody Poetry* which can fill 500 seater theatres if you will finance that kind of tour.' But they wouldn't. They would not upgrade the company and that I think in the end killed it.

REES: A lot of companies who are presently Franchise Funded are producing Shakespeare and Jacobean drama and dramatisations of novels on the mid-scale. Dead authors are in, and cheaper.

BRENTON: There is no reason why you could not now put together shows like Foco Novo have done on this scale and draw audiences. Writers would be interested like me, David Hare, Trevor Griffiths and Caryl Churchill. It would be great. Foco Novo, fifteen dates, at 400 seaters, terrific! Come into London at say the Royal Court. What's the problem?

REES: Both before and after the Berlin Wall came down what happened and is happening in Central Europe continues to hold a great interest for you?

BRENTON: I was a soft communist after 1973. I liked the Labour left and I was a member of CND. I admired Tony Benn. I wished he had been able to take over the Labour Party and become its leader. I never liked Militant or the Communist Party. British CP members in the theatre and the academic world always gave me terrible stick, and I always hated them. The reason I hated them was for all the reasons Gorbachev attacked the old regime.

We have been through many things over the last three years. First there was the dream that Gorbachev was going to revolutionise the old CPSU and found a new socialist party, transforming the USSR into what we always believed it could be. And he launched the most aggressive series of reforms in his own country and in foreign policy which was unbelievable. It was always something the Left in the west thought could happen – that the real Socialism will begin when the East starts to democratise itself. Under Gorbachev it did. But the democratisation made the USSR fall to pieces. There was nothing there. The communistical, egalitarian spirit died long ago in the CPSU. It's very difficult to live with that. I wrote a play some years ago called *Weapons of Happiness* about this very subject, and I got such stick from hard lefties in the theatre and the Labour Movement, particularly when I got an Evening Standard Award for it. With Gorbachev we thought: 'At last.' And now we begin to fear a new dark age. I certainly feel energised by these events. I'm sure you do. I went to Berlin when the wall came down and picked up some stories. But I fear the new dark age so I wrote a new play *Berline Bertie* which takes its strength from the notions of small scale – five/six actors. The pattern is oddly like *Bloody Poetry*. Take five people and look at their lives on a wide scale.

REES: I find that many writers continue to write as if these momentous events are at a distance from them. You continue to respond as if they were in your own backyard.

BRENTON: That's very kind of you. My generation has certainly tried to take the 'new history' on. Dave Edgar did *The Shape of the Table*. It was very good; but the trouble being you think: 'Look at these funny foreigners in mid-Europe. Let's judge their sense of morality.' It's very difficult to bring the bacon home.

REES: Theatre is getting more international. Like music – world music – world theatre. Do you think this is progress?

BRENTON: No I don't. I think it is highly retroactive. Like the plane that fell out out of the sky over Malaysia, it will blow the theatre out of the sky. *Moscow Gold* is now dated as a result of events, but it had a lot of energy. I went to see a production in Germany and it was given a Euro-style production. Terrific, mind-bending, post-modernist sets, audience packed to the roof, a lot of money spent and totally meaningless. Aestheticism. World theatre is about aesthetics. Pretty patterns. Dance at its worst. Its mildly pornographic. Like Peter Brook's work. It does not mean anything, but it is very sexy. It is very bankable and I hate it. That's why plays get so mashed-up done abroad. They think here's a radical playwright, so let's do our production in mud and have actors throwing raw liver at the audience. When you have tried to craft exchanges between actors on the stage, you go abroad and see this nonsense. I hate it.

Theatre has to be particular and go for its nights. Foco Novo was the middle ground. Wasn't prestigious like Shakespeare or, on the other hand, flashy like performance art, but it tried to capture the sounds and overtones of the mess of what was happening at the moment and anything good only comes out of that.

As a result of a legacy of a dear old uncle, I have heavily invested in CD equipment and I bought these Bach cantatas. They were composed for a particular church in Leipzig to satisfy specific longings and rituals of the day. Yet the music is eternal!

JOSHUA SOBOL

Joshua Sobol, Israel's leading playwright, has had his plays translated into many languages. *Ghetto*, the first part of a trilogy about Jewish persecution during the Second World War, has been performed in numerous countries. The production at the Royal National Theatre won Sobol the Evening Standard and Drama Critics Circle Award for the best play of 1990. In Israel, where he was an Artistic Director of the Haifa Theatre, some of his plays – in particular those about Israeli relations with Palestinians – provoked nationwide controversies, and the interference of the political authorities in the work of the theatre. Sobol resigned his position. He was one of the eight writers who contributed to Foco Novo's *Consequences* at the time the company closed.

SOBOL: I started writing plays quite late. My first was performed when I was 31. Previously I was a member of a socialist kibbutz in Upper Gallilee. I was a fisherman there. Then I became a teacher and started to write short stories. Later I went to Paris to study Philosophy at the Sorbonne. I was there five years. Only on my return to Israel in 1970, did I start to write plays.

REES: Were you influenced by particular writers?

SOBOL: When I was eighteen, I read Samuel Beckett and became so influenced, I was prevented for a period of time from writing. In Paris, it was Sartre and Camus. There was a community of exiled writers there – you could say Beckett and Ionesco were exiles.

REES: Did you feel you were an exile?

SOBOL: In a way. I was 24 and I wanted to stay outside Israel. I was opposed to the policy of the Government. And I was strongly influenced by existentialism. So Paris seemed the answer.

REES: You live with your family in Tel Aviv, but since 1986 you have spent a portion of each year working in London.

SOBOL: When I am here, I can be cut off and concentrate more easily. It is an intensive time for me, a condition I find good for writing plays. I feel secluded here.

REES: Where has *Ghetto* been produced?

SOBOL: First in Israel in 1984. Afterwards, in the same year, in Germany. Then in Austria, Sweden, Denmark, Norway, France and Belgium. The Los Angeles production in 1986 was the first English language production. London followed and then New York. The play is about a theatre company in Vilnius or in Jewish, Vilna, practising their craft in the ghetto during World War Two. The actors tried to make sense of their existence through political and then religious analysis. They finally came to identify their situation with their own art. And they performed a biting satire about the ghetto for the Germans, as a result of which they were all shot.

REES: How did you come across the material?

SOBOL: I was reading a book about the behaviour of the Jews in the ghettos during the holocaust and the relation of Jewish society to the Nazi occupation. First I studied the Youth Movements and, by accident, I read about the Vilna Theatre. Immediately it captivated my interest, probably because, I myself, was trying to find my way in the theatre.

I found out there were survivors from the Vilna Ghetto, still alive, in 1980, in Israel. Amongst these, was the former director of the Vilna Theatre, living in Tel Aviv. We had many conversations and they conjured up in him memories suppressed for many years. It took three years to research in Israel and then taking advantage of a vacation from a Drama School, where I taught, I wrote the play in three weeks. Now it is to be made into a film. Karl Francis is going to direct and produce it. All the material will be condensed into a two hour film.

REES: The majority of your plays, performed outside Israel, have been produced in Germany and Austria. *Ghetto* has been performed more in German than all of your other productions put together?

SOBOL: I don't know how many there have been. Fifteen or sixteen. I have seen six of them.

REES: Do you find this ironic, given the subject matter?

SOBOL: It *is* ironic. But it has to do with German guilt. They want to pry into their past, to cope with it, more than any other society I know. Israel is as obsessed with the past but Germany has put greater effort into examining it. They are very concerned with literature which shows the interaction between their society and other peoples.

REES: So here we have the situation of an Israeli writer performed as much in Germany as in his own country.

SOBOL: I find it very stimulating, provoking, this contact with German theatre.

REES: The theme of *Ghetto* is persecution. Are Jewish themes a preoccupation of yours, or do your plays also reflect contemporary Israeli themes?

SOBOL: For the first ten years of writing, all my plays were about Israel.

REES: In the Eighties, your interests turned to recent Jewish history?

SOBOL: To Jewish identity. Because I felt that the contemporary problems of Israel have their roots in Jewish history. In 1977, there was a political upheaval in Israel when the right wing party, Likud, won the elections and Menachem Begin came to power. To this day, I am convinced Begin was infested with the problem of Jewish identity and that he influenced the destiny of Israel by acting out his obsessions in public. He expressed something very profound in the Israeli collective psyche, for all Jews, European and Oriental. But still it was a terrible shock for me when he came to power. I thought this was our end. It was not, but he wrote some of the most tragic chapters in our history – the war in Lebanon, the prolonged occupation and domination of the Palestinians. That's when I turned to dealing with problems of Jewish identity, and that connects with my fascination with Germany. Jewish writers and intellectuals look back to the days of the Weimar Republic, with justifiable fascination because after that, there was a black hole in German culture and history. They look back with pride at Walter Benjamin, the Frankfurt School and the Bauhaus.

REES: How much is Israeli theatre dependent on British and American plays for its repertoire? How many new Israeli plays are produced?

SOBOL: Proportionately to the dimensions of the country, we have quite a few playwrights. But in the second half of the Eighties the situation changed. There was a lot of activity in the Seventies when new plays were put on. With the coming to power of the Likud, to be compared to the era of Margaret Thatcher in England, Israel became dominated by the Stock Exchange. People tried to become rich overnight and the Yuppie mentality prevailed. Theatre became commercialised.

Two leading Tel Aviv theatres came into the hands of people who knew nothing about theatre. The administrators were from the army and other similar organisations. A typical symptom of this development, was a production, one of these theatres staged, of *Les Miserables*. It was a carbon copy of the West End show and was, in my opinion, a catastrophe for Israeli theatre. The critics praised it. People went to see it. I was the only dissenting voice, writing an article criticising the way the production was made and saying it would lead our theatre in a damaging direction. In my view, that has happened.

Now both these theatres compete in producing large foreign musicals. They both have huge accumulated deficits in the region of two and half million pounds. And to recoup their money they have to become even more commercial. As a result of which, they produce English and American comedies from the Fifties – *Arsenic and Old Lace, Charlie's Aunt* – so our theatre has become very dreary.

REES: But you get your plays produced in Israel.

SOBOL: The success abroad has helped me at home. I wrote *Solo*, a play about Spinoza, for a big theatre in the Hague. In Israel, it was produced by the Habimah Theatre but in their smallest studio, The Cellar. Because the Habimah did not consider the play of importance, they hid it down there. To them, it was an obligation to fulfil – to be seen doing new Israeli drama.

REES: Have newer immigrants contributed to Israeli theatre?

SOBOL: In the latest waves of Russian migration, there are many people from St. Petersburg and Moscow, very remarkable artists. They are bringing a new tradition to Israeli theatre.

REES: What about Palestinian theatre?

SOBOL: At the beginning of the Eighties there used to be a Palestinian theatre, the Al Hakwaty, in Jerusalem. The director was François Salem – his father was Swiss and mother, Arab. At Haifa, where I was an artistic director, we started to collaborate with them. This was against the consensus both in Israeli as well as Palestinian society. We played in their theatre and they in ours. François came to direct a play in Haifa, written by one of our actors, dealing with the problems of the Druze community in Israel. The Druze are Arabic but not Muslim. They serve in our army. They are in the same position as the Jews who fought in the German army during the World War One against French Jewish soldiers. Because of the extreme politicisation of Palestinian society at that time, the Al Hakwaty theatre split up. Now some of them perform outside Israel and Palestine, in the USA. Their empty theatre building has become the meeting place for the Palestinian government-to-be.

REES: Whilst I realise you now translate your plays into English, is writing in Hebrew, as a first language, a problem?

SOBOL: Naturally, first of all, in Israel, it is an advantage to speak English because for most of our people, migrated from so many different places, English is the common language. However, with the large Russian influx this may change. Secondly, you need English immediately you leave Israel. Your plays must be translated.

REES: You are much produced in Europe, yet your eye is of one from the outside. Do you find that you share attitudes towards theatre with people in the UK, or do you find you hold different views.

SOBOL: Theatre in the UK has not influenced me. I have gained a lot more from conversations with people. But of the plays I have seen, I like those of Howard Barker. I identify his method of going back in history in order to reflect upon the present. I liked David Hare's *Racing Demon*. I could feel an affinity with a play about a religious professional who feels ill at ease in his profession and religion. I laughed a lot at *Kvetch*. I found the form of the play – the discrepancy between inner and outer speech – interesting.

There seems to be a prevailing confusion in theatre here. In isolation, people do something meaningful. You can say, here was a good production, there a striking play. What is absent from the theatre of the last decade and the early Nineties is a dialogue between playwrights, directors, theatres and the audiences. Everything is now an accidental encounter. Yet the world cries out for a different approach, a different dialogue as people look for answers at a time when ideologies have fallen apart.

REES: Perhaps recent events are too large and immediate. There is a paradox that whilst the English language is being daily more widely spoken, the centre of world events has moved away from the English speaking world. Elizabethan and Jacobean dramatists fed on the fact that their world was where it was happening. In the 1960's and 1970's British dramatists gained similar sustenance from their own soil. Now huge events are taking place before our very eyes on TV in other parts of the world, placing centre stage regions where English is not spoken. Do you think plays written in less familiar languages will become a feature of the future? Perhaps this is an explanation for the lethargy and isolationism you have found in our theatre.

SOBOL: What has happened in England is that theatre, as in Israel, has been forced to become more commercial, as a result of which playwrights have to write plays for three or four actors. If you are not careful, it confines dramaturgy to family dramas and marital problems. Large issues cannot be tackled.

Look at what happened in German theatre. There, theatres got support from the state and from their city to the extent that they allow 250 theatres throughout the country to produce what they want, how they want, and with casts the size of your National Theatre. It is a question of priorities in a society.

As a consequence of the city and state subsidy, German theatre has a strong sense of identity. You go to a German town and there are road signs directing you both to the Bahnhof [*Station*] as well as to the Stadt Theater or Schauspielhaus. This reveals the importance they attach to theatre and opera. In every city I have visited in Germany, the local theatre reflects the personality of that city. In Wiesbaden, the capital of Hesse, the theatre is very bourgeois and wealthy. In Essen or Dortmund, the theatres reflect the industrial, coal mining and beer brewing nature of the area.

REES: In Nuremburg, where I directed a Ken Campbell play, the car park was bigger than the theatre. Nobody walked or came by public transport.

SOBOL: It is typical for German theatres to be part of and to have a strong relation to their city. In England, it seems to me that theatre is a world apart from the city/town it is in, so that provincial theatres are no longer important. Perhaps in the UK, the notion of 'city' and 'town' exists no more. Here the theatre is separate and has its own flora, fauna and vegetation.

REES: Germany clearly holds a fascination for you. Brecht is one of the great German dramatists of this century. Did he influence you?

SOBOL: He used to. Nowadays I have a critical attitude to him. Brecht was obsessed with the idea of teaching in the theatre with the audience placed in the position of the learner. When you teach, you pretend to possess a knowledge or truth which you will share with others who do not yet possess it. This is a paternalistic attitude, similar to that adopted by religious authorities. The process of learning is democratic, teaching is not. You can learn by yourself but I believe the best way to learn is in a community with other colleagues through a process of trial and error and questioning those who pretend to have authority. Learning is a revolutionary procedure, teaching is conservative.

REES: What about the production values he brought to theatre?

SOBOL: Above all, he brought clarity and simplicity to the stage. I became aware of this when I saw *Mutter Courage* at the Hamburg Schauspielhaus. That theatre is a traditional, Italianate proscenium arch theatre, sumptuous and elegant with a magnificent curtain. The designer placed a Brechtian half-curtain within that space, cutting the height of the stage in half. None of the internal apparatus of the theatre was hidden. Immediately I realised what Brecht had been up to. He was reacting to his own times, and exposing the pretensions of those kinds of theatre buildings, very common when he was young. It showed how mystifying theatre had been.

REES: Yet many people, who regard his plays as old hat, have unwittingly adopted his approach to theatre and performance. He is part of our theatre vocabulary.

SOBOL: He stripped theatre of all its ornamentalistic overweight. This had to do with learning. You get rid of everything that is unnecessary or an encumbrance. In this way you sum up the essence for yourself. I think the theatre of the Eighties forgot this lesson and overindulged in the ornamentalistic overweight of unnecessary decor, scenery and lighting techniques.

REES: You say simplifying was a learning process Brecht adopted, yet you criticise him for teaching in his theatre. A contradiction?

SOBOL: Brecht was a man of contradictions. He believed in revolutionary socialism yet he was an ultimate individualist. He chose to live his last years in East Berlin running his own theatre, yet he kept a Swiss passport and bank account, since he trusted nobody anymore. He was a child of his time who excelled in contradictions. The contradiction of the teacher and the learner.

REES: He knew the wall was going to come down!

SOBOL: In 1985 I visited East Germany with a group of Israeli playwrights as guests of the East Berlin Writers Club. They were very generous, taking us to luxury restaurants in their fine cars. I felt privileged in a society of austerity. They were the princes of their society. When Brecht returned to Berlin in 1947, East Germany, having overthrown an aristocracy, required new princes and he accepted that mantle.

REES: Like you, he spent a considerable part of his life outside his country of origin, in his case exiled, and heard a number of his plays spoken for the first time in a language not his own. Brecht also lived through an unsettled period of world events. He called it 'the dark times.' How do you think playwrights will respond to the events unfolding in the world during the next decade?

SOBOL: I see the Nineties as a reactionary period, a replica of Metternich's Europe, a 'dark reaction'. I think that theatre in the Nineties will revert to the Paris theatre of the Fifties, becoming dissident, separated from mainstream society and will survive only in what is left of the Fringe. The big houses of culture built in the Fifties and Sixties, requiring large subsidy, are becoming more and more a cultural boulevard, a superior cultural boulevard from the point of view of acting and production values. They will not inspire new writing. The real new writing will occur in places where one can dare to fail.

The forms favoured and considered avant-garde in the Eighties were primarily physical theatre, dance, and performance art. Content took second place. By the end of the Nineties, I believe, we will return to the primacy of content. It will not continue to be sacrificed to form, as is happening nowadays, encouraged by the contemporary establishment and funding bodies. 'Get away from content, concentrate on form and we will support you.' Form is at present the message. But it is obsolete and decadent. Heavily subsidised but decadent. Today false gods are praised.

REES: How would you categorise the explosion of international theatre at the moment, international exchanges of theatre, World Theatre? Do you think a babel of languages is a desirable future for theatre?

SOBOL: It is a phenomenon I call 'Festival Theatre'. This type of theatre is important for theatre people. They come into contact with new forms, plays, playwrights, actors. But this activity is only for the small theatre community. It does not concern the wider audience. Putting on earphones and listening to plays via an interpreter is not for that audience. In the end, what counts is what happens within a culture, within its own language. Festival Theatre has to be approached with scepticism.

REES: What do you see as future developments in dramaturgy?

SOBOL: In 1987, at the Haifa Theatre, a political scandal followed the production of my play *Jerusalem Syndrome* about the situation in Israel. It met with such intolerance that I resigned. It became clear to me then that I had to write plays with small casts, but still try to deal with the same issues. It obliged me to look for new forms of expression in dealing with social issues.

REES: In the Seventies and early-Eighties, Foco Novo mounted productions with casts of ten and on two occasions of fourteen actors. By the Eighties, we were down to casts of six and four. As you said earlier this so often leads to plays about families and close situations. But we continued to look for ways to capture a social as well as an individual world with small casts.

SOBOL: In my last two plays, I have dealt with historical and moral problems with casts of three and four. I find it stimulating. I imposed the condition on myself.

REES: Apart from small numbers of actors being used to express scale, what other dramaturgical developments do you see as necessary?

SOBOL: In Tel Aviv University and at the Drama School where I taught, I experimented and searched for a form which would bring together the collective unconscious of society. To find out how you could make a stream of consciousness for an entire group of people through a chain reaction. Returning to Brecht, this is also why I am critical of him. His heroes had the position of Kings and Queens on the stage. Shen Te in *The Good Woman of Sechuan* is not a queen as such, but dramatically she is. Galileo is absolutely a king. The structures of his plays depended upon the large main part, a very traditional concept. To portray a community, you need a form which will give an equal voice to lesser members. I call this approach polyphonic. With Chekov, you cannot obviously point out the main character. There is no obvious leading part. He brings to the stage a very sharp observation of Russian society and history. He does not teach me, but he is someone with whom I can learn.

REES: Why polyphonic?

SOBOL: Plays like this develop like a musical orchestration. You cannot say one instrument is more important than another. For example, Jazz is a very democratic form. Every voice can take the place which it deserves according to its inspiration at a certain moment. Jazz is like an open platform on which each voice can speak out what it has to say. When you come to a Jazz performance, you do not know what will happen. Jazz is a polyphonic form. Every voice will act itself out fully without restraint.

TEARING DOWN THE CURTAIN
Design for Touring

Design was fundamental to Foco Novo. Why we chose to 'show' a play one way rather than another, was central to the question of 'why' we were doing that show. Visual decisions were then vitiated by the conditions of touring a great variety of theatres and venues.

The secret for us, as a touring company, was to come up with a design in which the whole play could flourish without once altering that set. Bold simplicity was paramount. In this way, an open space was created which, in design terms, allowed the spatial relationships of actors, one to another, to become the primary factor on stage rather than objects deciding how the space has to be used.

On tour there is often a limited acting area and few technical aids. Anything in a design that did not contribute to the core of the play was junked. Detail was a matter of selecting what was absolutely necessary. Ally this to a preference for a rawness, even a honed roughness, and an aesthetic begins to appear. It is conceptual in framework and realistic of selected detail. It is a poetic approach.

Directing new plays is not a matter of finding fashionable interpretations as you might, say, with Shakespeare. You have a bare blackboard and can write on it what you want. At the same time, you are looking for the essence of the play. I work on a play until an essential image emerges for me. That is what I start talking to the designer about. They, of course, bring their own ideas. From this moment the relationship becomes one of partnership.

English theatre practitioners like to talk about 'stylisation' and 'theatricality' as if these terms were the descriptive opposite of anything that is normal, representational reality – Naturalism. Naturalism is itself a style, particularly the studied naturalism of TV and Film. As Adrian Vaux says, the camera has taken over the designer's job of portraying representational reality, so they are freed to explore other regions of what theatre design could be. In the same manner during the last century, the camera wrested away from the painter, the practical need of recording an individual's existence.

The exciting challenge of using 'found' locations for performance, in comparison to the convention of theatres, is discussed; a desire to introduce into theatre, paradoxically, the 'cinematic'. To use the idiosyncratic atmosphere of an actual location – say an old industrial building – with the connotations of its former use, and make it play host to another use – theatre. In this way, an audience is made to re-appraise their perception of what theatre might be. The paradox is that by introducing one medium within another, you heighten the givens of theatre, making it more real and at the same time more theatrical.

231

James Snell and Trevor Butler in Foco Novo's 1984 production of John Constable's *Black Mas*, costume designs Sheelagh Killeen.

Dorien Thomas and company in Foco Novo's 1987 production of James Pettifer's *Needles of Light*, desinged by Ariane Gastambide.

DESIGN

Adrian Vaux, Tanya McCallin, Ariane Gastambide and Sheelagh Killeen have all worked in the subsidised theatre, both at National and Regional level, as well as with smaller touring theatre companies. Some have also worked on Opera and in Film and Television. All four have worked with Foco Novo and Roland Rees, covering fourteen different company productions.

Designs for Foco Novo:
Adrian Vaux: Brecht's *Edward II*, C.P. Taylor's *Withdrawal Symptoms*, Mustapha Matura's *Independence*, Nigel Gearing's *Snap*, and David Mowat's *The Guise*.
Tanya McCallin: Bernard Pomerance's *The Elephant Man*, Colin Mortimer's *The Free Fall* and Tunde Ikoli's *The Lower Depths*.
Ariane Gastambide: Kate & Mike Westbrook's *The Ass* & James Pettifer's *Needles of Light*.
Sheelagh Killeen: Costumes for *Snap, A Seventh Man, Puntila and His Servant Matti, Black Mas*, and *Bloody Poetry*. Sheelagh was a Board member of Foco Novo.

REES: The relationship between a director and a designer is essentially the same whether they are preparing a show for a building-based theatre or a tour. However, in the preparation of a touring set, there are parameters within which a designer must work and qualities they must observe, which make the experience different. What do you think these differences are?

VAUX: Touring is harder. It's more difficult to fit a show into a truck. To have a set made that will survive the rigours of being humped from venue to venue. You have to invent more because you have to leave so much out. You have to squeeze your brains harder.

McCALLIN: I find it the complete opposite. I suppose this could be the result of the way I design. I try to arrive at the lowest common denominator, by removing the large issues and coming to the essentials. I always find it a great burden designing for a big stage. Having to fill from pros stage right to pros stage left and all the way around the back. For a large opera, you have to put an enormous quantity of idea on stage. The space you have to fill is often bigger than the idea actually is. Whereas in a small touring venue, you can be so precise and dynamic, because you are forced to create out of simplicity. So the idea becomes much stronger, by the nature of being confined within a twenty foot square acting area. This distilling process is terribly helpful and it makes you focus tightly on the core of what you are looking for.

It seems more difficult to design for a smaller company, because you've got to say to yourself: 'I haven't got the money'. So even when you have your idea, you still have to make it work within that tight budget.

VAUX: There are so many more things you can't do with a touring set. If you've got a large canvas, you can splash ideas across it. You can take risks and play around with space in a much freer way.

REES: In a theatre building, you can rely on its infrastructure to supply the means to achieve sophisticated solutions. Whereas, I used to say to designers working for Foco Novo, you must be able to erect your set in a field. The only addition being the electricity supply. You have to break down the components of a touring set into a jigsaw to enable it to fit into the van.

KILLEEN: Even so, it is amazing what you can come up with!

VAUX: When you are touring a show, we, the designers, rarely know what every theatre looks and feels like, how the set will relate. So you are really working blind to some extent, and sometimes the surprise is not a good one.

I designed Mustapha Matura's *Independence* but I did not see it anywhere except at the Bush, [*Unusually opening in London, 1979, rather than touring first*] so I could never imagine how it looked in another space.

REES: I asked you for a Caribbean version of a Hockney swimming pool. And you produced an evocative and colourful trompe l'oeil painting of a Caribbean pool and hotel, which had seen better days, the canvas of which covered the floor and walls of the Bush Theatre. You painted it yourself. Our last venue was the Marylands Community Centre, off the Harrow Road, and they liked the set so much that we left it there. This Black Centre used it for years as a back drop for their saturday night bops!

VAUX: Pity I didn't have a percentage!

REES: The types of theatres and venues which touring companies visit are often converted buildings. They don't have fixed seats. The acting area is on the original floor of the building and the seats are placed on rostra. The perspective is the floor and the back wall. There are no wings, only the original walls of the building. Even a larger space like the Riverside, formerly television studios, does not naturally have wings.

McCALLIN: I remember the twenty foot square touring space had to include all exits and entrances. Actually that twenty foot frequently ran from the back wall to where the leg room of the audience began!

REES: A major factor was how an actor got on stage.

McCALLIN: Your actors might have to be stored in the back of the set and appear for their entrance from within the twenty feet. [As they had to in Tanya's design for Tunde Ikoli's The Lower Depths]. And then suddenly, next week, at another theatre the same set would be floating in a vast great space.

GASTAMBIDE: It is a very difficult problem. I have been working with Complicité Theatre Company. [The Winter's Tale]. They have no set at all. They just want a surround with a few pieces of adaptable solid objects.

REES: A surround is closer to the demands of dance.

GASTAMBIDE: Yes, it is like a dance floor and it means their lighting has got to be very precise: another problem because all the venues are different. They must also reorganise their moves at each venue, which the company are used to. They want to make sure they are always getting the maximum use of each space, regardless of what the designer has imposed. In fact, they don't want the designer to impose anything. I was left in the dark at the beginning as to what they wanted. I had to see how rehearsal turned out. It was not the conventional way a designer works. But it is exciting!

REES: That is very different to Foco Novo because we used to make the twenty foot square define the acting area, regardless. We did this to combat the immense differences between the size and feel of each venue. This avoided the need to re-rehearse. But I share the preference for an open space whose use can be choreographed in many different ways.

McCALLIN: That approach sounds more like the old Italian street theatre where two poles were set up, with a rope across, to hold up a curtain. There were always splits in the curtain. And if you needed a room, you just painted a window above. You could perform on the back of a lorry or on the street. Anywhere you could put your cloth up. That was based on a tradition of theatre, a form with which everyone was familiar.

REES: That is not necessarily an accurate analogy for Complicité's work.

VAUX: There was, as you say, a certain formula to that sort of travelling theatre, whereas the theatre which Roland was dealing with was something else entirely.

REES: Foco Novo means 'new starting point' and expressed both a desire to innovate and a determination to let each project, each text, itself be a new starting point for the company. We had no formula to fall back upon except our own approach, which we developed out of our experience touring small to middle scale theatres in the UK over many numbers of years.

Foco Novo had two full time staff – an Administrator and an Artistic Director. Only when the project had become a text, could the members of a company begin to be assembled. Whilst many of the same actors, publicists and stage management came back to work for the company, it was individual designers, as the fourteen shows covered by your presence here indicates, who most frequently returned to work for the company. This fact was bound to have an aesthetic input into our work. It exhibits the commitment to the central role of design even if the scale was small.

Let me put my original question another way. Would you have chosen different routes to solving a play's problems, if any of the shows you did with Foco Novo were to be presented in only a single theatre?

McCALLIN: We usually knew where we were ending up. We were designing for the final theatre in London, whether it was Hampstead or the ICA or the Riverside. The set was never built by that theatre, but its dimensions and feeling were born in mind, and in a sense you did work for that space.

REES: After all, a touring company, like Foco Novo, in the Seventies and Eighties, would play only two or three consecutive nights at each venue during one given week. Whereas we would play three or four weeks consecutive performances in the same London theatre.

KILLEEN: You would get the groundplans from each venue. They were put on tracing paper and by placing the London plan on top of all the others, you could work back through the tour and find the common denominators.

REES: Ralph Steadman designed the set for *A Seventh Man*, Adrian Mitchell's adaptation of the John Berger book about migrant workers. It consisted of a series of backcloths – a Turkish village in rich colour, and black and white cartoons of landmarks passed by the migrants on the journey from their village. However, the resources of the theatres we toured, did not allow us to use all the cloths. Only when we reached our final destination, Hampstead Theatre, could the whole vision of the design be seen.

McCALLIN: With *The Elephant Man*, the ceiling height had to be eleven foot three precisely, because that dimension was governed by the ceiling at Hampstead where we were to end up. That was not required by other venues but it was quite good that it was part of the brief. It meant the set would definitely fit in all the places you were touring.

What was alarming on tour were the get-ins. In a theatre you know your facilities, the size of the dock doors, the relationship to your audience – you can see them for yourself. But on tour that was an unknown. You might find the set had to go up three flights of stairs, and then through a regular sized door. Or your audience is suddenly in the round and not end-on. Those surprises could be alarming.

REES: Performing in the round never happened in Foco Novo productions, with one exception to which we will come. We liked to perform end-on or in the thrust. In small spaces, the round reduces the possibilities of design.

KILLEEN: Your audience might come into the auditorium through the same entrance to be used by the actors. Anyone arriving late or going to the loo during the performance, might bump into an actor making their entrance!

REES: Some people would ask: 'How come the touring company did not know all of these problems ahead of time?' The answer is that the burden of this research would normally fall upon the permanent Production Manager in a building based theatre. With Foco Novo, the appointment of such a post, for financial reasons, happened only after the designer had started work. Each designer had to research each individual theatre, and this could mean fifteen or twenty separate ground plans, many being indifferently prepared or just plain wrong or out of date.

VAUX: That's the thing which grinds you down. You look for the worst possible situation that you are going to find. And you find it out at the get-in – that everything has got to be four by two foot six and so cut down to size!

McCALLIN: Just in terms of carpentry that makes the set more expensive.

REES: Do you remember, Adrian, that your set for David Mowat's *The Guise* would not fit through the small dock doors of the Theatre Upstairs, at the top of the Royal Court. It came up in the hoist, outside on the street, and wouldn't fit through. So we had to cut it in half, get it in and stick it together again! Just as well it was the last port of call.

For your set for *The Ass*, Ariane, we had to make sure that the venues matched the width of the Riverside

GASTAMBIDE: Riverside has a special problem because it has no depth, but great width. A real letter box stage. You can make it smaller by changing the seating around.

REES: That at the Riverside is as costly as designing a new set. It is too expensive to consider altering the seats. With *Edward II*, Adrian, which visited what the Arts Council liked to call middle scale venues, basically 500-seater theatres, we played the now defunct Roundhouse.

VAUX: We thought about the design with the Roundhouse in mind, the most difficult space. Everything after that was a pushover. The sightlines and the physical disposition of the performance had to relate to the Roundhouse.

REES: You made choices because of the nature of the building – its special qualities, being in the round, and being a large, nineteenth century, former railway engineering shed in Chalk Farm.

VAUX: I liked the space. It was different from anywhere else we had done shows.

KILLEEN: And the production wasn't in the round anywhere else.

VAUX: The fact that we had to work almost in the round, made one think about it with a specific kind of energy, which related to the Roundhouse, and which worked very well in more conventional spaces.

REES: We determined to 'modernise' Brecht's play, as he had done to Marlowe. To do a Brecht on Brecht. I said: 'Take note of his theories on production values but do not become a slave to them. Take what you want and make it your own.' Whilst there is reference to siege engines in the text, it was surely playing at the Roundhouse with its great height, that made you think of using such monster structures?

VAUX: The Roundhouse was an inspiration for the play – a building left over from the Industrial Revolution – so my thoughts about the play related to that. It had that certain tacky, industrial feel. I drew from that. The effect of the set was as if we used bricks and stone shale. Tactile material which echoed the building. We used tall wooden pikes for the battles which again echoed the columns of the building.

REES: And we were not faithful to any particular period. We borrowed and chose from many periods, for each costume and prop. Whatever was appropriate within our concept of the play. The fourteenth century was there but so was the twentieth.

VAUX: Up to then, 1982, that was something you would have largely seen in European theatre. It is the kind of thing where a modern reference brings out more clearly the issues of a play. So *Edward II* was not history theatre but theatre with an historical context.

REES: We imposed a physical world of a medieval mafia – a melange of sight and sound. There were huge war machines, which the cast manoeuvred, and means of captivity and death – the pikes, thick ropes, chains and a 'Ned Kelly' pail in which Edward's head was imprisoned. The sound of percussion, a trumpet and a conch horn, whilst underfoot you had placed gravel and shingle.

GASTAMBIDE: It is more inspiring working in a big space not built as a theatre.

KILLEEN: For example, Ariane Mnouchkine and the Theatre du Soleil in their aircraft hanger outside Paris.

VAUX: At the Roundhouse the audience got a different perspective of the show, depending upon where one sat.

REES: I bump into our percussionist from time to time, Eddie Sayer, him of the hub caps and tins. All our music was by this Jazz percussionist, who had a collection of timpani the like of which you had never seen. His percussion produced all the battles.

KILLEEN: He had them strung on a rope between two poles and would rush up and down in a red Indian, horned headdress banging away on these instruments. I had just come back from India where theatre is often performed on a small, trestled rostrum with a backdrop curtain hung from two poles. Suddenly I was in a big performing area, with this percussive noise and an amazingly large set, which Adrian had contrived by using his versions of Leonardo da Vinci's war machines. I found it an exuberant and wonderful experience.

VAUX: It's a shame that there are not more spaces around like the Roundhouse.

McCALLIN: A terrible shame that the building will be sold. A lot of money was spent on it. Now it is being abandoned. It would cost a lot to renovate.

KILLEEN: It was a tragedy that it never became the multi-cultural and ethnic Arts Centre it was intended to be.

VAUX: These experiences make one realise, how very boring conventional theatres really are. You can do more interesting things in a given space. TV and films do all the picture making very efficiently now. It gives us room to do something else.

McCALLIN: We're still stuck behind the arch.

VAUX: When we went to see Edward Bond's *The Sea* at the National, you felt the writing and the form of the play suffered by being in the wrong space.

KILLEEN: The designer was faced with the terrible problem of filling one side of the Lyttleton stage to the other.

239

VAUX: If you had put that play in a small space, in a more oppressive relationship to the audience, you would have raised the temperature and made the violence more immediate. It would have made the play work better.

McCALLIN: But the designer has double the problem with the Olivier stage, where the distance from pros right to pros left is eighty feet. If you use the whole space, and there is no point in not using it, you spend most of your budget visually getting from one side of the stage to the other.

VAUX: Just masking the space off. Enclosing it.

McCALLIN: It is so vast that some plays never had a chance. This is not the designer's fault. They are just fulfilling a brief. If one considered doing one of the smaller cast plays done at the Olivier with Foco Novo, would it prove impossible because you did not have the facilities of the Olivier stage and that budget? The answer is, of course, you could. Of course, you could. We build so much vast scenery just to fill the stage, not only for visual interest but also to avoid leaving large empty spaces or having to fill them with black drapes. The Olivier is a very difficult stage. It's there for *Tamburlaine,* big pieces.

KILLEEN: It's epic theatre time.

REES: We did Bernard Pomerance's *Quantrill in Lawrence* at the ICA in 1980 and Marganita Laski, who was a member of the Arts Council Advisory Drama Panel at that time, used her position as a critic, to chastise us on BBC Radio's Saturday Critics Forum for spending far too much money on the set. Despite the fact that we mounted this production on money earned from Bernard's New York run of *The Elephant Man* and not through our Arts Council subsidy – these days a plus for one's entrepreneurial activity! She compared our apparent 'lavish' expenditure with the RSC's Barbican production of *Pericles* using only, as she said: 'Two planks and a mast'. And we all know, as your evidence has indicated, how much two planks and a mast could cost at the Barbican.

KILLEEN: We had been minimalist for years and this was our chance to show what we could do with design on a little extra money. So that nagging criticism was quite upsetting!

REES: Oliver Ford Davies told me that he did a show at the Barbican about the same time which, in his opinion, could have been eminently done with a table and four chairs. He remembered the designer saying: 'They've cut my budget from £25,000 to £18,000! What am I going to do?' The designer was in despair. Oliver thought to himself: 'Well, I could do this play for £30 and I think it would be as good a design as yours.' [*These are Eighties' prices. Nevertheless they illustrate the size of such an RSC budget compared to the £2000 Foco Novo spent on this special occasion*].

Quantrill was set in Kansas, in the town of Lawrence and amongst the woods and forests of the vicinity. It was an epic piece which Max Stafford-Clark had inappropriately suggested could fit into the Theatre Upstairs. I wanted a Kansan adventure playground to encompass the wild activities of Quantrill's gang which included Jesse James and his brother. Iona McLeish, the designer, provided wooden rostra of palisades, corrals and ditches.

You could not have done this play with a table and four chairs or with two planks and a mast. So when someone makes those kind of criticisms, they need to know how much sets cost, however simple they seem.

VAUX: Over the years, the big theatre space became a white elephant and, as designers, we are always looking for new ways to say things in new spaces.

REES: The first show we ever produced in 1972 was the play *Foco Novo* by Bernard Pomerance, which we performed in the premises of a large garage, situated in Gospel Oak. With the arrival of subsidy for the company, committing us to a policy of touring, we could not do shows in this way. I was always very keen to return to the use of undedicated theatre spaces for performance. They are, for me, the most exciting way visually, to undo the usual responses audiences have to plays and to reawaken fresh ones.

GASTAMBIDE: I think it is much more important when we can transform a space and the audience can be involved in the set and the atmosphere in a more direct way. It is much more exciting.

KILLEEN: That's one of the pleasures and achievements of this kind of theatre. I now rarely design sets, but I am always aware of being trapped in conventional theatre by the seating. Where the audience is placed, is such an enormous part of what you are doing. One of the great things about Fringe theatre is that you might be in the round, you might be in a pub, or you might be in an industrial building. That is what is exciting. You are not trapped by red plush seating and a pros arch.

REES: The origins of many companies' work in the Sixties and Seventies was based on the desire not to perform in theatres. A separate circuit was created, many of them being converted buildings – for example, The Traverse, The Roundhouse. However, there were one or two groups, who made performances for a special occasion – a one-off performance – and probably out of doors.

KILLEEN: You are not text-based with actors speaking words, if you are doing that kind of theatre.

McCALLIN: Nor are you design-based because it is the director's visual sense which makes such a performance work. Unless you build something for a space and this designed 'something' is maintained for the performance, we, designers would have to put ourselves in a different frame of mind for such a project.

241

KILLEEN: Welfare State did a piece in Docklands for LIFT [*London International Theatre Festival*] which had enormous set pieces comprised of floating boats with lights inside. The effect was Bosch-like.

McCALLIN: I thought you were referring to a more environmental approach in which the chosen location is the set.

KILLEEN: In a sense, it was environmental. It was not one focussed idea. It took place in different sections of this old dock with its locks, basins and cranes near Silvertown on the Thames.

REES: You designed *The Ass,* Ariane, for Foco Novo in 1985. This was a most unusual show combining music, choreography and the poetry of D.H. Lawrence. It was adapted by Mike and Kate Westbrook from Lawrence's poem of that name and was set in the town square of Taormina in Sicily. The background of the Westbrooks is Jazz. The nearest I can get to a description would be a Jazz Operetta. [*See Interview* The Ass] Ariane, clearly we needed an ass and you designed a larger than life donkey, whose head would move if its tail was pulled, in unison with its bray. And you made a life size ass's head, which Stephen Boxer playing Lawrence at one point wore, as did the saxophone player who was able to stick his soprano sax through the ass's mouth and continue to play it!

GASTAMBIDE: Because of the width of the Riverside, you either have to use the whole stage or focus the action very strongly for the audience by enclosing the acting area. We had a grand piano on stage to cope with. We also had a screen on which to project the slides of Kate Westbrook's paintings. I had been to Taormina in Sicily and was keen to match its setting by making an atmosphere which was filled with a huge sky, the sea and the rock towering over this very small village. The Westbrooks produced these photos they had of the old walls and entrance to the town. That entrance and the ruined wall, topped by tufts of grass, became the idea for the base of the ass. Both elements crystallised into the one object.

REES: What we needed was a piece of Sicilian show biz! You provided a gigantic ass dwarfing a miniature town, surrounded by a cyclorama of a huge, blue sky, set on a silver floor to reflect the light.

GASTAMBIDE: It was a great shame that *The Ass* was not more popular because it was a beautiful show. So many who saw it said it was so rich and enjoyable. Somehow, other audiences, encouraged by the critics, were not ready for that sort of thing. They were either coming to see straight theatre, to see D.H. Lawrence, or they were coming to listen to music. It was both, and they should have been open to this combination. It's such a pity nothing else has been done like that. You should do another one. But do you think more audiences will now be ready for this sort of theatre?

REES: Yes, in the future. It was ahead of its time.

KILLEEN: With the set of *The Elephant Man*, Tanya, I believe the paintings of Francis Bacon were a big influence?

McCALLIN: Well, they were one of the starting points.

REES: I wanted Merrick's head inside one of Bacon's cages.

McCALLIN: The set was an extraordinary mixture. It took a long time to evolve. The play seemed an awesome problem at the time. With most plays, there is a straight series of scenes but with *The Elephant Man* there was a central core – John Merrick in his room or bath – to which you kept returning. And then there were scenes in hugely different circumstances, such as Liverpool Street Station. At first, it seemed impossible but that is the sort of problem I like. It forces you to look for a solution which has not been achieved before and which, in its answer, is a statement for the whole play.

KILLEEN: Tanya's way of showing John Merrick's world was to choose a geometric shape, a twisted trapezium or rhomboid, made of metal, which acted as the only surround for Merrick's hospital room – the 'Bacon' cage. The room was a rectangular plinth serving as a bed and opened up to become a bath. All this was raised on a rake, giving the impression the whole set was floating.

REES: We had no idea how we would obtain the physicality of Merrick. Apart from a terse stage direction suggesting 'no make-up', the process involved with the naturalism of make-up would have made the business of touring very onerous, if not impossible. Watching the prosthetic preparation Dave Willets underwent for *The Phantom of the Opera* reminded me of this. So we looked for other solutions.

McCALLIN: That was what was so marvellous about doing it. I remember the first time I read the play and thought I have absolutely no idea how to design it. It's not stageable. But as you get into a subject and you embrace it for what it is, you find the central core. If the writing is strong enough in that central idea, it will carry the other areas. For instance, the Liverpool Street station scene worked so well because in the end the actors, being where they were placed on stage, made it live.

REES: With a little help from a smoke machine and the lights!

McCALLIN: It took me a long time to realise how to do the play. I was stymied. So I went back to source, to my researches. Again, I visited The London Hospital in the East End where Treves, a surgeon there in the 1880's, had taken in Merrick under his wing. There is a Hospital museum and Merrick's bones are kept in a glass cabinet. It was one of those grey London days when the curator showed me the actual room in which Merrick was housed.

I will never forget walking down those stairs into the dark London basement, walled with those white Victorian tiles, covered in grime from the Whitechapel Road outside. There were pipes everywhere. The room was horrendous. And suddenly, in that room, I realised what the play was about. Nobody could quite deal with Merrick!

REES: Many of our plays were historically set. The events of the past reflected back to our own time. So there are documentation and first-hand accounts about the subject. The set you designed, Adrian, for *Snap*, the story of Muybridge, the early photographer, who turned his 'stills' into 'motion pictures' by revolving them in his zoopraxiscope, was the inside of a camera obscura. In the darkened interior, you could not tell where the entrances were or the light came from. The four characters acted out their drama as if they were in a movie. There were many examples of the stills Muybridge had taken, of his wife and himself, with which to study his method of work. Oliver Ford Davies, who played Muybridge, said the important thing about researching an historical character is to know when and what to jettison.

McCALLIN: I am experiencing this at the moment. Visiting the locations where a play is set, you find it impossible to get rid of the experience. Visual research can be even more problematic than an actor's research. If a photo exists, you could reproduce that image on stage. So you warn yourself that you do not have to recreate that actuality.

VAUX: What research often does is throw up a lot about the background to the play, which in the end you don't need. Research is about finding out what you do need. It is about the process of selection. You might select everything or nothing.

REES: Tanya, you designed Tunde Ikoli's *The Lower Depths* which toured and played at the Tricycle Theatre, 1986. The play was set in the East End of the 1980's. [*An updated version of Maxim Gorki's original play. See interview with Tunde Ikoli*]. We visited Cable Street and Tunde showed us the house where a former Nigerian friend of his father's used to run a boarding house, such as exists in the play. We never gained access but Tunde described how the house was separated between the ground and upper floors, where the family lived, and the basement, which was subdivided into small rooms for the lodgers. The play's mode was poetic naturalism. Although you were asked to design the interior and backyard of a house, the solution was not straightforwardly representational. Your use of colour and shape denied this.

McCALLIN: If you start with the particular clothes actors need to wear and props they need to use, in real terms, you can develop outwards towards a set which can become an assimilation of all the requirements, but which is not a representation of any one scene. It is its own world. All plays which are domestically based, as opposed to those set on a broader or grander scale, are limited to people exiting and entering through a door. So with Tunde's play, you needed seven doors on stage to represent the seven cubicles where the lodgers lived, plus the doors into the basement!

REES: That worked very well because we decided to set them, unnaturally, in a straight line one next to another, facing the audience, and so gave the impression of a spartan cramped barracks. You found the lack of actual depth for each cubicle – eighteen inches – difficult to believe we would get away with. But we had to and we did! It was like a Meyerhold comedy, an essence of realism, but the perspective was resighted for us.

McCALLIN: It was a limiting situation. You had to have a working stove to cook the patties, you had to have the doors and the play became about these doors. In themselves they worked. They were wonderfully wrecked, covered in twenty layers of paint. But to me it was a rather conventional solution.

REES: Foco Novo was in the business of new plays. With a new play, you want to produce that play to exhibit its strengths as a piece of writing. Later productions have the opportunity to re-interpret a text, in another way.

Adrian was saying earlier that Television and Film excellently achieve the job of representing photographic reality back to us. It frees theatre to do something else. So the question should be asked of a play, can this text benefit more from a television production than from a theatre production? I would say that, by and large, Foco Novo's shows were theatre pieces first and foremost, constructed through the 'language' of theatre. Including *The Lower Depths*. That play could be done on TV, but I believe that this would cramp Tunde's language and would force it into becoming a soap opera.

Tanya is indicating a preference *against* plays set in interiors of people's houses and *for* those more epic in scope, containing many scenes in diverse locations. Unlike *The Lower Depths*, which had two acts with separate locations, the majority of Foco Novo plays consisted of many scenes and required a set within which everything needed to take place. Such as *The Ass, The Elephant Man, Foco Novo, Snap, Quantrill in Lawrence, A Seventh Man* and *Edward II*.

McCALLIN: In a set which serves many scenes, the actors themselves are part of the visual statement. They link the play to the visuality of the set. This allows for a much more creative process for actors.

REES: All our casts had to be their own stage hands and move scenery and props. In *Needles of Light*, a play about the Spanish Civil War, [*Riverside Studios 1987*] Ariane, you designed a set where the actors gradually filled the acting area with some large, irregularly-shaped rostra pieces, one in juxtaposition to another, like some giant jigsaw, until at the end of the play, the shape of

Spain was revealed. It was, of course, an image, fifty years on, of a country divided by war and forced to unite under fascism.

Again in *Edward II*, Adrian, your gigantic battle machines had to be manoeuvred by the cast, splinters and all, as the war between the Barons and Edward unfolded. The actors, by comparison to the machines, seemed like ants as they scrambled to push and pull the pieces from one position to another.

McCALLIN: At least the actors did it. They knew this was part of their job. At the RSC they would be unlikely to be involved in such a procedure.

REES: What do you see as future trends in theatre design? At the moment a backlash is developing against theatre which, it is claimed, is dominated by directorial quirkyness and by design awash with performance and visual priorities. Is theatre going international?

VAUX: There should be a move against establishment theatre, which is digging its own grave and stultifying the rest of theatre. Theatre is richest when it grows out of local situations. When people write against a background of social and political unrest, a concern about what is happening around them. The international thing is nice, but you only come to that after the hard work is done. Corporate cash may fly around for showy, high profile work. But what is important is the theatre which climbs up through the cracks in the pavements.

McCALLIN: We have been through an amazing twenty years for designers. What we did those years ago is very different from the immensely sophisticated work young designers now do. Design has changed from being the after-thought to being the essential element, beyond the text and sometimes beyond the performance. This contribution owes a lot to the world of opera. I admire the work there enormously. I go for the visual feast but I am not entirely sure what that approach has to do with theatre and language. Design was grossly undervalued before. But now it has taken on such a sophisticated level that the reason for it is not 'felt'. It's there only for its own purpose.

GASTAMBIDE: There is a huge difference between theatre and opera. We go to opera for the visual feast and the atmosphere of the music, but we go to theatre for a text feast. Theatre is poorer and does not have the scope to indulge designers. Actors play a greater part in the activity of theatre. Since the Seventies, there has been a slow but increasing trend towards equal proportioning of parts, which itself further encourages actor participation.

McCALLIN: The visual feast at the opera and the epic play at the National all end up looking the same to me.

VAUX: The National is the ultimate for many people's aspirations. They think it is the building where the excellence par excellence happens. When the idea was first mooted years ago, I thought the possibility of having many theatres, chained in repertoire across the country, exactly what a National theatre should be. New playwrighting, along the lines I have been talking of, may have difficulties in flourishing at the National Theatre we have ended up with.

McCALLIN: What has historically happened with design in France and Germany, we missed out on until recently. We are text and performance and actor bound. Our younger designers have found new approaches. We are all aware of what Peter Stein and Peter Brook have done. Even if we do not read the International Theatre magazines, this approach is part of what our theatre now is.

VAUX: Peter Stein realised that he had placed such grotesque impositions on plays with his production ideas that he has disowned all that he did, up until two years ago. He suddenly thought:'Who am I to do this?'

REES: Many British groups have been developing work along the lines you are talking about for a number of years. In the case of The People Show since the mid-Sixties. Appearing in small theatres, with very finite resources, this work has not been internationally recognised. Suddenly foreign directors and designers come here and it is all 'new', because it is high profile.

McCALLIN: Yes, a lot of what you did with Foco Novo, which we have been talking about, and Pip Broughton's production of Zola's *Germinal*, were examples of what British theatre could do with this kind of work on texts.

REES: I think many of our shows have achieved considerable visual impact even if they were confined to smaller theatres and spaces. Our approach to plays was to maximise the visual quality. However this never meant design for design's sake.

GASTAMBIDE: Foco Novo always allowed designers freedom to do what they really wanted, within the intentions it had for the production. You approached the designer as a partner.

VAUX: This marriage is the best way to achieve good results.

HE WHO PAYS THE PIPER
Subsidy and Sponsorship in the Arts.

In the late Sixties there was no structure for the distribution of funding to small companies. By the Eighties there were innumerable structures, administered by the Arts Council officers. The New Theatre movement had become institutionalised. Appraisals, business plans and three year franchises were introduced by the Arts Council, and many additional sources of funding, including commercial sponsorship, became essential ingredients of arts budgets. Funding had become plural.

This development made theatre change its spots. Producers had to respond. In this climate, new play producing companies were the most exposed. Thelma Holt says she was attracted by the 'kamikaze' attitude of Foco Novo's work and joined the Board in the early Eighties. She liked the fact that the company had no 'scaffolding' around it and were out there in the deep end.

John Catty, Graham Cowley and Dr Trevor Griffiths focus on how theatre administration has to respond to the variety and vagaries of funders and sponsors. Jenny Waldman provides a unique picture of working for the Arts Council as well as being an arts administrator, now Director of Arts Centre Projects at the South Bank.

THE PRODUCER

THELMA HOLT

Actress and Executive Director of the Open Space Theatre Company,
Director of the Roundhouse, Head of Touring and Commercial
Exploitation of the National Theatre, Executive Producer for Duncan
Weldon of the Peter Hall Company. Now Director of
Thelma Holt Ltd.

Thelma Holt was on the Board of Foco Novo.

HOLT: My first memory of something I wanted to do as a very little gel was that I wanted to be a priest. I didn't want to be a lady priest, I wanted to be a man priest. I wanted to wear that lovely frock! I am Roman Catholic. I learnt the *De Profundis* before the Lord's Prayer. I used to hold funeral services in the garden. Bury a doll in a shoe box. The name I always put on the box was my sister's. She was older than me. I thought it quite a good idea to kill my sister!

Then, and I'm sure a lot of people who go into theatre go in this way, but won't admit it, I suddenly found I got attention, got noticed and praised for doing things. If I did a little dance, people smiled and said: 'Isn't Thelma sweet?' If I sang, they would say: 'She can sing!' It seemed a nice way of getting applause.

My serious interest came when I was at school. I developed a tremendous interest in poetry. I am grateful for that because I have met people, who have left school recently, and who have no knowledge of English literature at all. It would have been perfectly alright with me if we had done nothing else but the Bard at the Open Space. That would have been quite okay.

REES: Charles Marowitz, Artistic Director of the Open Space, wanted to do a season of American plays in 1970 and asked me, because of my New York experience and my productions by American authors at the Ambiance, to direct two pieces by Leonard Melfi and two by Michael Weller. At the time he had a company presenting Shakespeare, which you were in. You were both an actress in the company and Executive Director of the Open Space.

It was an important time, the late Sixties for new theatre. In many instances, it was Americans who were instrumental in encouraging this movement. What did you see as the importance of the Open Space?

HOLT: I met Charlie an an actress. He had seen me in a production at Hampstead, and was casting *Hamlet*. He offered me Gertrude. I had been expecting to be offered Ophelia, but when I looked at it properly, I realised Gertrude was a much better part for me!

Having been so keen on classical theatre, suddenly I loved what he was doing with Shakespeare. I liked his interest in new plays. This boulevard Café Theatre thing was started by all these Americans. But with no disrespect, they could start it, their enthusiasms were great, but they did not have the discipline to carry it on. It applies to all of them – Ed Berman, Jim Haynes. We were the ones, people like you and I, who slogged away and carried it forward.

Charles approached me and said: 'If we cannot do the work we like, why don't we control our own destinies, start our own theatre and go in as partners?' I said: 'Why not indeed.' The original idea was that we would go

50/50. He would direct the plays, I would act and learn to run the place. I was on holiday with the family and he rung me up: 'We've got the building!' It was fortuitous that I was with my Father-in-Law because we needed £60,000 to build the Open Space and he gave me £3,500. We raised the rest from donations. Sean Connery gave us a bit of money, so did Sam Spiegel, Joseph Losey and Chris Blackmore of Island Records. It opened on 8th June 1968 with *Fortune and Mens Eyes*.

In 1976 the theatre moved up the road from our Tottenham Court address. We had one year there and during that time I left. Lots of things were said about what happened between Charlie and me. I'm very fond of Charlie. But nobody said what really happened between us, including him and his book. What happened was that the pupil bought the idea more than the tutor and we began to go different ways. Charlie was finding it tiresome that we did not have money, that things were not working out for us. So when our partnership ended in a blaze of publicity – the bathroom suite became the little drama neither of us cared to cope with.

☐ *Marowitz procured for personal use a bathroom suite cheaply or free, depending on the story you believe, from one of the suppliers to the Open Space.*

The thing which people forget is that three months after I had gone to the Roundhouse, one of the first things I did was to invite him to do his production of *Hedda Gabbler* there with Jenny Agutter. We had reversed our situation.

REES: The Open Space was about starting something from scratch. The Roundhouse had a history. It is a miraculous piece of architecture in Chalk Farm, originally built by British Rail as a locomotive engineering repair shop. I remember wandering around the building in 1968, before any conversion had begun, and marvelling at its possibilities.

HOLT: Centre 42, based at The Roundhouse, was formed in 1960 by a group who succeeded in getting the TUC to pass a resolution, Resolution 42, supporting the Arts. Arnold Wesker was the original Artistic Director. He and George Hoskins, the administrator, persuaded the owner, Louis Mintz, to donate the sixteen year lease of the Roundhouse to Centre 42.

REES: Hoskins ran it as a Touring House for all sorts – music, theatre, speak-ins. You inherited this. And developed your own policy. And it was from this period that your interest in bringing international companies to London found expression.

HOLT: We brought over many foreign companies. We had a policy of doing half a year of regional work. I did not want to be a rooming house. I certainly did not want to be a landlady. And the other half of the year, I would bring in things from overseas. I wanted Roger Planchon and Antoine Vitez and Brook, naturally.

But the great thing which changed my life was the Rustaveli Company. [*From the state of Georgia in the then Soviet Union*]. And that made a big, big change for me. It made me realise how terribly important international work was, and what it could do for us. It became my raison d'etre. My artistic relationship with Robert Strua [*Artistic Director of Rustaveli*] is still going ten years later. He recently did *The Three Sisters* for me. [*With the Redgraves*].

A big part of the policy at the Roundhouse was the two hugely successful seasons with the Manchester Royal Exchange. Michael Hordern, Vanessa Redgrave – *The Lady From the Sea* – and Eddie Fox were all in plays. When Michael Elliot died, [*one of the Artistic Directors of the Exchange*] for me the impetus went off the boil. It was that relationship which worked for me.

We had Foco Novo in with Brecht's *Edward II* which was one of the ten best uses of the space in my entire time at the Roundhouse. It gave the chance for Foco Novo to go into a rather awesome space and spread around it. It was artistically enormously successful.

REES: It was one of the shows I was most proud of, and since the days I had seen The Living Theatre perform there, I had always wanted to devise a show for the Roundhouse. Did Centre 42 have any control over your policy?

HOLT: No. The only connection with the original Roundhouse was George Hoskins and the fantastic Council of Management of the Roundhouse Trust. They were unbelievable. Wonderful, wonderful men. Ellis Birk, husband of Baroness Birk, at one time Labour Party spokeswoman on the Arts in the House of Lords, Louis Mintz, Barnett Shine, Eddie Kulukundis, Toby Rowland and Robert Maxwell, who was the Treasurer. They were hugely supportive. They put their own money on the table when I was desperate. They supported all the schemes I came up with. Without them, I would never have done it.

REES: After you left the Roundhouse, there was an attempt to turn it into a Black Arts Centre.

HOLT: Why should Black actors go and act where only other Black actors are working? That's a ghetto. It is a beautiful building. And if it is going to be an Arts Centre which concentrates on minority work, then I would have been very happy if we had a predominance of plays, new plays preferably, by Black writers with Black actors and Black companies coming in, as long as we were also going to let the Irish in.

That building required more than expertise to run it. It is a weird, weird building. I love it. And those who worked there loved it. But you cannot just walk in and expect to run it. From Stephenson onwards it has been defeating people. The idea of an Arts Centre for Black artists ultimately is correct and should happen, but unless the building is very, very handsomely funded, it would be better they went for a purpose built building.

REES: You then went to the National Theatre. To continue the work of bringing foreign companies to the UK?

HOLT: I had the oddest job at the National, as Head of Touring. This meant I had to take us out around the country. In fact, there were lots of other people to help with that job so it wasn't something that needed a bucket and spade merchant like me.

But the other job I was given by Peter Hall, who was very clever at recognising skills, was to get us on over the river, to do the transfers. The first year there, I transferred four plays which were financially very successful for the National. And in my opinion, the West End received plays that still had life and were value for money. Then, at the end of my first year, I was on a plane with Peter and he said I had done 'frightfully well' and 'was I happy?' and I said, ' Yes', and he said: 'You can have your reward. Go and organise an International Season. That's what you like to do.' What he didn't say, in typical Hall fashion, was that I also had to go and find the money to do it!

So I went back to Maxwell. It was he who gave me the seed money for what became International '87 at the National Theatre [*Stein's* Hairy Ape, *Bergman's* Hamlet *and Ninagawa's's* Macbeth *and* Medea *and the Mayakovsky Company from Moscow*]. He gave me £50,000 and that kicked it off. All I ever did is write and shriek for help. He never refused.

I had been introduced to Cyril Stein who ran Ladbrokes. He let me use the Ladbroke Hotel at Lords for the companies visiting the Roundhouse. So I went back to him and said: 'Now I am bringing tours into the National.' So I was thrilled when he bought the Hilton because I would have even more space to spread myself around. He's a Roundhouse contact. Like Maxwell, he is someone whose generosity seems to be boundless.

REES: In the early Eighties, you joined the Board of Foco Novo. You provided very valuable advice. What made you want to support the company?

HOLT: Largely your kamikaze attitude, which I have always admired in your work. You were doing very innovative work, and unhappily by the time I came to the Board of Foco Novo, so many of you had disappeared. Everyone had gone either as a result of Arts Council decisions, or had gone under because they were fatigued and tired, which was what happened to

Charles. You can only do that sort of thing for a number of years. Anyone who works in a situation like Foco Novo needs the stamina of an ox. You get worn out. So maybe everyone was worn out. And you seemed like the only one left at a certain stage.

New companies are not springing up any more. They are only able to spring up and survive when they have got scaffolding around them. You had no scaffolding at all. You were out there in the deep end. And the support you had from people like Howard Brenton, [Dr] Trevor Griffiths, Nigel Williams and Mustapha Matura indicated the importance of the work. But it is a suicide mission trying to do the kind of work you did. I'm interested in suicide missions. I like them a lot. I've done it recently with *Tango in Winter*. [*With Alan Rickman at the Piccadilly, directed by Ninagawa*].

REES: Joint Stock and Foco Novo, both companies with considerable reputations, had their grants withdrawn on the same day in 1988. In Foco Novo's case, this means the Board had to take the decision that the company must immediately cease to trade, whilst it was in rehearsal for a show. The Arts Council knew of our financial circumstances and, therefore, presumably knew that their decision would force the Board to have to take theirs. What did you think the Arts Council thought they were up to when they made that decision?

HOLT: I think the Arts Council was looking to save money. I wonder how many of those who sat round the table and made the decision to withdraw the grant, and indeed give increased grants to others, and who talked and expressed opinions about the work, had actually seen the shows? You need people working in the real world who can find time to discuss with an Artistic Director their work and future plans for a company. So I think the Arts Council were laissez-faire in their attitude when this was happening to Foco Novo.

When they are going to axe something they obviously get worried. Trying to decide whether a big organisation is cost effective is always somewhat daunting. Whereas with a small company, they can see very clearly if you are making the books balance. Indeed, if you are going to have any chance to do so in the future. Every time they kill off a small company, the amount of money they save is minimal. It is very shortsighted and a piece of philistinism from people promoting the arts. If we want innovative work, such as Foco Novo did, we have got to let these companies reserve the right to fail.

REES: The argument went that the older touring companies on Revenue funding had to go and make way for the newer ones.

HOLT: The idea that they had to get rid of the older touring companies to make way for new ones is absolute rubbish. Where are the new companies? Are they going to kill off the old flagships and create new ones?

REES: The Project funded companies who had not yet become annually funded.

HOLT: That's the lazy way. That's the lazy way! The harder, but more fruitful way to do it, requiring more work, would be to look for money elsewhere. To see how much support for the bigger companies, who quite rightly take a huge slice of the cake, could come from sponsorship and how much they could get from abroad. Remember, when you went down, any conception of the extent of sponsorship the RSC and the National are now able to command, would have been unthinkable. Unthinkable. Now it has happened! But it was never explored by the Arts Council then. Nor was the exploitation of what could come from overseas or promotional possibilities. These were never explored. It's all happened in the last few years.

REES: Do you think sponsorship is the way forward for the future?

HOLT: I think it is an absolutely necessary evil. I am not a hypocrite. So I cannot say you can do without sponsorship. I have just produced a play in the West End, Ninagawa's *Tango*, in the middle of a recession with 25 actors. It is technically extremely complicated with fifteen crew at one point lifting a wall. We could not have done that, and it was important to me we did it, without sponsorship directly from Japan.

REES: From Japanese companies?

HOLT: Yes. [*Fujitsu, Itoh, Shimizu and Shiba Corporations, and from Maxwell's company Great Britain-Sasakawa Foundation*].

REES: Can sponsors be relied upon?

HOLT: They get bored with you. There can be a man at the top, who for a time has a yen for certain art forms. If he goes, it stops. Then it gets harder. When I did Peter Stein's production of *Hairy Ape*, I raised the money. But I don't think I could do it again. I did try to raise money to bring his production of *Cherry Orchard* over. But I wasn't new anymore. I was new the first time. Also, I was doing something that had not been done since Peter Daubeny died and I was doing it at the Lyttleton, a prestigious theatre. But then I became not very 'interesting' anymore. It's a rocky road to go down but I would rather go down it than not do the work.

REES: I was also thinking how sponsors react to the occasional failure, falling flat on your face. Subsidy can and should allow this. Can sponsorship?

HOLT: I am a very dangerous person to talk to about that. I am blinkered. I believe in the nobility of failure. I don't even believe in the right to fail, but the nobility of it. Do you only measure success and failure financially? I didn't make money on *Tango* but it opened a lot of doors for people who don't normally go to theatre. Many of the audience came because they were Alan Rickman movie fans. They came round to the stage door afterwards and indicated very clearly that they will now go to the theatre in the future. So I see that as a success.

REES: Prestigious companies naturally have a high profile which attracts sponsors. The National, I believe, became the 'Royal National Theatre' exactly to enhance its opportunities for sponsorship?

HOLT: I imagine so.

REES: Small companies, unless they produce work acceptable to the sponsor, such as the classics or educational work, cannot provide that cachet. To find sponsorship to tour new work is the most difficult task. It is untried and it has no regional base. Sponsors like something tried and tested?

HOLT: They do indeed. They want something that gives them a high profile. They cannot have a high profile if the show hasn't.

REES: So a mixed economy – subsidy and sponsorship is the way forward?

HOLT: Yes.

REES: Another buzz word is, 'Appraisal'. It has become part of the Arts Council's new glossary of terms. It is an administrative apparatus to monitor companies' work by outside observers – professional and academic. This provides a means of executing decisions on behalf of the funding body through the conduit of an 'objective' eye, as well as the means of cloaking a decision, even from the observers, including the decision to eliminate you .

HOLT: Appraisal is an awful word. If that is going to become the norm, then okay, providing it is done properly and is executed by people equipped with the skills to make judgements.

I don't think they should get rid of anybody. I think they should do like they do with Drama Schools to accredit them. If you see something that was very good two years ago but is not now, you say in a courteous and delicate way, that this particular area is not as good as it was. And that you should tidy up your act. But the accreditation cannot be removed. That isn't done. You come back another year and hopefully things are better.

So I think there are ways for artists, amongst themselves, to sort things out. I would not object if I were running a subsidised theatre, to half a dozen of my peers coming and looking and, if it was done properly, saying: 'I don't like the way you do this and this is the reason'. I may not buy what they say, if that is how I operate, but I would listen.

REES: There has been argument in recent years whether public subsidy for the performing arts should exist at all. You obviously think it is important?

HOLT: Yes I do. I don't think we are in danger of having too much subsidy like German theatre before the Wall came down. I don't think we are going to have that problem in this country. Dreadful. Dreadful that we have kids unable to go to opera because they cannot afford the price of a ticket. If you can find money to make bombs, to make some of the things we do in this country, which are so utterly, utterly frightful, then I don't see why you cannot find money to fund the Arts.

I do think that the interests of economy have in the past few years taken precedence over the interests of the quality of human life. I do think that. That is true of our hospitals and our education system.

REES: You have gone into commercial management now. Previously with the Peter Hall Company and now for yourself.

HOLT: I'm not commercial. Well I am. But I'm a maverick. I go out and get sponsorship and then raise the rest. Supposing your show costs £300,000 and you have one third from a sponsor, you can go to your investors and say we need £200,000 and the remainder is sponsorship which they know does not have to be recouped. That is attractive to them.

My first show – *Three Sisters* – with the Redgraves, was sponsored by Switzerland. I found two thirds of the money and a third was sponsorship. My second show *Tango* was sponsored by Japan and I had to provide a fifth of the money. My third, Deborah Warner's production of *Electra*, with Fiona Shaw, is being sponsored by France. We are going to Bobigny. They are providing one third of the total pre-production costs.

[*Bobigny is an exciting performance space situated in a suburb of Paris.*]

The investors on *Three Sisters* laughed all the way to the bank. I had money then for *Tango* which I spent. Then I lost it.

REES: Subsidised theatre provides, with increasing regularity, commercial theatre with tried and tested productions. With actors, directors, designers and writers who have cut their teeth in the public sector. I wonder if the cost of the original production plus the invisible cost of the back-up and infrastructure, which any large subsidised institution provides, gets remunerated?

HOLT: The subsidised theatre benefits from the commercial exploitation of their show. There is no conflict of interest. You do a show at the National, where it is tried and tested, done well, and the National gets money out of it.

REES: Do individual actors get more, working for the same show which starts its life at the National, if it moves across the water into the West End?

HOLT: It depends how successful they are. Obviously you earn more if the life of the show is extended. Whether your weekly wage is greater is up to your negotiating position. Everyone always thinks they will, but often they do not. There is no pot of gold.

REES: The stars/leads will earn more than in the subsidised house?

HOLT: They will get a wage as well as royalties. [*A percentage of the Box Office receipts*].

REES: At the National you get a wage and a performance fee. So actors in the middle hierarchy of a cast will probably earn less in a transfer.

HOLT: Probably. That depends on how good their agent is. An agent will make sure they get it rounded up. It would be terrible if they earned less than in a subsided house. And remember there are eight performances in a week so you are working harder for the same money. Everyone else gets the basic Equity West End minimum.

□ *The National Theatre and the RSC work a repertoire system in which an actor does say eight performances in a row and then does not perform for two weeks, whilst they continue to be paid.*

REES: You mentioned Peter Daubeny. You have the same quest to promote international work. What is 'International Theatre'? Does it mean theatre from other countries or is there an approach which is international?

HOLT: I prefer the term 'World Theatre'.

REES: Like World Music?

HOLT: Yes. Something you can make accessible to anybody. You can take a Greek tragedy, *Medea*, played in Japanese, and make it accessible to English speaking people. You can take a little-done American play, O'Neill's *Hairy Ape*, played in German, and play it to an English audience. That is exciting.

However, there is one danger. Quite a lot of people have asked me: 'What's so special about international theatre and working with foreign directors who cannot speak English?' I tell them: 'I have now gone a step further, I am bringing over those directors to work with English actors in English.' 'Why do that?' they say. 'What's different about them?'

Well, they are not different. The reason I work with Robert Strua is not because he is Georgian but because he is very good. If he was English, it would have excited me just as much. Having worked on three productions with Ninangawa, I longed to see how he would work with English actors.

REES: Have Ninagawa and Strua found English actors to be what they expected?

HOLT: They cannot wait to come back. They love working with them.

REES: What features do they value?

HOLT: Discipline. They are very aware of the kamikaze attitude of English actors. Willingness to jump in at the deep end. Don't mind falling flat on their faces. They are engaged by the way English actors are democratic and bolshy and so think for themselves. That they will go from rehearsal and come back next day, showing they have done three or fours work overnight. They come with new things, new ideas. That excites.

REES: The other difference .surely is that actors working with say Strua's Rustaveli company in Georgia are not constantly beckoned by a large TV and Film industry. Actors remain for a long period of time with a single company. They are state employees. When you first brought over the Rustaveli Company, they gave an afternoon's question and answer session at the Roundhouse. They sat in a semi-circle and looking at them, apart from a sense of formidable physical presence, what struck me was their ages, ranging from 35 to 55, with the majority in the 40/45 age range. Completely different to an English company. In the UK, actors, at the height of their powers, would not be exclusively working for a theatre company over a long period of time. The earnings they would make in TV and films would prejudice this. So Ninagawa and Strua are coming to work with market orientated actors.

HOLT: Very much. Very much. I don't say here is an actor. I say here are ten, choose one. And indeed which one wants you. So that's exciting. For instance, Alan Rickman has not been asked to read for a director for a very long time but he was aware Ninagawa knew nothing about our actors. So he was very willing to do this. Ninagawa was absolutely horrified. 'If he reads for me and I want him, he will ask to come over to Tokyo to see my productions, to see if he wants to be directed by me!'

REES: I suppose grass is always greener. But it is an irony that we are struck by the discipline, the willingness to do unusual work and 'be' in the same production that the company work of Ninagawa, Strua and Stein exhibits, work born out of a climate of subsidy. Yet they desire those same virtues and presume that they can best be obtained from the market place.

Jon Catty (left), Dr. Trevor Griffiths.

Jenny Waldman   Graham Cowley

THE MANAGER, THE ACCOUNTANT & THE CHAIRMAN

JON CATTY

GRAHAM COWLEY

DR. TREVOR GRIFFITHS

Graham Cowley, original Administrator of Foco Novo and Joint Stock in the mid-Seventies, General Manager of the Half Moon Theatre in the early Eighties and of the Royal Court Theatre since 1987.

Dr. Trevor Griffiths, Director of Media and Interdisciplinary Studies, Faculty of Humanities and Teacher Education, University of North London and Chair of the Board of Foco Novo during the Eighties.

Jon Catty, Accountant for the Royal Court Theatre, 1966-76, subsequently started his own accountancy firm and is now production accountant for twelve shows currently running in the West End. He was also accountant and auditor for Foco Novo.

The interview took place in the offices of the Royal Court Theatre.

REES: Jon, you work as a production accountant with commercial theatre companies in the West End. What are the primary financial differences, the different motives and goals, between commercial and subsidised theatre production?

CATTY: Primarily, the objective of a commercial manager has to be to make a profit from the shows he puts on. Obviously, he wants to do something good as well, but since he has to raise his money from backers, he is obliged to put on only those shows which will have a reasonable chance of making a profit. To do that he has to run a show for as long as possible to maximise the financial investment. One of the objectives of subsidised theatre is to be successful at the box office, but it is not the primary objective. The primary objective must be to do interesting plays, depending on the particular programme of the theatre concerned and the budget that company has. Subsidised theatre is not obliged to put on shows for long runs.

REES: Do subsidised theatres who originate a production, which is subsequently put on by a commercial management, get from that exploitation a return on their original budget for that show?

COWLEY: The answer is a great deal less, if the theatre sells the show to a management, than if they exploit it themselves. To do this, you can either keep it running longer at the original theatre or you can transfer it yourselves. To do your own transfer, a subsidised theatre needs a commercial subsidiary company because subsidised theatres are usually of non-profit making charitable status. We already had such a company, Royal Court Theatre Productions, sitting on a shelf, ready to be used. When we wanted to exploit Caryl Churchill's *Serious Money*, we thought why don't we, instead of selling the show off to a commercial management, do it ourselves? It's just like putting a play on and we do that all the time. The only difference was that we had to raise the money and produce the show in somebody else's theatre. In fact, raising the money was a piece of cake. It came in in about a week.

CATTY: The Royal Court is an ideal sized theatre, 400 seats, to assess what a successful run might mean in a small, 600 seater West End theatre. Going from 200 seats at the Tricycle or the Hampstead, to 600 in the West End is a very different proposition and does not allow that judgement to be made so easily.

REES: Are wage structures very different in the West End in comparison to subsidised theatre?

CATTY: There is a bigger range in the West End. The stars get much more, but the minimums are roughly the same, depending on which particular contract the subsidised theatre operates. The minimums are around £220.

COWLEY: This year we are paying £225 across the board.

REES: However illustrious a name is in lights on the front of the theatre?

COWLEY: Yes.

REES: When your shows go into the West End what happens?

COWLEY: A completely different situation. You have to acknowledge that, because a management, which could be ourselves in the form of our subsidiary, is exploiting a play, it is doing so in order to make money. No need to be coy about that and pretend the show is still at the Court. There is no justification for preserving an equal pay situation, if there are parts in the play that are bigger than others, or actors in the production of different status in the business. So a different wage scale comes into operation.

CATTY: The star in the West End expects to get up to ten per cent of the gross weekly box office returns.

REES: Many of the subsidised companies, and I imagine many subsidised theatres, adopt a policy of equal wages, either through a principle of equity or, more probably, as a means of eking out budgets which never expect to be augmented with profit from the commercial run of a show. However, it is illuminating that, when transferring a show, the same actors, all paid across the board one week at the Royal Court, can expect the next week in the West End to experience a hierarchic wage structure, as a result of 200 extra seats.

CATTY: It is to do with the marketability of each individual actor and how good their agent is. And the intention then is to run the show for as long as possible.

REES: Graham, you were administrator of both Joint Stock and Foco Novo at the same time, operating from an office in the basement of David Aukin's house in St John's Wood. What are the main differences in running a touring theatre company and running a building-based theatre?

COWLEY: We do tour from time to time here, but obviously the building is the main difference. If you are building-based, you have a building to look after, and so you have a much bigger staff. A touring company is pretty free. It is rather a luxurious situation. You are one remove from the exigencies of the box office because when touring you get a guarantee from each theatre you visit.

REES: However there is a maximum level of guarantee on the circuits. Guarantees rarely contain an element of profit. They are there to cover costs.

COWLEY: On the small scale circuit, the venue seating capacities are such that the guarantee far exceeds what could come in from the box office. There are so many bits of different subsidy coming into play.

□ *The guarantee is contributed to from the subsidy of the venue/theatre, the local Arts Association and the incoming company is itself subsidised.*

Running a theatre is much more complex because there are more people. You run a touring company with three permanent staff. Here there are 35 people. That means management skills. You don't need much management skill to run a touring theatre.

GRIFFITHS: The Arts Council wouldn't agree with you! One of the things we found when we were touring was that the interface with the building we were visiting was actually a very difficult part of the process. Quite often the loyalty of the building staff was to their own programme, and we seemed to get the sense from our companies that we were regarded as cuckoos in the nest.

COWLEY: I think you have put your finger on a real difficulty about touring. We find we have to make an exceptionally conscious effort to welcome a touring company to avoid those things Trevor has mentioned. You take it for granted in your own productions that the commitment and pride is there. A touring show is totally separate in its origin. I agree the welcoming is often not done.

REES: Trevor, when you first came onto the Board of Foco Novo in the late Seventies, what were the factors that most immediately made an impression on you of how a touring company had to work?

GRIFFITHS: I think it was the relationship with the Arts Council. I did not know whether that was peculiar to the position Foco Novo found itself in when I arrived. In retrospect, the arms length principle was being used *to keep us* at arms length from the Arts Council, rather than to keep government interference *from us* at arms length! I always had the sense that we were operating in a fog which was not our fog, but someone else's fog, and that was difficult.

This also goes back to Graham's management skills. Small scale companies cannot offer the financial skills, book keeping skills, on the day-to-day level that a larger organisation can. This was the result of the level of salaries we were able to offer and, therefore, the lack of experience and training which people we could employ came with. This inevitably led to problems at the financial level.

We would come to the moment when we wanted to commit ourselves to a project and the Arts Council demurred, and you did not know what the 'urr' was about. But you did know there were a whole range of people at the Arts Council with very sophisticated financial skills, who were actually keeping themselves at arms length, and even though they saw the problems, they were not going to tell us what they were.

REES: To return to Graham's three personnel running a touring company. You have to remember they were each doing two or three jobs. That's how administrators learnt their trade. Companies like Foco Novo were a training resource.

COWLEY: Yes, that is inevitable. Given the funding structure, working for a touring company is an early step on the ladder. The difficulty in a small situation is that there is nobody else to learn from. In the case of Foco Novo, there was Roland who provided the continuity over the years. But that's not universally true in all touring companies and small theatres.

GRIFFITHS: We did not expect the administrators to stay more than two years. We got ambitious people who wanted Foco Novo on their CV, and they wanted to move on to a more permanent post. You had to build that into your calculations. If they were any good, somebody else would want them. If they were bad, you would not want them for more than two years.

COWLEY: It is all too rare for the Arts Council to provide guidance. Jean Bullwinkle was an exception, an example of an officer who would guide you. She made herself available to be constructive, help the administrator grow, even without formal training, and that availability is all too rare at the Arts Council.

REES: The Arts Council used to be the major, if not the only subsidy provider. Now it is one among a number. From what sources and institutions does subsidy come?

COWLEY: The sources of funding are many and varied. There are quite a lot of statutory sources, most of which are easier to come by if you have a building, because you are based somewhere. Therefore, there is at least a ghost of a chance of obtaining local authority support. In London there was the GLC and now there is LBGS [*London Borough Grants Scheme*] and LAB [*London Arts Board – formerly Greater London Arts*]. There are also Social Service funding agencies. For example, if you do a play about HIV, there are Health Service agencies who will provide funding. Many companies started their life through the Manpower Services Commission or the Enterprise Allowance. The drawback with the Enterprise Allowance is that it only lasts a year or so.

Then there is the private sector. Charitable Trusts and Foundations. It is practically a full-time job to keep applications going into Trusts. They create their own funding criteria. You have to study such criteria very carefully and make sure your application fits their guidelines. Then there is commercial sponsorship. There are Patronage schemes, again much easier to set up if you are a building, rather than a touring company. Theatres also set up Friends organisations.

CATTY: Charity and Foundation money is only possible to obtain if you are a building-based company, almost impossible for touring companies.

REES: Is it true that touring companies depend far more on a single source of funding in comparison to building-based companies – namely the Arts Council and its various arteries?

GRIFFITHS: Yes it would be true, although there are other sources, but these originate from the Arts Council via Regional Arts Associations. One of the things which always struck me was how much effort we were required to put into chasing commercial sponsorship as a touring company. Yet for all the reasons Graham has mentioned, we knew that the chance of getting anything was very limited. But we had to be seen to be doing it, so that the Arts Council could satisfy its political masters, that they in turn were seen to be asking us to do it. Quite a lot of time and money was spent on this exercise producing a glossy brochure and employing extra staff when, rationally, it would have been much better to spend the money on an extra actor. We got samples of Caribbean rum for one show!

REES: It was solely for audiences on the opening night of John Constable's *Black Mas*, a show about carnival! No money was forthcoming.

GRIFFITHS: A lot of effort went into that!

REES: Ironically, I believe Foco Novo was one of the earliest touring company recipients of sponsorship – from the NUM – for our tours of the Welsh, Yorkshire and Scottish minefields. This was in the mid-Seventies, long before sponsorship was a favoured idea. But I don't suppose non-commercial financial support from that quarter counts as sponsorship!

Yet in 1987, when we did a show about South Africa – Michael Picardie's *The Cape Orchard* – I wrote to forty companies who had recently devolved their business from that country. I congratulated them on their principled stance and welcomed their sponsorship of a play which echoed their action. Hardly any replied. Those that did said they never got involved in this sort of sponsorship, and subsequently I discovered that many of them continued to trade in South Africa under a different name!

COWLEY: I have made fundraisers redundant here because they were not even raising their own salaries. Not that the work they were doing was valueless, not at all. But a recession is an impossible time to raise money from private sources.

GRIFFITHS: It takes a special kind of commercial sponsor to want to be associated with the kind of work the Court produces.

COWLEY: We have attracted commercial sponsors, quite substantial ones, but they have been windfalls. We stumbled on them rather than it being the result of long and patient wooing, the kind of work implied in having a sponsorship officer. I think the chase after sponsorship as such, as opposed to other private sector sources, has been a wild goose chase for companies like Foco Novo. A complete waste of time and effort. The Arts Council should have known that.

GRIFFITHS: I think that they did.

COWLEY: It was a cynical exercise.

REES: Do you think, given the political bias of potential sponsors, that the content of plays, which theatre companies like Foco Novo presented, would have prevented commercial companies from considering sponsoring such work?

CATTY: Yes. Most commercial companies would not want to be associated with a company that was known to produce plays with a radical viewpoint.

GRIFFITHS: The commercial company is looking for a publicity bonus and enhanced image, so there is no benefit in financing a theatre company that might be critical or controversial. You couldn't easily take your corporate guests to some of the more rough-and-ready venues we toured to.

REES: When sponsors do provide, they expect a high profile in the company's publicity. As a result, the public often believe the sponsor has paid for the whole production when, in fact, they may have only paid a fraction towards the cost. Do you think that the Arts Council or the Drama Panel ever considered withdrawing subsidy from companies because they objected to the content of the work in any way? Do you think such an equation ever entered their thinking during the Thatcher years?

CATTY: I don't believe it was specifically the content of the work that caused companies to have their subsidy withdrawn. However, I do think that the Arts Council became gradually more craven in accepting the prevailing Thatcherite economic principles and that this fact led to some companies losing their grant.

COWLEY: One might not agree with all their decisions about artistic quality, value for money and administrative skills, but I think those are the criteria they use.

GRIFFITHS: There was clearly a move away from political companies towards more performance/live art orientated companies, which did match the atmosphere of the times. But I suspect that there would have been all kinds of complex mixtures of pressures pointing in that direction. I doubt if anything as overt as the equation you are suggesting came into it.

REES: An increasing amount of documentation arrived on our desks from the Arts Council in the Eighties accompanied by a new vocabulary of terms. Apparently only since the last election have the Labour Party finally permitted the use of one example of the new vernacular – targeting – into its own publications!

GRIFFITHS: That kind of language, I used to experience in a meeting at the Council for National Academic Awards, only to arrive at a Foco Novo Board meeting to hear the same language being used by the Arts Council!

REES: A member of the Drama Panel told me they were asked onto the Panel for their particular expertise on theatre, yet they found they were spending a lot of time talking about business plans.

COWLEY: The emphasis on sharpening up your act was bloody uncomfortable at the time. But a business plan for an organisation like this is a good thing. In the climate of shrinking subsidy, if you simply regard the application of a business plan as a threat, not as an opportunity, then it is depressing and your own morale suffers. We made ourselves see the business plan as an opportunity.

Going through the exercise makes you focus on things that previously you had not focussed on. We discovered that in establishing bar prices, we thought we were competing with the pubs in the area. Actually that was a nonsense. We were competing with other West End theatres where the bar prices are much higher. So we raised our prices.

CATTY: You need the size of administration to cope with a business plan.

COWLEY: Exactly. You have to be large enough to cope with the concept of a business plan. And to put it into action when you've done it.

GRIFFITHS: We were unsuccessful in achieving our three year Franchise Funding when the scheme was first started. But I know other companies, who were successful at that time, who are now feeling that they are in the exact position we were in, because they do not have the expertise and financial control larger organisations have. They are now terrified that when the next plan comes along, they are going to have to reveal financial problems which will mean they will be cast off.

In this kind of scenario the Royal Court is big enough to take care of itself. But for a small operation it is much more difficult to jump through those hoops and do those plans realistically.

REES: Since the introduction of the three year Franchise Funding scheme, five companies have lost that status of which we were one, twelve have gained that status. The five who lost it were, with one exception, new play producing companies. Of the twelve new ones the percentage is weighed against new writing. The most recent plays of Paines Plough, Shared Experience and the David Glass Mime Company were dramatisations of novels. Two of these three adaptations were written by writers – Nigel Gearing and John Constable – whom Foco Novo first introduced as playwrights, with a production of their own play, *Snap* and *Black Mas* respectively.

GRIFFITHS: The last years of Foco Novo consisted entirely of meetings to write Appraisals and business plans. That's my recollection. Nothing but Appraisals and business plans. What I enjoyed was going to see a show which we somehow produced in the middle of this.

CATTY: You wondered whether the Arts Council judged the work on the business plan rather than the show you did.

COWLEY: A company of your scale with that few people working for it, having to produce the same amount of documentation as a large company, was set an impossible task.

REES: That was the original point I was raising. You are doubling and trebling up on jobs all the time and not concentrating on the things even the funder would say was most important – the real work.

GRIFFITHS: Because people get so tired, there comes a point where exhaustion is reached. This happens to your permanent staff, the volunteer Board, and to the goodwill of your accountants. When Foco Novo finally stopped, although it was very sad, it was a great relief since we were not banging our heads against that particular wall any more. The artistic endeavour had become subordinate to survival and the preparation of Arts Council plans. In fact the planning called for was not real, it was the re-arrangement of deck chairs on the Titanic!

CATTY: The Arts Council wasted that period of time and the resources they had by only funding Foco Novo and Joint Stock to do two shows in a year. With a little more money they could have had companies working three quarters of the year. Just 30/40 per cent more could have achieved this. You already had the core costs of the office and small staff and that seemed to me the greatest waste of all. In the last year of Foco Novo, 1988, we had funds to do only one production.

GRIFFITHS: At one point we were positively encouraged by the Arts Council to find co-productions until someone woke up to the fact that this concept was based on double subsidy. The artistic reasons for co-productions were good, but suddenly for the Arts Council the economic reasons were not good, because now they were being asked to demonstrate value for money. So they changed the policy and we were back to the cost effectiveness argument.

REES: We followed the success of our Haymarket Theatre, Leicester co-production of *Bloody Poetry* in 1984 with one of Genet's *Deathwatch* with the

Birmingham Rep in 1985. This also worked very well and Birmingham agreed to co-produce Tunde Ikoli's *The Lower Depths* in 1986. It had a cast of ten and so needed the additional financial input. It seems that in the light of the changed policy on co-productions, the incoming Artistic Director of the Rep felt that it was unwise to honour what we considered was an agreement. So we lost the co-production and thereby, committed to the show as we were, started to accumulate the deficit which became our albatross.

GRIFFITHS: I remember the most famous disputation was over the question of whether Croydon was part of London as far as touring went.

CATTY: You couldn't visit Cardiff and count it as playing weeks because it was in the Principality of Wales. [*Wales had its own Arts Council which in turn received money from the Arts Council of Great Britain*].

GRIFFITHS: The Croydon question was resolved by the Arts Council stating that the Ashcroft, Croydon was not in London but the Warehouse Theatre, Croydon was! It was a way of indicating to us that we should not go into middle scale touring – the Ashcroft. Your kind of theatre, the Arts Council implied, is the Warehouse. A visit there is fine by us, and you can count it as an out of London touring date. This was part of the arms length principle which would never say, 'we don't want you to do this,' but finds all kinds of other methods of indicating what the Arts Council does not want you to do.

COWLEY: This was a misjudgement on the part of the Arts Council. This whole scale argument made no sense. There were other companies, like Temba, who were discouraged from going into the middle scale. Really discouraged from it. And now there is utter shortage of new drama on the middle scale. The Arts Council Touring Department, notably while Jodi Myers was there, were absolutely desperate for good quality plays.

CATTY: Not new plays.

COWLEY: Given the fact that it was difficult to get new plays on in the middle scale, I would have thought that the companies who got the bookings should have been encouraged.

CATTY: The five companies who have come off Franchise Funding were new play companies. That is not just the Arts Council's rejection of new plays. It is their reaction to the fact that they know the audiences for such new plays are dwindling and more conservative.

REES: Do you like the renewable three year Franchise Funding scheme, Graham?

COWLEY: I have never really taken much notice of it.

REES: To us, as you can understand, it loomed as the major factor.

GRIFFITHS: We were at the beginning of the experiment and it was clear there was an agenda in which some were being rolled off and some were being rolled on.

We put a proposal forward for our three year Funding Franchise that we would like to take modern classics on the middle scale and to combine this with the kind of techniques we had honed on the small scale. That did not fit into the correct pigeon hole either. If you wanted to get out of the pigeon hole, you were not allowed to, and if you stayed in the pigeon hole, you would be shot.

COWLEY: The annual increases in subsidy built into this scheme, were so microscopic they were meaningless. Granted you knew you were going to be there in three years, but you would hope that anyway. So the security it offered was not very important.

GRIFFITHS: When they first introduced Franchise Funding, it was a method of getting rid of what they perceived as dead wood at a time of great financial stringency. Newspapers tell me since that time more money has been put into the system and, therefore, has reduced the pressure. There is now a cushion. The real problem, in 1987, was there was no cushion. The only way to change was to do something, and that something was to cut companies, a bureaucratic way of asking people to commit suicide rather than having to murder them. Once the financial situation improved, even slightly, it was no longer important. That's my reading of the situation.

REES: Do you fit the correct pigeon hole? We did Bernard Pomerance's *Quantrill in Lawrence* produced solely at the ICA – no tour – as an additional show to our programme on the money we earned from our cut of the box office receipts from Pomerance's *The Elephant Man* Broadway production. The Arts Council criticised us for not touring it. It was a thirteen-hander and would have proved far too expensive. Then they said to us: 'You did three shows last year, why are you not doing three this year?' It seemed such gall when we had showed enterprise.

GRIFFITHS: That was in the nature of a windfall, and was not going to be repeated. If you only do two shows in a year, you are in an entirely different situation to a theatre producing eight. That's four years of Foco Novo work in one year! So the perception of your work is different. If you do one good one and one bad one, they stick out equally. A theatre doing eight shows can obliterate its bad by its good shows.

REES: Robert Petty, then of the Midlands Arts Centre, was on our Appraisal team in 1987. When he discovered what the Arts Council had decided about our future in the next year, he wrote to Ian Brown, the Arts Council Drama Director, protesting at our treatment and asking whether their Appraisal had

271

been a complete waste of time. He said the suspicion has to be that this Appraisal was not what the Arts Council wanted to hear. So it was ignored. He asked: 'Had they discovered something that eluded us?'

COWLEY: The great value of the Appraisal is that you are talking to your peers, who, because they work in the theatre, may well understand your problems better than the officers at the Arts Council. There are moments during the process when you can have a really sensible, honest discussion with people who understand the issues. But the final version does not always reflect those discussions. If you have an Appraisal team who are very tenacious with what they want to say the final document can be very valuable.

REES: In our case, Robert Petty's remarks stand for themselves.

CATTY: The Treasury has set aside funds within the Arts Council grant this year so that the recommendations of the various Panels and Appraisal teams are implemented, instead of lack of money always remaining the excuse for inactivity.

REES: Are we taking the American route to the funding and support of the Arts? And would it alter the kind of plays produced?

COWLEY: There is such a resistance by the British public to contribute to theatre, except through the box office. It would be an incredibly long term project actually to turn the English system into the American funding system, however much the government would wish to do that. The Arts Council was at one stage bringing over American fundraisers to demonstrate the infallibility of the pyramid-selling approach to private contributions. When you listened to them talk it was plausible, and rather exciting in a way. You thought: 'We can crack this and get in first and nab all the people who will give money.' But actually nobody wants to do that. Because it feels very foreign to the English theatre-going public.

CATTY: The American system is based on tax relief. In the UK, tax relief is only available on donations of over £600. That is quite a lot of money for an individual. It is not even attractive for the rich because, with the tax rates so low, there is no incentive to give. And there is no ethic of doing that here either, as Graham was saying. Occasionally there is a case, such as the Young Vic, when they were in trouble and they made a particularly good appeal, raising £250,000 with lots of people giving £100.

COWLEY: The one-off appeal works. People are generous *once*. But after a couple of years you run out of people who will give.

So I would say that the Arts Council might have toyed with the American approach to supporting the Arts but it has changed. The last two annual grant-in-aid awards were really quite substantial. Whether it was an election ploy or whatever, it was still money – subsidy.

GRIFFITHS: In America there are quite a lot of theatres heavily into subscription ticket sales. That has never really taken off here. I couldn't see people taking out a subscription to the Court.

COWLEY: We have never seriously considered the idea for the reasons you stated. When you look at theatre abroad in the States and Australia, subscription sales have an effect on the work you produce. We took a show to the Sydney Theatre Company a few years ago and their funding pattern is entirely different from ours. They got only a small proportion from public sources and a high proportion from private sources, so they relied heavily on their subscription audience.

REES: So the choice of material in their seasons was accordingly....

COWLEY: Had to be conservative. In order to attract people under their subscription schemes.

GRIFFITHS: Audiences are becoming much more compartmentalised. There are clearly people who go the ICA, who would never dream of going to the Royal Court, and vice versa. People who go only to the Drill Hall or the Oval House might visit the Court if there was a Sarah Daniels on. Otherwise they would think the Court had nothing to offer them. That segmentation is increasing. Just look at the ageing of a West End audience in comparison say to the audience at the Drill Hall.

COWLEY: What we are sorriest about is that we cannot hang onto the ageing audience, quite honestly, because they are the ones with a bit of money! But the audience profile is still young here which is good. But we are regretful that our audiences sometimes view the Court as a stepping stone before they go to the National.

REES: The National Arts and Media Strategy paper, I read in my newspaper, is recommending that the new Department of National Heritage, which has subsumed the old Office of Arts and Libraries, should seek alternative entrepreneurial sources of funding – loans, guarantees and capital injections. This surely is an American approach. It also proposes, I learn, that there should be new contractual arrangements between 'clients' and funder with the basis for the terms of funding being openly stated. I quote from my newspaper, 'the clients ability to fall in with the Department's overall objectives,' and 'resources will go to those who best meet these needs.' This would seem to get rid of any myth about the arms length principle.

CATTY: I don't think the arms length policy ever existed. It was a bit of nonsense. What does it mean? That the Arts Council will never interfere in what is done? On what basis do they give money? It has never been stated.

GRIFFITHS: Nudges and winks not absolute statements. If one had had a clear statement – you can do this with your money or you may not do that – it would have been of great benefit. Policy was so obscure that until you came up against it, you did not know it was there – like Croydon being London or not. If it was said, 'we have a history of national culture and we want all the theatres this year to do Shakespeare,' we would all be appalled. But we would all know where we were! The Court would get Timberlake Wertenbaker to write a version of one of the Bard's plays and Foco Novo would have got Tunde Ikoli to write a version of *The Tempest.* You'd have done that because you knew the rules of the game. My experience has been that the rules constantly change, the goalposts are moved, not by those whom you are talking to in the room, but by somebody else who you will never meet. So if the terms of funding become openly stated between funded and funder, I am all for it. I would welcome it!

REES: A well-known politician came, a few years ago, to the local church to address the people of Peckham. Standing in front of the altar, he described how he made and lost a million before he was 26, and went on to make another million. His advice to everyone was: have more than one job and always clear your desk at the end of each day. Afterwards, looking around at the faces of the locals during the book signing, I wondered what they were making of advice which was about as appropriate as our company was receiving from advisers in the Arts world at that time.

Foco Novo did enjoy a number of years of funding from the Arts Council. But when they decided that companies must find an equal amount of their income from sources other than subsidy, and it was clear commercial sponsors favoured particular kinds of work rather than others, then certain companies lost out. The Eighties was a seductive decade in which form came to dominate content. The agenda for the Arts was altered without resort to heavy-handed tactics. Pressure, administrative manoeuvres and the introduction of the values and taste of the market place did the trick.

This policy was politically motivated. Conventional political language was not employed in arguing the case; in its place a new vernacular was created. As Jon Catty said, the Arts Council and their advisers were craven in accepting the prevailing Thatcherite economic principles. Instead of keeping government at arms length, funding bodies became the arm of government policy. Foco Novo could not conform to the new priorities, so we went under.

THE ADMINISTRATOR

JENNY WALDMAN

Administrator for Foco Novo 1983/86, Arts Council Drama Officer 1986/89, now Director of Arts Centre Projects, South Bank Centre.

REES: In the Seventies and the early Eighties, there was an entirely different climate in the Arts compared to the end of the Eighties and Nineties. What do you think are the main differences?

WALDMAN: Administrator of Foco Novo was my first job in the early Eighties and so my awareness of arts funding occurred at the moment the circumstances were starting to change. Change occurs in a cyclical, not in a sudden, rapid way. It goes round and round repeating itself. According to whether devolution is in or out, or how important the regions as a factor are, is in or out.

It is very hard to have new ideas. Usually people have ideas they think are new but really they are fifteen years old. They don't realise this because they are a part of a new generation. It is also to do with the whole structure of funding bodies and Government – trying to second guess Government views. The Arts Council for quite a long time now has been fighting for its survival, concerned to remain in the forefront and not be overtaken either on the one hand by the Regional Arts Associations, now the Regional Arts Boards, or the Government on the other. It is caught betwixt and between.

REES: You have named one big change. The Arts Council, from being a primary or even the sole source of funding, is now one among many equals.

WALDMAN: That's an enormous change. And the many, it is now one among, includes the commercial sector, sponsorship, Trusts, Foundations, donations, ticket sales – all of those kind of other income sources which for emerging theatre companies make up a far smaller proportion of their income. In the late Eighties, the Arts Council decided that theatre companies should derive 50% of their income from sources other than their funding. Suddenly that was a decision. It was a nice equal equation but there was no particular logic to it. It had not been mentioned before.

REES: Was that a principle which the Arts Council adopted and made absolutely clear or did it develop internally within the Council?

WALDMAN: It developed internally. It was made clear first to building-based companies who had more of a chance of achieving it. And much later to touring companies. And even with touring companies a lot of exceptions were made. Some heard sooner than others. A company like Foco Novo or IOU would never have a chance of making up 50% of their turnover from earned income.

REES: You came to Foco Novo as Administrator in 1983. What were the factors that most made an impression upon you about how a touring company had to work?

WALDMAN: The main thing which intrigued me was that Foco Novo, like other companies who created new and challenging work and who sought to disseminate that as widely as possible, had got caught in a problem where the demand to tour was regarded by the Arts Council as equally important as the desire to produce new work. The Arts Council was funding Foco Novo both to tour and do new work. Yet the company had grown in its artistic ambitions, as most companies of its generation had. It wanted to do things that were technically very difficult to put on in smaller halls around the country. [*Small scale touring circuit*] It also wanted to go to larger theatres. The economics of that were becoming unviable and nobody was admitting that because nobody could.

Foco Novo could not say to the Arts Council, 'all we can do is tour three weeks and then play three weeks in London', because it feared that the Council would cut it. It probably would have done. So the company was struggling to create an eight weeks required tour without there being enough places that could provide the technical and financial resources to make it worthwhile.

The Company was also caught in a change of attitude towards theatre that was part of the shift in funding. The Arts Council created, through its funding of touring companies, a loose network of venues interested in taking that work. These venues were funded by the Regional Arts Associations and the Local Authorities. Having their own funding, the venues began to develop an autonomous attitude with their own idea of what they wanted to do and what their audiences wanted. In effect creating their own artistic policy. These soon diverged from the artistic policies of those touring companies funded by the Arts Council, for which many of the venues were originally created.

This autonomous policy making, combined with their own financial pressures to generate larger audiences, made the venues seek out more 'populist' work. For example, ATC and Cheek By Jowl, doing Shakespeare and the classics. That was an enormous change.

REES: When the Fairfield Hall, Croydon booked our production of Brecht's *Edward II*, it was, they said, because the title was 'royal' so they could sell it to their audiences!

WALDMAN: Shared Experience did it by doing novels that were well known. Even on this scale, you needed a known name or writer to sell a show. Preferably a dead writer.

At the same time, to compensate for the higher charging shows, the venues needed cheap product as well. They paid a lot less for student shows and companies who did not operate Equity rates. Red Shift, before they got funding, and a lot of the mime companies, with very little funding, went out at much lower fees. They were cheaper.

So, many of the older and original touring companies, through their natural artistic growth, ambition and interest, priced themselves out of the market, both financially and technically. At the same time they were doing work that was not drawing in large crowds. Perhaps this was a development that had to happen.

REES: Sponsorship has become a very important way of raising money for the Arts. Michael Billington said in *The Guardian* that it was not now the icing on the cake but a substantial part of funding. Where do you see us going?

WALDMAN: I think people in sponsorship are now very dismal about the immediate prospects. The recession. Companies are pulling in their horns and spending money even more carefully than before. They need to know very clearly the benefits they will get for their money. The negotiations are getting tougher and tougher. A colleague of mine has just come back from the States and says arts organisations there are very worried indeed because sponsorship is drying up. And there it plays a much larger proportion of arts funding.

It is quite hard to see the logic in which it is said that sponsorship should be the icing on the cake, but every company should try and get more and more of it. I don't think there is a company in Britain, who once they have developed sponsorship sufficiently to put it into their budget, can really manage without it. Nobody's budget has icing on it! You could say that the National puts on an educational tour of one of its shows as a result of finding sponsorship. I don't think educational tours by the National are icing. They are an essential part of what the National is doing. Arts Council policy is quite muddled about sponsorship for small companies. If the middle and small scale companies had banded together and said in concert, "it is not worth our while chasing sponsorship, we are not the kind of companies who will be found sponsorable," then I think the Arts Council would probably have taken that position seriously.

When I was administrator of Foco Novo, I went to see Mary Allen at ABSA [*Association of Business Sponsorship of the Arts*]. She has now been appointed Deputy Secretary General of the Arts Council. She said then that there are some companies, and Foco Novo is one of them, for whom it is not worth making the effort to find sponsorship, not worth employing someone to chase it.

Such a touring company goes to different places in the country at different times. You cannot say to a potential sponsor with an HQ in Nottingham that you promise always regularly to visit that city. You cannot know that. Such a company plays to 150 to 500 a night. That is not worth the sponsors while. You can get a number of companies to give you a few hundred pounds from their charity fund. You can call that sponsorship if you like. But actually persuading sponsors to part with big money because they might think it a market advantage to associate their name with a small scale touring company producing new plays is a crazy prospect.

But whatever Mary Allen said, the problem is some companies got it. Woman's Theatre Group got a number of hundreds that added up to a thousand or so from WH Smith and Marks & Spencers. Paines Plough did a little spurt, often through personal contact. If you have dinner with the right person you could get £5000. But then you expect to get it next year and you don't.

REES: Given the political bias of sponsors, would the content of plays companies such as Foco Novo presented, have prevented them from considering sponsoring our work?

WALDMAN: Possibly. Where the content might have been off-putting is in the context of a sponsor paying for a staff social occasion. Foco Novo shows would not have provided the 'jolly' event required for that.

It's like the British Council who used to take abroad only companies containing one of four names in their title – National, Royal, Oxford and Cambridge. That's all changed now, but it still helps enormously.

REES: Sponsorship officers are very well paid. Do they get back in sponsorship what they cost the company?

WALDMAN: There is always a tension in arts organisations between those who do the art, who are three a penny, and those getting the money in, who are hard to come by and so are sometimes paid more. Some companies get it wrong and pay sponsorship officers more than the Artistic Director. Meeting the actors after the show cost nothing but once you start offering sponsor hospitality, parties, free drinks and tickets, those are actual costs and mount up. There are some organisations, like the Royal Opera House and here at the South Bank, for whom it would be stupid not to offer sponsors the space for corporate entertainment.

Smaller companies, with only two full-time staff, cannot afford to devote half that company's resource to chasing very small and annually variable if nil amounts of money. Foco Novo got money from *The Elephant Man* and from the GLC. If you had started building that into budget assumptions it would have been quite dangerous.

REES: The Arts Council is by no means the only funding organisation to refer to those it supports as 'clients'. Normally in the business world, which the arts world wishes to emulate, a client is the one with the clout and the money who wants a job done. Clients normally employ. So the Arts Council is turning on its head a very fundamental fact about the basic relationship between funder and funded.

WALDMAN: It should actually make it possible to get the relationship on another footing. As a word it should project that the client has some power which we know most companies do not have. What else can we use?

REES: I don't take to the new vernacular, so I have no formula word for funder and funded or giver and receiver. But I do find it contradictory if a word is used in a manner which is meant to follow the relationships found in the business world being, employed in this way.

WALDMAN: Mary Allen of the Arts Council thinks there should be the kind of relationship between client and funder where there is negotiation. You negotiate what the funding is for, what is expected of both sides. This would be clearly set down on paper and then funders could assess you on the basis of what both parties know. Rather than now, where something is left far too vague or is kept secret or the funder changes its mind without letting you know.

The main problem was that the Arts Council was not being straight with Foco Novo. They wanted more touring, but they did not spell it out. They should have been specific and said we want so many weeks touring and so many shows for that money. They found it embarrassing to say we want you to use less actors and do more touring weeks.

REES: Do you think the Arts Council ever considered withdrawing subsidy from companies because they objected to the content of the work?

WALDMAN: No, not at all. One of the things which impressed me when I worked at the Arts Council was that the political nature of a company's work was never an issue.

REES: What do you think will happen now that the Regional Arts Boards are receiving some 150 devolved former clients of the Arts Council? This is going to change the landscape enormously. Some large orchestras have complained that they do not want judgement from local Arts Boards but from the central Advisory Panels of the Arts Council which contain, they consider, the proper expertise for artistic judgement. They say: 'What will bookers in Europe think if we are not funded from central Government?"

WALDMAN: I don't agree with that. You don't refuse to book the Chicago Symphony Orchestra on the basis that they receive city funding rather than government funding. You book them because they are a brilliant orchestra. In Spain and Germany, arts organisations are funded locally and are of the highest excellence. It's a red herring. What it shows is a mistrust of the 'local' because this country is so centralist. London is so important and the Arts Council is a central body.

What is really worrying large arts organisations, like orchestras, is that if you are a middle sized fish in a very large pond, there is always the opportunity that you could gain more money and be upwardly mobile. But if you are a middle sized fish in a rather small pond you look big. Your money is stuck at a limit and can only shrink, not grow.

REES: Will the Regional Arts Board's be independent of the Arts Council or will they execute the policy of the Council in the regions?

WALDMAN: With David Mellor as Minister of Heritage, it will be up in the air. In the long run the Arts Council will diminish more and more. Central Government will take on responsibilities for the larger organisations and oversee the funding of the rest through the Regional Arts Boards.

REES: An example of one of your cyclical changes! Foco Novo, along with other companies were, put on 'Project Status'. That is they could, like anyone else, apply for a Project grant. Have there been recent priorities for Project funding?

WALDMAN: Project funding developed a set of priorities which revolved around approaches to theatre not well represented within the majority of theatre, which receives most of the funding. New plays per se were already being done in some of that majority – Regional Rep. studios, the RSC – producing playwrights Foco Novo had often discovered and helped on in their careers. The kind of innovations that Project funding prioritised were innovations in form rather than content. Text is used by the vast majority, so the argument went: 'Let's support other forms.' Although that does not mean Project funding did not support text-based work. I think it was right to change the balance in a climate dominated by text.

REES: This seeming division into text and non-text based work is most bizarre. Theatre is the collaborative art par excellence. Many of the early companies did not just do texts. They introduced the concept of collaboration between forms. It has not just suddenly happened. For example, Foco Novo, who usually did do texts, also produced something like the Music Theatre piece *The Ass* with Kate and Mike Westbrook. Performance art and visual theatre also has a 'text'.

WALDMAN: I profoundly disagreed with the decision to cut Joint Stock and Foco Novo. I was not a party to the decision. I thought it would have been best to renegotiate what you were doing. The basis on which any company is funded is that it is doing excellent work, providing a resource to the artistic community and is providing excellent product on the scale you work, for appropriate numbers of people.

Joint Stock and Foco Novo were not getting in the audiences in sufficient numbers because you were both concentrating on doing larger and larger shows. You had all reached an age that going on one night stands around the country, for however many weeks at a time, was not what you wanted to do. You wanted to concentrate your work on London where you saw your artistic excellence being greatest, and on a few key centres and audiences who genuinely appreciated what you were doing and were keen to have you back. Centres who were able to offer you a run of several nights, so that the work was seen at its best.

With regard to the other two criteria – excellence and resource – maybe with regard to providing a resource for theatre, you were not quite fitting the criteria, doing only two shows in a year, not doing writers' workshops etc, whatever you could contribute as Foco Novo the resource. You liked to use your energy concentrating on producing two or three shows a year of the highest innovation and quality.

REES: Our resource was training young writers, actors and stage managers and, may I say, administrators to be excellent at their job and invigorate the theatre at large. I cannot think of a better 'resource'.

WALDMAN: So it comes down to whether your work was excellent and whilst I thought it was, others in some cases did not. And another thing. Those companies that still exist from the Sixties and Seventies have new people running them. They changed those companies' outlook and policies. Not that they are without morality, but the companies have actually changed much more. The people who continue to develop and explore the same area of work are in trouble at the moment. Funding bodies don't like it.

REES: That's the style of our time. Don't stay anywhere long or people will think you are not ambitious. People start a new job and immediately begin to think about when they will move on. Career is what it is about. Not creation.

ENTRANCE AND EXIT

ENTRANCE

JOHN ASHFORD

Photo: Peter Trievnor. © *The Times*

Reviewer and Theatre Editor, *Time Out*, 1969-73. He has been involved with many varieties of theatre from the presentation of playtexts as General Manager of the Theatre Upstairs at the Royal Court, 1974-76, to inter-disciplinary experiments as Director of the ICA Theatre, 1977-84, and, since 1986, dance as Director of The Place Theatre. Ashford talks about the origination of the Fringe and the future of performance.

REES: Throughout the period covered by these discussions, you have been working in the Fringe and the experimental area of theatre. Does how you saw the Fringe in the early days, and how you see it now, differ greatly? For instance, when you reviewed for *Time Out* in its early days, was it the intention to popularise the cause of the new theatre?

ASHFORD: *Time Out* did not have that view. For a long time it was just me. The magazine was a three weekly guide to London. The theatre section was divided between the 'West End' and 'Outer London, club and studio theatres'. I introduced the title 'Fringe Theatre' to the listings, adopted from the Edinburgh Festival Fringe. Edinburgh has 'invitees' at the main Festival and a Fringe of the uninvited who shack up in any old village hall. The latter was an appropriate model for what was happening in London, where people were taking over spaces not designed for theatre. This was 1969.

I started by doing a couple of reviews a week. Then as the magazine quickly expanded, they needed an Editor. It was a part-time job. I was also the magazine's Production Manager! There were only twelve of us. Everyone had a voice in the design, lay out and editorial content of each issue. So I put reviews into the Fringe listings because in those days there might be only twelve things on.

REES: *Time Out* was the only paper reviewing that sort of theatre?

ASHFORD: Yes. In present day terms it was a good marketing ploy to go to the then Editor, Tony Elliot, and say we must address this type of theatre. None of the national papers are. *Time Out* was primarily a listings paper. Editorial content came second. From the outset I wanted to address the casual reader who bought the magazine for the rock listings. I wrote theatre reviews in a language 'as if spoken' to engage that casual reader. At the same time I wanted to interest the well-informed theatre-goer and also the company presenting the play. Quite difficult to do that in 150 words!

REES: I draw a distinction between New theatre and Fringe theatre. New theatre had a coherent philosophy, however loud the slanging matches at parties were! Whereas Fringe suggests being on the outside wanting to be on the inside. The coherence disintegrated into separate skills, Fringe was swallowed up in the mainstream.

ASHFORD: That is important. On leaving *Time Out* I tried to change the listings title to 'Spaces and Events'. As you say the coherence disappeared and the word Fringe marginalised the importance of that theatre. It should have been central, not peripheral. But it was too late in 1973. By that time the title had stuck.

At *Time Out*, I did not have to review anything I did not like! I wrote bad reviews of West End shows and those produced by newly subsidised companies, whose work I thought should have been better. But I always wrote only good reviews of the area of work that was vital, growing and unsubsidised. I did not regard myself as a critic. I felt someone had to get in there and use this new, attractive magazine to proselytise that area of work. The caption review was an important innovation in *Time Out*. You could convey double the information by accompanying the review with a picture. I wrote six reviews a week. At midnight I would return from a show, choose the picture, type the 150 words and then, as Production Manager send it off to the printers!

REES: What were the venues you visited?

ASHFORD: Oval House, Open Space, Arts Lab, first in Drury Lane, then on Robert Street, lunchtime theatres like the Ambiance and Soho Poly. There were very few regular spaces. Sometimes I would go to an *ad hoc* space set up for a show.

REES: What were the characteristics of this theatre?

ASHFORD: Experimental theatre not based on text, physical theatre making use of text, performance art proceeding from a fine art tradition where the artist was often the subject of that performance, new writing, theatre with a direct political motivation, community theatre geographically based and community theatre interest based, eg for Old Age Pensioners, TIE. [*Theatre in Education*].

REES: The word 'group' was used in the same way rock bands were called groups in the Sixties.

ASHFORD: I remember putting up a notice at Oval House describing the work of a company I was in – 'A theatre group which works like a rock band!' The word 'gig' was also borrowed from rock music.

REES: What did being a member of a group imply?

ASHFORD: Collective responsibility. If a group did not themselves devise their shows, each member bore equal responsibility for what went on on that stage. Ensemble creation was at the root of it. This meant the existence of a continuous membership of a group. If someone left, you lost the piece. And even where companies like Portable Theatre used writers, writing at that time structurally drew and learnt from the groups. As a result, writing was more cinematic and free flowing in approach to narrative. There was a time when Howard Brenton said his favourite company was The People Show!

REES: Some groups specialised in bringing a physical approach to their textual work, others liked to make events outdoors in an environment. What do you remember of the practice of some groups?

ASHFORD: Granada Television asked me to make a youth programme. I got the group, John Bull Puncture Repair Kit, who did very exciting outdoors work, to make a show on the tarmac of Blackpool Airport, against the background of a World War Two Lancaster bomber! They did a flying display with wheelbarrows, beautifully painted with camouflage and RAF insignia. Donning flying helmets, kazoos in their mouths, trails of vapour coming out of each handle of the barrows, they did formation flying! Very spectacular to look at and completely silly. This work came out of the Bruce Lacey *An Evening of British Rubbish* tradition.

Then there was the whole physical theatre area inspired by American models, particularly through the influence of Grotowski. The actors whole physical presence was engaged in the intentions of a performance instead of the actor as the talking head. Nancy Meckler's Freehold did this. Berkoff also, but from a different angle. At the time of Peter Shaffer's *Equus*, people said that the play and production of it could not have been conceived in that way without the work of Freehold. So the Fringe did have an influence on the mainstream. Clearly and demonstrably the physical work of the groups on the one hand influenced production and the collage and construction work on the other influenced playwriting.

Subsequently the work of people like Meckler has been itself altered by the conventions and practice of working in mainstream theatre. She has moved from group creations to Sam Shepard plays to more conventional interpretations of classic texts. I don't know whether that's giving up or growing up!

A lot of those who worked in visual and performance theatre moved not into mainstream theatre, but into video. Both the commercial side of rock videos and the less commercial art videos.

REES: Many people moved into theatre, who at other times would not have.

ASHFORD: Very important that. There was a rejection of trained actors. The intellectual approach of those trained at university and college, who had done student acting, was closer in spirit to this new, flourishing theatre than were drama school actors. There was a divide. It reinforced the distinction, for example, between Portable Theatre [*Started by David Hare*] who employed 'actors' and Pip Simmons whose people were not Drama School trained and would probably not have got a job in 'proper' theatre. Similarly The People Show came out of the mixed discipline courses of Trent Park Polytechnic, now the University of Middlesex.

REES: How do you describe the shared philosophy?

ASHFORD: Very difficult to hive that off from the cultural politics of the time. I don't know if you remember but some years ago you provided me with a revelation during a conversation with you. I have been quoting you ever since! – 'The '68 generation was the first post-war generation who did not need to work or go to war.' Coming out as adults from our Further Education, we had time to think and to challenge the received wisdom of our elders. That's what produced the underground movement, which sometimes had American models but always had a distinct British accent. There was Paris '68. The Vietnam experience. The response to it in America, Germany and Japan. There was a feeling world wide amongst the young for the need of change.

One of the reasons I became interested in theatre was the desire to articulate those things. The cheapness of production of newspapers and theatre made these forms immediately available. The diversity of forms under the umbrella of Fringe may have only been coherent for three or so years, but it was joined to a much larger sub-culture which articulated its ideas through political demonstrations, drugs, rock and roll, the underground press and an attitude to the world wholly in opposition to its parents.

Originally Fringe theatre was driven by a need to articulate these ideas. Rapidly the vitality of the area was recognised by those who wanted to showcase their talents. Throughout the Eighties, Fringe theatre increasingly became a 'showcase'.

REES: How would you characterise the different approaches to the work? I find the current distinction drawn between text and non-text based work very unhelpful. It deceives.

ASHFORD: There is a catholic and a protestant model. The catholic model is 'There is the word'. It is interpreted by the Pope – the director – and made flesh through the actors. The protestant model is much more to do with individual responsibility and the joint creation of work. One works from the bottom up and the other from the top down. That is still observable.

The catholic model is authorship as a result of a single person sitting in a room conceiving something, the production process of which is to do with the explication of the author's intention. However if you want authorship to be a joint sharing of all the contributions, the protestant model, made by the participants – design, text, music, choreography and performance – then it is a very different authorship. In the first model, there is singularity of meaning In the second, there is a multiplicity of meaning, with as many interpretations of the piece as people who see it and the number of times it is performed. Certainly there is an area of authorship in the second model, but the intentions in terms of meaning are very different. One process is a construction of different viewpoints towards authorship. The other is the given of authorship, that is then deconstructed in terms of meaning during rehearsal in order to get it on stage, the factor which best articulates that authorship. The processes are very different.

REES: I accept that the processes are different. However, unless the performance continues to be formed and re-formed through, for example, improvisation or individual intervention, I do not think there is a difference ultimately between your two models. In the end there is a text. You have a solid object which is lodged in the performers brain cells, released through the performers physical means of expression during each performance.

In your collective model there is always, I believe, a dominant eye, ear and mouth, or one that becomes dominant, as the process moves from an original babel of voices to the position of an acceptance of one way as opposed to another. I may be cynical, but I do not believe a performance is achieved democratically. It is the result of benevolent despotism. This is obvious, as you point out, in your first catholic model. When a playwright comes to you with a script. That is the author. They have copyright. More difficult to perceive is the authorship in your collective model, but I believe it is there. And it is also singular. There is a clandestine author. Usually this is the person whose company it is. They have put themselves in a position of choice. This choice is authorship. After all, to carry on your religious metaphor, someone has to be the first person to start something off. That person chooses the next person and so on.

Catholic and protestant are also muddling as a metaphor. You can say someone is catholic of taste. This would, as an expression, surely be more appropriate for your collective model. Remember the Protestant, Martin Luther, declaring: 'Here I am. I can do no other!' What can more admirably sum up your catholic 'singular' author?

ASHFORD: Let me put it another way. Text-based theatre has a narrative which makes fictional use of time and space. It adopts the mask of character. It employs design which is representational. The tradition of the Fine Arts is different. Here the use of space and time is real. Objects are only themselves. If this tradition is used for performance often the material is the person, the being, the physical presence of the artist. They are not pretending to be someone else. These are the two traditions and they are different. Although they may mix freely in the area now known as Live Art, the theoretical distinctions can still be usefully applied.

REES: Up to your time at the ICA, your work had been in theatre. Six years ago you moved here to The Place dedicated to dance? Why?

ASHFORD: I now see quite a clear progress from one peak of pure form, a play – my work prior to the ICA – through a verdant valley of multi-media and inter-disciplinary performance, now known as Live Art – my time at the ICA – to another peak of pure form, dance, at The Place Theatre, where I now work. My work at the ICA brought different forms, performance, music, dance, text, design, together to meet as equals. That seemed the most productive area of theatre work at the time. That challenged the supremacy of authorship, the singularity of meaning of text-based work and so pushed theatre into finding new ways of expressing ideas.

Mark Long of The People Show said that their form of theatre was forced to put on display its paint rags alongside its masterpieces. In today's conservative climate, that's tough for audiences. It is difficult to engender the same level of skill with each experiment. In more generous times audiences were interested in sketches. Now people only want to see masterpieces because they are a surer bet for a night out. With the kind of collaborative work I was presenting at the ICA, you cannot create masterpieces all the time. The public became disenchanted.

Dance is an ensemble creation. With companies like DV8, Lea Anderson's companies, the Cholmondeleys and the Featherstonehaughs, there is no author trapped in a room. The work can only be created in a studio with the dancer's bodies. So this was a natural progression for me. Audiences like the demonstrable skill of dance, particularly when choreographers took greater risks. The skills became more spectacular. So audiences came. As plays retreat into a naturalism, readily recognised by audiences reared on television, dance brings back the poetry to theatre.

Many of the ideas developed by multi-disciplinary work are now finding expression in dance. Sometimes the work produced by independent dance companies is dismissed as fashionable. But each new generation makes its own mark. So there is a quick turnover of styles. This may seem as if it is merely fashion conscious. But over six years, I have noticed that dancers move in different ways as a response to the way people are on the street and in life, as the world moves them. Abstract movement is no longer an end in itself. That's as honourable a 'content', reflecting the way the world is, as say, a politically correct play preaching to the converted of fifty seats at the Edinburgh Fringe.

REES: Is World Theatre the same thing as World Music in another form?

ASHFORD: No. In World Music there has to be an element of cross-over. For instance, Rai music from Algeria. It is a mix of traditional Algerian music, put through a political filter with radical lyrics and then amplified like a rock band mixed with hip hop!

REES: A music produced in pre-electric conditions then crossed with music in post-electric conditions.

ASHFORD: The World Theatre seasons at the Aldwych in the Sixties did not contain this sort of cross-over. They were productions of text-based plays from many different countries in the language of that country. That is still largely what World Theatre is.

REES: Do you think an increasing amount of contemporary theatre is 'Festival' theatre?

ASHFORD: I'm against 'Festival' culture. Culture is not for holidays, it is for every day. With the decline of organised religion, the congregation which makes up the audience at a theatre is an extremely important part of of the moral and social fabric of life. That's exclusive to live presentation. Going to three shows at LIFT [*London International Theatre Festival*], good as it is as festivals go, is a jolly good thing, but it is much better to have an interest in that culture as part of your daily life. Western culture is being festivalised in an unhealthy way.

REES: Colonising that which lies outside of it, by embracing it as part of the dominant culture through festivals, is very like, in my opinion, what often happens with World Music. It becomes general, abstract and not specific and for its time.

ASHFORD: 'This is a great show but it won't work in my Festival!'

REES: The recession lengthening, new age sturdy beggars nomadically trailing through the countryside, urban underclass burning and joy-riding. All this and more, dance can respond to in the next decade?

ASHFORD: In that dance is a participatory activity. Yes. Dance is exemplarily multi-cultural, appealing to young audiences. I rarely notice the tone of a skin on stage with dance, unless that's the point. Anyone from any culture or country can have access to dance. Asian and Caribbean dance forms have had an observable effect on the contemporary mainstream of dance. This relies on funding and the will of the people of this country to recognise that culture is central to all our lives. Britain's many cultures will only hold together if they can represent themselves to each other. Then there's a hope that the honourable history of a thousand years of integration in this island will hold, that the centre will hold.

The way I now see the last ten years is that Thatcherism determined to tackle the hearts and minds of the people of this country. To change their views on how the country should work by first recognising the influence of the chattering classes. They are largely found in the arts and the media. Thatcherism then put a squeeze on the arts so that all the arguments would be debated in the high profile arena of the national media. Having won the argument about financial accountability, three year business plans, marketing, all those new buzz words, that dreadful vocabulary we had to adopt, they would then do the same with the Universities, the Health Service and Education. The debates were honed by practising them with the intellectuals in the arts. Now the arts will be left alone during the next decade. This leaves them free to articulate all the conflicts to which you referred and to heal those conflicts.

EXIT

ROLAND REES

On September 15th 1988, a letter arrived by private messenger from Luke Rittner, Secretary-General of the Arts Council of Great Britain, to the offices of Foco Novo theatre company addressed to Dr. Trevor R Griffiths, the Chair of Foco Novo Board. The letter stated that: 'The Drama Panel did not feel justified in recommending a return to revenue funding status to Foco Novo.' The company would not be receiving subsidy in the next financial year 1989/90.

Rittner realised that this news would come 'as a considerable disappointment.' The Council's decision was made on the basis of 'established Council and Drama Panel priorities.' The company would in future be on 'project applicant status'; one which allowed us the eligibility, along with many others, to apply for individual Project funding. We were offered the solace of a meeting with the Drama Director, Ian Brown, if we wanted to discuss the matter further. Unlike the commercial world, whose methods the new arts mandarins champion, a 'client' of the Arts Council is at the receiving end of recommendations.

Hastily a meeting of the Board of Directors was called that evening. We were in rehearsal for a newly commissioned play *Consequences*, a work by eight contributing writers. The company had already suffered a 25 per cent slash in subsidy in the current year, 1987/88, and it had a bank overdraft. So the news of that day placed Foco Novo in immediate jeopardy, particularly because the collateral customarily required by the bank to continue to let us trade on an overdraft was the knowledge, in the form of a letter-offer of subsidy, that the Arts Council would continue to support our programme.

The Board had been forced to meet a considerable number of times in the last eighteen months; continuously to reconsider the stark facts of survival, in an age when public subsidy to the Arts was dwindling in favour of attempting to obtain income from other, often non-existent, sources. In view of the company's financial situation, the Board could have been held to be trading recklessly under the terms of the Insolvency Act, if it had continued with its programme now that Arts Council support was no longer guaranteed. At the end of a long meeting, a frustrating and sad inevitability forced itself on the Board. Foco Novo would cease trading the next day, September 16th 1988.

This decision meant the cancellation of *Consequences* and would probably lead to the eventual liquidation of the company. To delay such a decision would mean the exchange of one body of creditors for another. They along with the theatres who had booked us would immediately be informed. After sixteen years and thirty eight productions, the denouement was very sudden. We were in no position ever to use the name of the company again. It brought home to us what an endangered theatrical species the small national touring company is without capital assets in these times.

Nine months later I received a phone call from Detective Constable Boggis of Holborn Police station asking whether I was Roland Rees? Did I once rent an office on Alfred Place, off Tottenham Court Road? Wondering what was coming next, he said that in April, 1989, during redecoration, an AK-47 rifle had been found at the back of our former office! It had been handed into them, tested in their labs and found to be a model unable to fire 'real' bullets. I said it was a prop for a play about South Africa. He said: 'You can fetch it any time.'

I held a shotgun and firearms license, for theatrical purposes, over many years and knew the complexities of fulfilling police requirements for carrying imitation firearms around on tour. The models had become so real they were being used in hold-ups. Chains attached to concrete and locked boxes were required. At the time of the phone call, I was watching events unfold in Beijing on television and thought an AK-47 was probably not too different to the arms carried by the Chinese soldiers we saw there in the square, facing unarmed students. It made me reflect how many of our productions had required the use of firearms and the ability to fire 'blanks', in plays which show people's struggle to free themselves from a yoke.

FOCO NOVO
PRODUCTIONS 1972-1988

1972
FOCO NOVO
Bernard Pomerance
The Roxy & The Oval House
Director Roland Rees *Director* Roland Rees *Percussion* Nigel Morris
Lighting Dick Johnson
Cast: Glen Beck, Stephen Bradley, Laura Esterman, Mona Hammond, Oscar James,
Neil Johnston, Judy Monahan, Richard Pendrey, Bernard Sterlin

1973
DRUMS IN THE NIGHT
Bertolt Brecht
Adaptation C.P. Taylor
Traverse Theatre, Edinburgh Festival & Hampstead Theatre
Director Roland Rees *Designer* Moshe Mussman *Music* Andy Smith
Cast: Irene Bradshaw, Bill Hoyland, Petra Markham, Ken Morley, Brenda Polan,
Stephen Rea, Andy Smith

1974
COCK ARTIST
Fassbinder
The Almost Free Theatre
Director Roland Rees *Designer* Norman Coates

1975
DEATH OF A BLACKMAN
Alfred Fagon
Hampstead Theatre
Director Roland Rees *Designer* Bernard Culshaw
Cast: Mona Hammond, Gregory Munroe, Anton Phillips

A MAN'S A MAN
Bertolt Brecht
Adaptation Bernard Pomerance
UK Tour & Hampstead Theatre
Director Roland Rees *Designer* Di Seymour *Music* Dave Brown
Cast: Dave Brown, Jack Chissick, Alan Hulse, Terry Jackson, Stefan Kalipha,
Peter Marinker, Jestyn Phillips, John Salthouse, Sheila Reid, Tricia Thorns

THE ARTHUR HORNER SHOW
Phil Woods
UK Tour
Director Roland Rees *Designer* Bernard Culshaw
Cast: Kevin Costello, Carl Davis, Pat Gerrard, Stafford Gordon, Alan Hulse, Paul Teague

1976
THE NINE DAYS AND SALTLEY GATES
Jon Chadwick and John Hoyland
UK Tour & Oval House & ICA Theatre
Directors Jon Chadwick, Roland Rees *Designer* Central School of Art
Cast: Aviva Goldkorn, Stuart Golland, Ian Heywood, Alan Hulse,
Terry Jackson, Stewart Preston, Mary Sheen, Robin Summers, Gareth Williams

A SEVENTH MAN
Adrian Mitchell
UK Tour & Hampstead Theatre
Director Roland Rees *Designer* Ralph Steadman *Costumes* Sheelagh Killeen
Music Dave Brown
Cast: Dave Brown, Aviva Goldkorn, Stafford Gordon, Alan Hulse, Terry Jackson,
Stefan Kalipha, Joan-Ann Maynard, Paddy O'Hagan, Stewart Preston

1977
TIGHTEN YOUR BELT
Jon Chadwick and John Hoyland
UK Tour & Oval House
Director Jon Chadwick *Designer* Sarah Paulley *Music* John Greaves
Cast: David Bradford, Aviva Goldkorn, Tony Gower, Sue Glanville, Carrie Lee-Baker,
Maureen Sullivan, Colin Tarrant

THE ELEPHANT MAN
Bernard Pomerance
UK Tour & Hampstead Theatre
Director Roland Rees *Designer* Tanya McCallin *Music* Pat Arrowsmith
Lighting Alan O'Toole
Cast: David Allister, Arthur Blake, Judy Bridgeland, Ken Drury, William Hoyland,
David Schofield, Jenny Stoller

1978
WITHDRAWAL SYMPTOMS
C.P. Taylor
UK Tour & ICA Theatre
Director Roland Rees *Designer* Adrian Vaux
Cast: Anne Godley, Mary Maddox, Anthony May, Anthony Milner, Anthony O'Donnel,
Gordon Reid, Rowena Roberts

ON THE OUT
Tunde Ikoli
UK Tour & Bush Theatre
Director John Chapman *Designer* Caroline Beaver
Cast: Michael Feast, Alan Ighon, Ade Ikoli, Hugh Kwachi, Lynn Pearson, William Murray, Roderick
Smith, William Vanderpuye

THE FREE FALL
Colin Mortimer
UK Tour & ICA Theatre
Director Roland Rees *Designer* Tanya McCallin
Cast: Peter Acre, Beth Ellis, Chris Hallam, Sharmian McDonald, Tim Myers,
Maggie Shevlin, Peter Wight

1979
INDEPENDENCE
Mustapha Matura
UK Tour & Bush Theatre
Director Roland Rees *Designer* Adrian Vaux *Lighting* Chris Ellis
Cast: Malcolm Fredericks, Michael Howard, Mary Jones, Stefan Kalipha,
Shope Shoedeinde, Ewart James Walters

LANDSCAPE OF EXILE
David Zane Mairowitz
The Half Moon Theatre
Director Roland Rees *Designer* Iona McLeish *Lighting* John Hallé
Cast: Martin Black, Jeff Chiswick, Michelle Copsey, Carl Davis, David Hargreaves, Michael Howard,
Vera Jakob, Brigitte Kahn, Joseph Peters, John Phillips, Frances de la Tour

THE GUISE
David Mowat
UK Tour & Theatre Upstairs, Royal Court
Director Roland Rees *Designer* Adrian Vaux *Music* Cliff Burnett *Lighting* Chris Ellis
Cast: Cliff Burnett, Andrew Berezowski, Carl Davis, Ken Drury, Caroline Hutchison,
Neil Johnston, Tom Marshall, Michael McVey

1980
WOYZECK
Georg Buchner
Translation Peter Hulton
UK Tour & Lyric Studio Theatre, Hammersmith
Director Neil Johnston *Designer* Alberto Bali *Lighting* Gerry Jenkinson
Cast: Ken Bones, Andrew Berezowski, Jack Elliot, Nigel Harris, Karl Johnson,
Jill Richards, Gwyneth Strong, John Vine

PLEASE SHINE DOWN ON ME
Olwen Wymark
UK Tour & Theatre Upstairs, Royal Court
Director Rolan Rees *Designer* Iona McLeish *Lighting* Alan O'Toole
Cast: Sheila Burrell, Alan Devlin, David Howey, Veronica Quilligan,
Pauline Munro, James Saxon

QUANTRILL IN LAWRENCE
Bernard Pomerance
ICA Theatre
Director Roland Rees *Designer* Iona Mcleish *Lighting* Gerry Jenkinson

Cast: Ron Cook, Don Fellows, Penny Fischer, Eugene Lipinski, Dan Meaden, Patrick Moore, Richard
Moore, Joe Praml, Mary Ellen Ray, David Schofield, Harold Saks, Joi Staton, Dikran Tulaine

1981
CITIZEN ILYUSHIN
Kevin Mandry
UK Tour & Tricycle Theatre
Director Roland Rees *Designer* Bernard Culshaw *Lighting* Alan O'Toole
Cast: Carl Forgione, Dione Inman, Richard Kane, Maureen O'Brien, Reginald Stewart,
Jenny Stoller

SNAP
Nigel Gearing
UK Tour & New End Theatre, Hampstead
Director Roland Rees *Designer* Adrian Vaux *Costumes* Sheelagh Killeen
Music Steve A'dor *Lighting* Alan O'Toole
Cast: Johnathan Burn, Lucinda Curtis, Oliver Ford Davies, Colette Hillier

1982
EDWARD II
Bertolt Brecht
UK Tour & Roundhouse Theatre
Director Roland Rees *Designer* Adrian Vaux *Lighting* Gerry Jenkinson
Percussion Eddie Sayer
Cast: James Castle, David Dixon, Ian Hogg, Karl Howman, John Joyce, Roderic Leigh,
Billy McColl, Vincent McLaren, Beth Morris, Matthew Scurfield, Reg Stewart,
Robin Summers, Dorien Thomas

SINK OR SWIM
Tunde Ikoli
London Tour & Tricylce Theatre
Director Roland Rees *Designer* David McHenry
Cast: Brian Bovell, Janet Key, Trevor Laird, Pat Leach, Tony London, Mary Zuckerman

CONVERSATIONS IN EXILE
Bertolt Brecht adapted Howard Brenton
&
FOUR HUNDRED POUNDS
Alfred Fagon
UK Tour & Theatre Upstairs, Royal Court
Director Roland Rees *Designer* Wallace Heim *Lighting* Ace McCarron
Cast: Gordon Case, Stefan Kalipha

1983
PUNTILA AND HIS SERVANT MATTI
Bertolt Brecht
UK Tour & Tricycle Theatre
Director Roland Rees *Designer* Peter Hartwell *Lighting* Andy Phillips
Costume Sheelagh Killeen
Cast: Dallas Cavell, Kim Clifford, Craig Crosbie, Sara-Heliane Elliot, Carol Harrison,
Anna Manahan, Bunny May, Penny Ryder, Barry Stanton, Robin Summers,
Charles Wegner, Peter Wyatt

SLEEPING POLICEMAN
Howard Brenton and Tunde Ikoli
UK Tour & Theatre Upstairs, Royal Court
Director Roland Rees *Designer* Wallace Heim *Lighting* Dick Johnson
Cast: Carrie Lee-Baker, Trevor Butler, Craig Crosbie, Alfred Fagon, Mary Ellen Ray,
Ella Wilder

1984
BLACK MAS
John Constable
UK Tour & New End Theatre, Hampstead
Director Roland Rees *Designer* Peter Whiteman *Costume* Sheelagh Killeen
Lighting Steve Whitson
Cast: Trevor Butler, Carol Harrison, Ian Reddington, James Snell

BLOODY POETRY
Howard Brenton
UK Tour & Hampstead Theatre
Director Roland Rees *Designer* Poppy Mitchell *Costume* Sheelagh Killeen
Lighting Richard Moffatt
Cast: James Aubrey, Sue Burton, William Gaminara, Jane Gurnett, Valentine Pelka,
Fiona Shaw

1985
DEATHWATCH
Jean Genet trans Nigel Williams
UK Tour & Young Vic
Director Roland Rees *Designer* Andrea Montag *Lighting* Richard Moffatt
Music Andrew Dickson
Cast: Sean Bean, Jimmy Chisholm, Garry Lilburne, Vicenzo Ricotta

WEEK IN, WEEK OUT
Tunde Ikoli
London Tour
Director Tim Fywell *Designer* Bunny Christie
Cast: Peter Attard, Maria Charles, Harry Perscy, Debbie Roza, Cindy Shelley,
Larrington Walker

THE ASS
D.H. Lawrence devised/composed, Mike & Kate Westbrook
UK Tour & Riverside Studios
Director Roland Rees *Designer* Ariane Gastambide *Choreography* Pat Garrett
Lighting Richard Moffatt
Cast: Trevor Allan, Stephen Boxer, Lesia Melnyk, Kate Westbrook, Mike Westbrook,
Peter Whyman

1986
THE LOWER DEPTHS
Tunde Ikoli
UK Tour & Tricycle Theatre
Director Roland Rees *Designer* Tanya McCallin *Lighting* Richard Moffatt
Cast: Maria Charles, Ram John Holder, Joy Lemoine, Janet Palmer, Robin Summers,
Rudolph Walker, Sylvester Williams, Colin Tarrant, Tilly Vosburgh

BANGED UP
Tunde Ikoli
UK Tour & Young Vic
Director Roland Rees *Designer* Andrea Montag *Lighting* Richard Moffatt
Cast: Trevor Laird, Tilly Vosburgh

1987
NEEDLES OF LIGHT
James Pettifer
UK Tour & Riverside Studios
Director Roland Rees *Designer* Ariane Gastambide *Choreography* Pat Garrett
Lighting Richard Moffatt *Music Director* Robin Canter
Cast: Martin Gower, Harry Landis, Richard Mayes, Stephen Oxsley, Gengiz Saner,
Dorien Thomas, Hilary Townley

THE CAPE ORCHARD
Michael Picardie
UK Tour & Young Vic
Director Roland Rees *Designer* Norman Coates *Lighting* Richard Moffatt
Cast: Norman Beaton, Claire Benedict, Pauline Black, Naomi Buch, Joseph Charles

1988
SAVANNAH BAY
Marguerite Duras
London Tour & Battersea Arts Centre
Director Sue Todd *Designer* Iona McLeish *Lighting* Geraint Pughe
Cast: Faith Brook. Alexandra Mathie